AMERICA THROUGH FOREIGN EYES

AMERICA THROUGH FOREIGN EYES

JORGE G. CASTAÑEDA

OXFORD
UNIVERSITY PRESS

OXFORD
UNIVERSITY PRESS

Oxford University Press is a department of the University of Oxford. It furthers
the University's objective of excellence in research, scholarship, and education
by publishing worldwide. Oxford is a registered trade mark of Oxford University
Press in the UK and certain other countries.

Published in the United States of America by Oxford University Press
198 Madison Avenue, New York, NY 10016, United States of America.

Library of Congress Cataloging-in-Publication Data
Names: Castañeda, Jorge G., 1953– author.
Title: America through foreign eyes / Jorge G. Castañeda.
Description: New York, NY : Oxford University Press, 2020. | Includes index.
Identifiers: LCCN 2019044724 (print) | LCCN 2019044725 (ebook) |
ISBN 9780190224493 (hardback) | ISBN 9780190224516 (epub) |
ISBN 9780197660072 (paperback)
Subjects: LCSH: Exceptionalism—United States. | National characteristics,
American. | United States—Foreign public opinion. |
United States—Politics and government. | United States—Social conditions.
Classification: LCC E895.C38 2020 (print) | LCC E895 (ebook) |
DDC 973—dc23
LC record available at https://lccn.loc.gov/2019044724
LC ebook record available at https://lccn.loc.gov/2019044725

1 3 5 7 9 8 6 4 2

Paperback printed by Marquis, Canada

CONTENTS

---�---

ACKNOWLEDGMENTS

I am deeply grateful to the many friends and family members who contributed to making this long-desired endeavor come to fruition. Firstly, to Alejandra Zerecero, my friend and co-worker, whose research, editing, organization, fact-finding and -checking, and overall management of this book were invaluable. To Daniela Silva, who worked tirelessly with Alejandra and myself on these same challenges, mainly on research and fact-checking, I am also greatly indebted.

Alan Riding, whose 1985 book about the Mexicans served as an inspiration and model for this one, not only read the manuscript twice, but edited it thoroughly and suggested detailed improvements for several sections. My thanks, once again. My son, Jorge Andrés, my brother Andrés, and my sister Marina all plowed through various versions of the final draft; their comments, suggestions, critiques, and encouragement were priceless. John Coatsworth, Ken Roth, Jose Luis Alberro, Dudley Ankerson, and Sheerly Avni also read the entire text, suggested improvements, detected confusion or mistakes, and provided encouragement. My thanks for taking the time from a hectic schedule to do this. Rebecca Bill Chávez, Krissie Dahr, Alan Tonelson, and Daniel Wilkinson read parts of the text early on, and were especially helpful in starting me off on the right track.

Lastly, I owe a great deal to David McBride, my editor at OUP, who believed in this project from the very beginning, waited patiently for it to get underway, and then acted even more patiently in dealing with my constant pestering and stubbornness, in addition, of course, to carrying out the best possible job of editing. My thanks for all this effort.

Introduction

FOREIGNERS HAVE BEEN WRITING about the United States ever since its foundation. Now it is my turn. But please don't hold this against me: the United States itself is at fault. Like a great many people on earth, I've long been fascinated by this remarkable phenomenon which calls itself America. My fate—or perhaps good fortune—has been that of a foreigner who for half a century lived the American experience—as a child, as a student, as an author, as a recurrent visitor, and as a university professor. Being Mexican places me in a special category: having lost half its territory to the United States in the nineteenth century, having found itself caught up in the maelstrom of America's current identity crisis, Mexico can never ignore what happens north of the border. Further, while serving as Mexico's foreign minister from 2000 to 2003, I had the privilege of peeping inside the machinery of power that makes this great nation tick.

That said, this book is not written from a Mexican perspective but rather from that of a sympathetic foreign critic who has seen the United States from both inside and outside. And its hope is to contribute something to how Americans view themselves and are viewed by the world.

Before embarking on this journey, I naturally looked back at some of my forebears, earlier foreigners who were drawn to visit or live in the United States and who then went on to offer their version of America to their home readers. Some like the French traveler Alexis de Tocqueville, author of the early nineteenth-century classic, *Democracy in America*, felt European nations had much to learn from the

American democratic experiment. Others like Charles Dickens left dismayed by what he considered to be the country's singular obsession with money. But they are just two of dozens who have tried—and continue to try—to find a magic key that unlocks the complexities and contradictions of American society. Indeed, it is as if the United States seeks to challenge foreign writers to explain it, confident they will fail. And in taking it on, these outsiders have variously experienced frustration, hope, anger, excitement, disappointment, and enlightenment—but never indifference.

I have varied my references to previous authors by country and language, but they are inevitably concentrated in Western Europe and to a lesser extent Latin America. These are the regions I am most familiar with, as well as where most of this type of writing was rooted. There are fewer references to Asian and African sources; the explanation lies in my own ignorance of their work. Perusing more carefully what Japanese and Chinese travelers concluded about America might be especially valuable, for example.

In the early nineteenth century, many European travelers struggled to come to terms with "the land of the free" where slavery was entrenched. The English writer and poet Rudyard Kipling was one who simply disliked Americans from the moment he landed in San Francisco. In the late nineteenth century, the Cuban poet and revolutionary José Martí, who spent fourteen years in exile in the United States, was fascinated with the American work ethic and prosperity but also deeply depressed over his host's obsession with money and the imminent conquest of his homeland. In 1906, Werner Sombart, a German sociologist, was puzzled why there was no socialism in the United States. Later, the German novelist Thomas Mann and the French philosopher Jean-Paul Sartre fell in love with the United States on arrival, then either left their temporary exile in disgust or became irreparably hostile to it later. Others responded anecdotally. The Russian-born novelist Vladimir Nabokov, a long-time resident in the United States, once quipped that cars are the only place in America where there is neither noise nor air current. More unusually, the Swedish sociologist Gunnar Myrdal wrote not for other foreigners, but for Americans: his classic on race, *The American Dilemma*, was commissioned by the Carnegie Corporation in 1942 and written in English. More recently, the Norwegian novelist Karl Ove

Knausgaard and the French thinker Régis Debray have published their own reflections, either in English or for the folks back home.

"This kind of traveler is not really a discoverer," wrote V. S. Naipaul, the Nobel Prize–winning West Indian and English novelist and essayist about his own trip through the American South in the 1980s. "He is more a man defining himself against a foreign background: and depending on who he is, the book he writes can be attractive. A book like that can be written about the United States only if the writer, taking the reader into his confidence, sets himself up as alien in some way. Generally, though, this approach cannot work in the United States . . . . It is too well known, too photographed, too written about; and, being more organized and less informal, it is not so open to casual inspection."[1] The travelers' notes about an America rapidly visited is a sufficient fixture of literature on the United States that Sacha Baron Cohen spoofed it in his now classic *Borat: Cultural Learnings of America* film from 2006. It is not Tocqueville, but it can be extraordinarily amusing.

I recognize that I am following in well-trodden footsteps, daring to presume that Americans might be interested in another foreigner's point of view. That said, this effort *is* essentially different from the older ones. For starters, it is intended for an American audience, not readers in my own country, Mexico, or in my own language, Spanish. I hope they will one day see it in translation, and that for them as for others it will contribute to the understanding of its giant neighbor. I do not seek to explain America to others, but to share one foreigner's view of the United States with Americans themselves.

Nor is this a travel book, the product of a few weeks or months crisscrossing the United States by car, boat, train, or carriage. This book is the result of many years of growing up, studying, residing, teaching, and speaking in the United States. It springs from dealing with American authorities on a government-to-government basis, and civil society to civil society. I have enjoyed the close and lasting friendship of dozens of Americans for the past half century and observed with them evolution of their country from within and without.

I am doing so at a critical moment in American history, one in which Americans are questioning both the working of their own society and political system and their place in a fast-changing and conflict-ridden world. The country's latent insularity, fed by the belief that its nation's size, might, and wealth offer it immunity from developments abroad, has again resurfaced. So has its instinct to lash out at perceived foreign threats, albeit more often now economically when in the past a military response was frequently preferred. Yet this has only underlined the new vulnerability to outside forces of what for so long was considered the global model of a successful Western capitalist democracy. In sum, the inescapable presence of the world *inside* the United States today has persuaded me that the moment is ripe for a foreigner's assessment of what is going wrong and how it might be fixed.

The agenda that lies before me is immense. It must incorporate history and economics, the legacy of slavery and the Civil War, the rush of industrialization and the emergence of the world's first middle class, America's critical role in two world wars, its emergence as the sole super-power after the collapse of Soviet communism, and the new challenge posed by China. But beyond these global headlines, I also aim to explore how the United States is now engaged in a difficult, painful, even traumatic self-examination in which the very tenets of the American Dream are being questioned. And to this, Donald J. Trump has added fuel by stirring age-old racial tensions and deepening class conflict through his policy of "divide and rule." Drugs, immigration, race, and religion are old topics that must be addressed in their new wineskins, with a new label.

What can I add to what has already been written? This book does not pretend to be a scholarly work, but rather an impressionistic, analytical, and intuitive review of what I have learned over more than fifty years of direct contact. Foreign writers have often asked the right questions, but in my view they have not always provided the right answers. To cite just two questions often posed by foreign writers which I will examine with fresh eyes: has consumer society stamped a "sameness" on Americans? Can the perennial claim of American "exceptionalism" still be justified? Or is America becoming more like everybody else? Isn't pining for a lost and glorious past as American as it is British, Mexican, Chinese, and Italian today?

It is of course fair to ask, can a foreigner see what Americans over-look? Is there a special *regard* that can only be directed from afar and abroad and that elucidates what the locals cannot? Today, practically every inhabitant of the planet has heard of the United States, consumes some type of American good or service, and watches daily events in America on television, cell phones, tablets, or laptops. For better or for worse, everyone has an opinion about the United States. When scholarship, through translation and cultural exchanges, is global, and the English language is too, what can one foreigner add to what Americans know about themselves, especially given the vast resources available to them and to no one else?

To begin with, a certain distance. Numerous books written by Americans—or other foreigners—about nations as varied as China, India, Italy, Spain, and Mexico have enlightened myriad readers from these countries. No one is transparent to oneself, and even today an external view can be insightful. It can offer a crucial ingredient which domestic scholars, journalists, or *literati* rarely contribute: context.

I also believe these pages can be useful precisely because I share Americans' affection and concern for the state of their nation. But I remain a foreigner, neither emotionally committed nor directly engaged in the near-existentialist struggle now gripping American society. I am no more than an observer, albeit one who has spent many decades monitoring the changing American way of life. Guiding me have been Americans too numerous to name who have shared their knowledge and experience with me. In the process, they have taught me a great deal. In these pages, I set out to share what I have learned.

I

American sameness, or the world's first middle class

MANY OF TODAY'S STEREOTYPES about American uniformity were born nearly two centuries ago. Take Dickens: "The people are all alike, too. There is no diversity of character. They travel about the same errands, say and do the same things in exactly the same manner."[1] This tells us more about Dickens and other foreigners who were discovering America in the early nineteenth century than it does about the Americans they met. But it also underlines how many of these judgments live on. Karl Ove Knausgaard, the Norwegian author of the monumental—in size and sales—*My Struggle*, was contracted by *The New York Times* in 2015 to write what the paper surely hoped would be two-part, original road reportage. It was of course beautifully written but repeated the customary reflections: "I had never really understood how a nation that so celebrated the individual could obliterate all differences the way this country did . . . . The most striking thing about the United States was its sameness, that every place had the same hotels, the same restaurants, the same stores."[2] Dickens and the author of *My Struggle* did not make this point critically, or even condescendingly. Nor did Lord Bryce, the British ambassador to the White House toward the end of the nineteenth century, whose two-thousand-page *The American Commonwealth* leads his readers through a meticulous review of everything anyone would want to know about the United States: "But uniformity, which the European visitor begins to note when he has travelled for a month or two, is the feature of the country which Englishmen who have lived long there, and Americans who are familiar with Europe, most frequently revert to."[3] In fact, these and other observers were not really talking about uniformity, but rather about the world's first incipient middle-class society. Foreigners found the United States to be uniform, and Americans to be "all the same" because what they saw was a middle-class society non-existent in their own countries. The country's extraordinary diversity, then and now, was not visible to them, or they did not seek it out with sufficient zeal.

There are few places on earth as diverse as the New York City subway. Each autumn I travel the Manhattan lines several times a week. How can anyone dwell upon, let alone emphasize "sameness" on the 8th Ave Express or the Lexington Ave Local? In fact, quite easily, but in a positive fashion. Everyone—the Park Avenue executive (albeit few), the UWS writer, the Mexican construction worker, the African American young woman going to Hunter College, the Asian American returning to Queens—is on board. In the morning or at rush hour in the afternoon, they are all going to or returning from work.

They all pay the same fare—weekly or trip by trip—fill up the same dilapidated cars, stand clear of the same closing doors, wear pretty much similar clothes, especially in winter. All have iPhones in their hands and earphones around their necks and avoid eye-contact at all cost. I find my fellow subway travelers all the same in their situation, and tremendously diverse in the color of their skin, their age, their station in life, and their rank in the happiness index published around the world every year. The "different ones," the "others" are those without work, unable to buy a Metrocard, cold in winter and suffocating in summer, with nowhere to go. This may be a better way to understand the foreign comments on American uniformity. Everyone on the train possesses one overriding common trait in spite of their subsidiary diversity: they all take the subway. As do their subway or elevated train colleagues throughout the United States: in the other coastal or cosmopolitan mega-cities, or parts of the "fly-over" country.

The first middle class ever

Today's foreign visitors reach similar conclusions to those of their predecessors, but with a more aggressive, denigrating tone. Perhaps like Dickens and Tocqueville (in the United States, "society is one single mass."), they miss one of the main features that distinguishes the United States: a uniqueness that only becomes apparent when they compare it with their own countries.[4] Perhaps the first foreign visitor to what became America to put his views on paper was French explorer J. Hector St. John de Crevecoeur. He wrote in 1782: "(American society) is not composed, as in Europe, of great lords who posses everything, and a herd of people who have nothing . . . . The rich and the poor are not so far removed from each other as they are in Europe."[5]

From the outset, given the colonial past, the frontier and the endless land available for settlement, along with what recent authors have called the "Middle Class Constitution," and a national character that contributed to and sprang from this inimitable configuration, America was a congenitally different society.[6] Different from other colonies, different from the European colonizers, different from the older Asian, African, and (Latin) American civilizations.

During its first two hundred years as an independent nation, the United States evolved as a society where a great commonality existed among its "citizens," with class differences smaller than in Europe or in other former colonies. Two economists recently reconstructed Gini coefficients—the most common measure of inequality, where 0.0 is perfect equality and 1.0 is total inequality—for the thirteen colonies in 1774. They discovered that eighteenth-century society was less unequal—even including slavery—than its equivalent in 2012.[7] Excluding slaves, and before taxes and transfers, the United States only attained a comparable level of equality to 1774 . . . in 1982, just after Ronald Reagan took office.

These approaches must be taken with reservations. Bryce exaggerated when he claimed that Tocqueville's *bon mot* about Americans being born equal was not far from the mark. According to one calculation, by 1831 half of the private property in the United States was in the hands of just 4 percent of the population.[8] The Englishman strangely mused later that "Sixty years ago, there were no great fortunes in America, few large fortunes, no poverty."[9] Not quite. He evidently overlooked the more than two million slaves, equivalent at the time to one-fifth of the population of the United States. By the beginning of the Civil War, the number of slaves would reach four million, or roughly one eighth of a total population of 31 million.

Hyperbole or not, most observers since then have attributed this undoubtedly real, though nuanced "original virtue," to the infinite availability of land through the vastness and constant extension of the western frontier, and to the legal status of the ensuing expansion, even before the Homestead Act of 1862. The colonies were egalitarian, if one discounted those who were not equal. On examining voting records before Independence, for example, when property was strongly attached to electoral rights, just after the French and Indian War (1756–63), two-thirds of white males were entitled to vote. In England at that time, only 20 percent could.[10] The colonies were much more egalitarian than the colonizer, as long as slaves and Native Americans were excluded from the calculation, which, of course, they could not be.

Equality, but not for everybody

The comparison with the independent nations that emerged in Spanish and Portuguese America just a few decades after the American Revolutionary War was dramatic. Those societies were, and remain today, some of the world's most unequal ones. The stark contrast between rich and poor, noted by the great German explorer Alexandre von Humboldt in Mexico as early as 1810, was never that visible in North America. This was partly because it wasn't that glaring, but also as a result of constitutional, legislative, and political smoke and mirrors. The original thirteen colonies, and their additions over the first half of the nineteenth century, accomplished this by excluding from "citizenship" (in the Athenian definition) all those who were different.

Fewer class differences prevailed among white males in the American nineteenth century than in the Old World or the Latin countries to the south, precisely because "others" were shunted away or separated from the mainstream. Along with slavery, there was the destruction, in one form or another, of a diverse or heterogeneous Native American population, indentured poor whites, the slotting of recently arrived immigrants at the bottom of the ladder, and the exclusion from suffrage of women and frequently of non-property-owning citizens. The Constitution did not establish property requirements for suffrage, but many states did. Then, as now, except for the reforms of the mid-1960s, it was the states that determined electoral rules. At the beginning of the nineteenth century, thirteen of the sixteen existing states restricted voting rights to property owners or taxpayers, though most of those specific restrictions were rapidly abolished and most white males were allowed to vote.[11]

After Emancipation came segregation, more immigration, and growing accession to "citizenship": the rights to vote, to hold public office, to own property, to expanded public education, but again, with new forms of exclusion. Until the Great African American Migration during the first half of the twentieth century, northern cities all mostly resembled each other, because the differences were in the South. Even after World War I and the beginning of mass entries from Mexico, Californian and Texan urban centers were still "all the same" because the "differences" were in the countryside. They could only be witnessed in far-removed rural camps or urban ghettos. On occasion, once the First War ended and subsequently during Operation Wetback in the early fifties, the "differences" were shipped back to Mexico. The mass deportations often included US citizens who "looked" Mexican, largely because their parents *were* Mexican.

Visitors during those years and again today experienced the same sensation. The United States appeared to be as close to a classless society as any on earth. Mass consumption, housing, schooling, public spaces, higher education, sports, culture, and communication were the norm, in contrast to a highly differentiated Europe. Leon Trotsky's recollections of his months in New York before the Russian Revolution are symptomatic: "We rented an apartment in a workers' district, and furnished it on the installment plan. That apartment, at eighteen dollars a month, was equipped with all sorts of conveniences that we Europeans were quite unused to: electric lights, gas cooking-range, bath, telephone, automatic service-elevator, and even a chute for the garbage."[12] After World War II, the Old World's immensely successful welfare states created increasingly egalitarian societies, enhancing their own impression of sameness, albeit without the social mobility enjoyed by the United States until the 1980s. Yet if impressions of American uniformity were paramount and up to a point valid, they all sprang from and depended on an indispensable condition: that the observer only took into account whatever confirmed those impressions, and either ignored or dismissed anything else. It allowed everyone to emphasize the classless nature of American society. Seventy-five years on, the novelist Anurag Mathur from Bombay was equally amazed: "The business of living was made easy, so you could get on with doing more than surviving. Ye gods, the very phones worked. Food, drink, transportation, communication, housing, clothing, the essentials were cheap and easy."[13]

All one had to do was to focus exclusively on the strip malls, or the Levittowns, and on the similarities of dress, language, recreation, cultural production and enjoyment, and workplace. In order for the Levitts's homes to be built quickly—180 per week, when they began outside Manhattan—they were necessarily built the same. Everyone who labored on a "Taylorized" assembly line in Henry Ford's Michigan plants after 1914 was identical to everybody else and could all (eventually) purchase identical Model Ts. But if an observer directed his glance elsewhere (and beyond the obvious and visible), those Americans on Main Street or in *Leave It to Beaver* were terribly different from the sharecroppers—black and white—in the South in the first half of the twentieth century, or the African American and Latino slum-dwellers in the sixties or today.

Given the way market economies function, the Europeans, who until the 1950s managed without ethnic, racial, or even linguistic minorities concentrated in mid-size pockets of poverty, would with time be obliged to introduce immigrants from abroad. Capitalism demands those pockets, or what Marx called the industrial reserve army. In the long run, its existence is indispensable for the economic system. Initially Italians, then Turks and Yugoslavians, subsequently Spaniards and Portuguese, Arab inhabitants of the Maghreb, South Asia and the Caribbean, and finally sub-Saharan Africa, partially replicated the American system. By the end of the twentieth century, almost every wealthy country in the world, excepting Japan, boasted a similar social configuration. It combined relative middle-class *equality* among its light-skinned, strongly rooted, Christian-faith and national majority, with gaping or modest *inequality* regarding minorities of color, ethnic origin, religion, nationality, and legal status.

Superficially, the *status quo* in the United States seemed similar to Western Europe's. In fact, it diverged radically, and should encourage Americans to count their blessings. Ideally, no nation would willingly exclude between a fifth and a quarter of its members from the welfare enjoyed by all. But if this disgrace constitutes an unmovable fixture of modern capitalist societies, better the American option with all its shortcomings (exclude Americans, who can one day be included) than the European one (exclude foreigners, who will never be included; Algerians in France from the early sixties, Indians in Britain, and a reduced number of Turks in Germany after the turn of the century are exceptions). The United States, one of the world's *youngest* rich countries comprises, in its African American population, one of the world's *oldest* excluded minority, descended from seventeenth-century slavery. It is also one of the least "different" minorities among the rich countries, insofar as, despite discrimination, it comprises exclusively American citizens. That minority's characteristics, in contrast to Europe, for example, are more *diverse* than *different*, in the legal, religious, and cultural sense of the word.

Whatever myriad foreign authors have noted, the United States is, with India, Brazil, and the Democratic Republic of Congo, the world's most diverse nation: socially, regionally, ethnically, linguistically, and culturally. It is also the quintessential middle-class society: less than before, but for a longer period than any other, and the first of its kind. It continues to convey an impression of geographical sameness, of physical monotony, of endless, uninterrupted treaches of desert, mountains, plains, and rivers. Jean Baudrillard, the renowned French sociologist who fulfilled his necessary pilgrimage to the United States in the 1980s, got it just right: "Drive ten thousand miles across America on the road, and you will know more about this country than through all the social science institutes put together."[14] Along with Nabokov, the Indian novelist Mathur is our third foreigner to focus on cars, Americans, and distance: "The car in which they (his friends in college) moved seemed a little world in itself, racing silently through the night. No rattles erupted in the engine, no blasts of outside air made their vicious and victorious way through minute gaps. His ears began to feel numb in the unaccustomed silence."[15]

Unlike Tocqueville's obsession with equality in the land he began touring in 1831, Baudrillard perceived everything in the United States tending toward equality, but also to authenticity and diversity. Possessing and adequately managing these two occasionally contradictory attributes is no easy chore. Nearly two decades into the twenty-first century, many Americans wonder if the goal is still attainable or if the country's earlier achievement is sustainable. The numbers are discomforting. A first glimpse at why Americans are worried, and should be, at least as far as maintaining high levels of equality, is worth interjecting here, especially insofar as there appears to be a correlation between more equal countries and happier ones.[16]

According to one measure based on the Gini coefficient and before taxes, the year of American society's broadest *income* inequality during the twentieth century and the start of the twenty-first was 1930, as the Great Depression got underway.[17] That moment was also the worst from the perspective of *wealth* inequality. Before then, the situation was not disastrous. The end of World War I brought a distribution of income and wealth that somewhat corrected the excesses of the Gilded Age. From 1930 onward, matters improved until 1970, which together with 1945, was the year of greatest *equality* in the United States. By 1975, American before-tax income inequality began to rise and nearly reached Depression-like levels in 2009: the year of the Great Recession.[18] This evolution tends to confirm French economist Thomas Piketty's thesis, whereby high inequality is the "normal" state of affairs for modern capitalism, except when vast swaths of wealth are destroyed by war (World War I and II) or depression (1929 and after).

If during the first half of the nineteenth century all things and people mistakenly appeared alike to foreign inquisitors, today that impression is far stronger and superficially more justified. The acute mass nature of virtually everything in the United States during the years after World War II inevitably produced a banality of daily existence. Most consumption goods and services became available to the entire population. Again, to all *included* "citizens," as defined before, and not in the fifties and sixties, for example to blacks in Mississippi or the projects in Chicago, nor Mexican-Americans in south Texas. Consequently, through the 1980s, the entire universe of Americans representing a significant majority of the population (except the excluded ones, at any given time) ate the same food, dressed in the same fashion, drove the same cars, watched the same movies, resided in the same type of home, took the same vacations, spent hours viewing the same TV shows and news programs, and listened to the same music. However much foreigners decried this, and certain Americans denied it, there was (and still is) a great deal of truth to it.

Even as intelligent, sophisticated, and at the time sympathetic an observer as Jean-Paul Sartre fell into this trap, aided, it must be said, by the vicissitudes of wartime. He marveled at what he saw: "Life is so standardized here that I found no significant difference between the menus of the luxury restaurants and the canteens. In restaurants, you pay mostly for the cutlery, the service and the atmosphere, but no matter where you go you find, whether it is in the 'automats' or the dining room of the great hotels, the same green peas whose color is so garish that you think they were hand-painted, the same unsalted white beans which are served in little dishes, the same brown and odd-looking gravy; it is semi-sweet, semi-salty and they spread it on a refrigerated piece of beef, and especially the same canned foods Heinz provides to all of America—its fifty-seven varieties of canned foods allow it play a great role as equalizer. To finish up, the worker, just like his boss, eats a big piece of sponge cake with cream or an 'ice cream,' they drink the same chlorinated ice water and the same bad coffee."[19]

The gradual process of inclusion of the excluded extended to every realm of life. Music is a good example and worth mentioning, regardless of how often it has been documented by other writers. As African Americans began to slowly enter the country's social, economic, and cultural mainstream after World War II, whites not only began to read Baldwin, Richard Wright, and the Harlem Renaissance writers. They started listening to jazz and blues. Then, black music started penetrating white musicians' rhythms and lyrics. Elvis Presley was the best-known case, but neither the only nor the earliest one. Soon there was no longer just black or white music, but also the combination of both—US syncretism, I might name it—which rapidly became dominant in American society. Before, Americans, whether part of or removed from the main body of society, did not sing or listen to the same songs. After the fifties, a slow and partial convergence occurred and continued.

The Motown explosion sealed the deal, at least to the extent of black production entering the white music industry. Once again, if we set aside those left out(side), the similarities among those inside grew remarkably. A parallel process has been underway for the past thirty years or so with Latino music. As Hispanics slowly joined the mainstream of American society, their music began to fuse with previous tunes and topics, from the Miami Sound Machine to Shakira, Ricky Martin, and Marc Anthony today. *Despacito* became a hit in the United States non-Latino establishment when Justin Bieber appropriated it.

It should have surprised no one that in the eyes of the foreign beholder, this homogeneity sublimated an underlying diversity, which until very recently overlapped with exclusion, whose victims were by definition invisible. Dickens and Tocqueville were well aware of slavery and were horrified by it. They were equally conscious of the existence and attrition of Native American communities. But they were unable to engage with African American slaves or Native American peoples (Tocqueville's *Two Weeks in the Wilderness* with what was left of the Iroquois nation was a brief exception) nor consider the diversity they represented. It was much too alien for him to fathom, although his more than fifty pages on "The present day state and the probable future of the three races which live in the territory of the United States" are remarkably insightful, albeit on occasion odious or simply mistaken.[20]

An analogous phenomenon occurs today. The European or Latin American visitor to the American heartland, or its more cosmopolitan shores, knows well what percentage of the population is of Hispanic origin. He or she is even familiar with the fanciful notion whereby some observers refer to the expansion of Latino culture in the United States as a type of *reconquista*. But only rarely will they devote a few days or nights to the Salvadoran neighborhoods of the Mission district in San Francisco, the Ecuadorean corners of Los Angeles, the Mexican barrios in Houston, or the Honduran ones in Queens. The travelers from abroad inevitably focus on the uniformity of everything else, to the detriment of the heterogeneous social, cultural, and economic landscapes inaccessible to the naked (extraneous) eye. As recently as 2012, in one of the more thoughtful and substantive travelogues published by a foreign visitor, Dutch historian and journalist Geert Mak remarked, "The very thing we Europeans deplore has been a great plus point to the

American traveller since the 1950s: wherever you stop, the rooms in a Holiday Inn and the taste of a McDonald's are precisely the same. The consistency and uniformity of the product—its dullness, if you like—, are fundamental components of the formula."[21] Maybe the non-travelers, those who have lived years in the United States, are more susceptible to the nuances involved. Witness the Mexican novelist Carlos Fuentes, who lived in Washington, DC, as a child, but also in dozens of universities until his late seventies: "American space imposes a series of generalizations about uniformity, emptiness, the immense and tedious plains, ignorance and the lack of information, provincialism . . . . But all of this becomes an incentive to search for anything to deny the cliché."[22]

Inequality, for more and more

None of these traits of "sameness" are absent from other rich countries, or even from the large middle-class contingents of many poorer ones. They just took hold first, faster, and more prominently in the United States. Until 2016, 1970 was the last year in which wages or household income grew along with productivity and the economy as a whole.[23] After 1970, salaries for the large majority of Americans stagnated, even if the economy continued to expand. The proportion of income corresponding to labor fell gradually but consistently. The share of income of the top 1 percent of society increased; that of the lowest 20 percent shrank. Today, the United States "has the most unequal distribution of after-tax income in the world for people under 60," according to Peter Temin's *The Vanishing Middle Class*. By one measure, the American middle class received 62 percent of national income in 1970, and 43 percent in 2014.[24] The era of the great, white, American, and unique middle class came to an end around 1980. Figure 1.1 illustrates this trend unequivocally.[25] The year the richest 1 percent of Americans received the smallest share of national income was 1976; the highest, 2012 and rising. The year the bottom half of Americans received the largest share of national income was 1968; the lowest, 2012 and dropping. Conversely the bottom 50 percent of the population received its highest share in 1968 and the lowest in 2012 with: 12 percent.

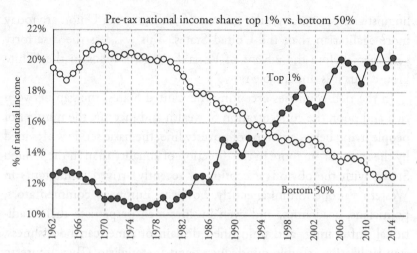

FIGURE 1.1. Shares of total pre-tax income 1963–2014

Source: Piketty, Saez, and Zucman. "Distributional National Accounts: Methods and Estimates for the United States." NBER. December 15, 2016. https://www.nber.org/papers/w22945.

The trend toward consolidation of the middle class and the ensuing onslaught of uniformity emerged differently on the western side of the Atlantic, but in the long term, convergence on both sides was the rule. The main difference can be found in Tocqueville's previously quoted quip whereby all of America's inhabitants were born equal, instead of eventually becoming so. By the 1960s much of Western Europe, Canada, Japan, and a smidgeon of other countries had become mass-consumption, middle-class societies. Some of them had possibly become so just before World War II, although the Great Depression masked previous progress. Television, the automobile, jeans, and rock 'n' roll invaded and spread throughout those societies very much like in the United States, often flagrantly mimicking the American precursor. The difference, however, lay in historical origins and process. Few in the mid-nineteenth century commented on French, British, or German "ordinariness," nor marveled at the degree of equality prevalent in those societies.

Hence, perhaps, today's contradictory evolution. Thanks to the European welfare state, to working-class conquests over the past hundred years, and to initially far more homogeneous societies (ethnically, linguistically, culturally), the nations of the European Union are today more egalitarian than the United States. This was less the case forty years ago, before the advent of Ronald Reagan's 1980s in the White House, but it is undeniable now.

In the rich countries excepting the United States, the gap between rich and poor, the concentration of wealth and income, the number of people living below any type of poverty line, the basic services provided by the state, all are more in the direction of equality than in the United States, with the obvious exception of recently arrived immigrants in Western Europe. Simultaneously, however, European commentators, politicians, academics, and even businessmen perpetuate their traditional, infuriating, and unjustified disdain of American boorishness, standardization, simple-mindedness, and materialism. They refuse to acknowledge that Europe's impressive achievements in social welfare and mass culture took place decades after they occurred in the United States, as the French anthropologist Claude Lévi-Strauss discovered after living in New York during World War II: "We sensed that all these relics (architectural, fashion and historical) were being assaulted by a mass culture that was about to crush and bury them—a mass culture that, already far advanced in America, would reach Europe a few decades later."[26] If anything, their societies resemble America more and more each day. They value their egalitarianism, which is largely consensual or non-partisan, at the same time as largely despising or mocking the American version.

It is as if they never resigned themselves to the fact that the Americans arrived at the promised land of a middle-class society well before Europe. German sociologist Werner Sombart calculated, with data from the end of the nineteenth century, that US working-class monetary incomes were two to three times higher than German salaries, decades after the great German migration. The cost of living in the two countries, for workers, was roughly the same.[27] The Europeans never fully accepted that such a society is the promised land. In their definition, that society and its welfare state are perceived largely in political or ideological terms: as Christian Democratic or Socialist, based on solidarity, equality, and the welfare state, rather than sociologically.

Perhaps this is due to the fact that the notion of a middle-class society is still partly alien to the Europeans. In America it means that class differences are narrower, and that everyone aspires to be something else and better, rather than continue to be a worker, employee, or successful professional . . . blessed with better wages, benefits, and social security. The political reflection of this state of mind was evident from the onset of the twentieth century, when a perplexed Sombart lamented the American socialists' approach to labor activism: "Now it is not infrequent that a 'social democrat' who is demanding the overthrow of the social order simultaneously has the picture of a fat sinecure hovering continually before his eyes. He is unselfish enough to be able to preach to his followers in the evening about the emptiness of the prevailing social order and the necessity for a Socialist movement, while in the afternoon immediately preceding that evening the boss of one of the major parties offered him the candidacy for a lucrative electoral office or promised him a fat proportion of the spoils of the next election victory."[28] This might have also been said about socialists elsewhere, but largely it wasn't: Sombart was undoubtedly referring to the lightly "ideologized" version of American socialism. Not every visitor resigned themselves to the inexistence of socialism in the United States, though. Liang Qichao, one of the most influential Chinese writers of his time, concluded in 1903: "I look at the slums of New York and think with a sigh that socialism cannot be avoided."[29]

Materialism forever

After uniformity, a second notable trait often cited by foreign authors is money, or the birth of *homo oeconomicus*, whom many visitors considered to be the quintessential American. Obsessed with wealth, driven by the search for monetary success, measuring success only in relative economic terms, materialistic to a degree unheard of elsewhere in the world, inhabitants of the United States are viewed by visitors, analysts, and pundits as a peculiar breed. They care about nothing but becoming, remaining, or aspiring to be rich. José Martí, the father of Cuban independence, lamented that "American laws have given the North a high degree of prosperity, and also a high degree of corruption. They have monetized everything to make it prosperous. Prosperity at what cost?"[30]

This theme surfaces time and again in virtually all of the writings of travelers to or observers of the United States since the early nineteenth century, and perhaps never as much as today, with a businessman in the White House. Many Americans, probably a majority, see Donald Trump as an anomaly. Foreigners who have dwelt on the American penchant for ostentatious wealth and its subsequent equivalence with achievement and happiness, however, view the current president as a logical, though regrettable, consequence of this penchant. From this perspective, Trump simply verbalizes what all Americans think. He flaunts what they all believe, even if on occasion they feel too embarrassed to express it. When he appoints a cabinet whose net worth is far superior to that of any previous administration, and its members brashly transfer their life-style and habits to government, Europeans, Asians, and Latin Americans conclude that this is the true self of the American character. It demonstrates the eccentric but deplorable nature of that character. They are not surprised: just bemused. Witness Bertolt Brecht, the German poet and playwright exiled in Hollywood during World War II: "Remarkable how in this place a universally depraving, cheap prettiness prevents people from living in a halfway cultivated fashion, i.e. living with dignity . . . . Mercantilism produces everything, but in the form of saleable goods, so art is ashamed of its usefulness, but not of its exchange value."[31] It might be worth adding that the extraordinary author of *The Three Penny Opera* did not fare well professionally during his American sojourn.

If these stereotypes were accurate, two large universes that should not get along are Mexicans and Americans. Their relations have been studied to death where and when they coincide inside the United States, but much less so, if at all, in Mexico. Most people ignore the fact that over one million Americans reside in Mexico, more than in any other country in the world. If Americans are the most materialistic people on earth, and Mexicans among the least, it would stand to reason that their encounter, in any case on Mexican soil, would be uncomfortable, if not downright hostile. Not at all.

They come from all over the United States, not just the coasts or Texas. They lean toward middle or retirement age, are well off but rarely wealthy, and are clustered in a dozen or so small or mid-size Mexican communities: San Miguel de Allende, Ajijic, Mazatlán, Guadalajara,

Puerto Vallarta. They blend in with the landscape and the people of those communities, which are anything but gated. There are virtually no incidents of any type involving them. They are good neighbors, friendly hosts, generous donors to local causes, mixing in with other "natives." Nothing in them replicates the caricature of the ugly American: to the contrary. Mexicans like them, respect them, and get along with them. Materialistic? Uncouth? Blustery and bullying? Nothing of the sort. For what it's worth, this is a real-life, real-time experiment that gives the lie to the wealth-seeking, self-interested stereotype. All of this in a country that is known for its hospitability, but not so much for its open-mindedness and lack of resentment. Mexicans may not always enjoy the presence of certain categories of American visitors—spring-breakers or coke-heads, for example—but even these are welcomed and appreciated.

The more complex question is whether the over-valuation of success and material riches is specifically American, or whether it reflects the underlying mechanics of two indispensable components of capitalism, or market economies. These are the accumulation of capital, and the expansion of a middle class large enough to consume what the capitalists produce and market. Is conspicuous consumption an American phenomenon or simply part of modern society? Is middle-class extravagance—whereby everything is gauged by the possession of luxuries transformed into basic necessities—exclusively the centerpiece of contemporary American life? Or does it reflect typical middle-class existence itself, both in wealthy countries with a broad middle class, and in poorer nations with a narrower one? Are Marx's memorable words at the beginning of *Capital*—*De te fabula narratur*—addressed to all nations and workers of the world, valid for all middle classes, in addition to the United States? And is the arrogant repulsion felt by the spokespeople, businessmen, politicians, and intellectuals of other successful economies a consequence of their hopes and fears, dismay or despair, with regard to a future that can be plainly discerned across the Atlantic or below the Rio Grande? Witness a Japanese historian, who had studied in the United States, in 1925: "The United States is a materialistic country. It seems like a gathering place for money-grubbers with neither high ideals nor moral behavior."[32] Needless to say, not all foreign and knowledgeable observers of the American scene shared these opinions. Jorge Luis Borges, the great Argentine writer and poet, saw things differently: "I found America the friendliest, most forgiving and most generous nation I had ever visited. We South Americans tend to think in terms of convenience, whereas people in the United States approach things ethically."[33]

Since Tocqueville first took note of the aforementioned peculiarity in 1832, the reason Americans have equated wealth with success was possibly that affluence was within reach. Other forms of socially acknowledged achievement—nobility, military prowess, religious rank— were either less attainable or not gratifying. Given the high degree of social mobility available to white American males since the beginning of the nineteenth century, prosperity was achievable for many. In aspirational terms, it could be seen as open to all: I myself might not be rich today, or even tomorrow, but my children can be, or I will be some time from now (even though this may no longer be true). It seemed far more reasonable to identify success with a goal that could be accomplished, and that was realized by many around one, than to correlate it with social standing, cultural recognition, or professional performance. This was not especially materialistic. It was ordinary math, convenience, and pure pragmatism. As a Chinese scholar reflected in 1926, "Americans . . . are the first among nations in their emphasis on money. Even when friends haggle there is a commercial motive . . . this is due to their love of money."[34] They are this way because they can be; money matters because other standards for success are unavailable or irrelevant. Money is accessible to enough wannabes for everyone to dream of it.

Did Americans define wealth as the only scorecard for success? Not really. Tocqueville realized that material prowess was a singular American standard for measuring advancement: "Love of wealth is at the bottom of all that Americans do."[35] He explained it by the absence of hierarchical rank or any type of aristocratic structures. With time, however, it became clear that many other metrics also mattered. By the second half of the nineteenth century, the United States had created a professional meritocracy, whose late birth perhaps explained why Tocqueville did not detect it. It functioned not only in business, but also in government and the military, in civil society, academia, and later in culture: sports, entertainment, the arts. Like all meritocracies, despite its best intentions, it rapidly proved highly elitist; merit mattered only among those who possessed it. The "best" attended the best schools and universities, where their parents had also graduated. It is interesting to note how scholars familiar with China's millenary Mandarin bureaucracy idealized the American one, as late as the mid-1920s. Xu Zhenkeng knew the American university system well, having studied at Cornell, but could nevertheless not avoid comments like the following: "Students with motivation and ability are admitted regardless of race, age or sex . . . . They are white, black, red and yellow . . . . All students are treated the same, without distinction."[36]

Meritocracy, mobility, or both?

At first, most of the meritocracy's members were mainly from Ivy League universities, and that meritocracy in general reigned supreme over certain professions—law, medicine, the sciences, even sports—and was almost always, at least indirectly, indexed to wealth. One was, indeed, a better lawyer, doctor, or engineer if one made more money; and better lawyers, doctors, or engineers did make more money. Granted, some dentists, scientists, or Hollywood directors have always been more accomplished and acknowledged than others. And the mythically "equal opportunity" American meritocracy was and is today more than ever class-, race-, and gender-biased. But it is a *complement* of the country's proverbial obsession with wealth, not simply its reflection.

Lastly, the American pursuit of wealth and its materialistic ethos cannot be dissociated from the notion of social mobility. Americans seek financial gain because . . . they can. The frontier in the nineteenth century, immigration since the 1850s, the Great Migration to the North in the twentieth century, the phenomenal expansion of the middle class after World War II, the myths and realities of self-made magnates for two hundred years: all contributed to the perceived quasi-certainty of eventually achieving prosperity. Low-income Americans have occasionally opposed tax increases on the rich, because they believe they may one day be rich themselves and have to pay those taxes. Polls vary on this matter, but a long-term Gallup survey of Americans' opinion of whether government should or should not redistribute wealth by heavy taxes on the rich tends to confirm this view, at least at certain moments in time.[37] In 2011, 2008, 1998, and 1939, a majority considered that they should not. Americans in all walks of life seek monetary improvement because—rightly or wrongly, at different points in time—they deem it accessible, unlike other forms of social escalation.

In the United States, one cannot become a lord or a member of the French Academy, since there are neither lords nor academies of this sort. It thus makes a great deal of sense to value more what is feasible, rather than what is non-existent. As Spanish-born, Harvard-based philosopher George Santayana put it once, "The American talks about money, because that is the symbol and measure, he has at hand for success, intelligence and power . . . ."[38] Whether this assessment is accurate or simply aspirational is less important than its ubiquitous implications as an idea. Until recently, Americans have been largely convinced that theirs is a truly mobile society, where anyone can get ahead, become affluent, famous, or powerful. Since the mid-nineteenth century, there have been sufficient demonstrations of this for it to appear true and sensible, and certainly difficult to disprove.

It is no less true that the expectations and real-life consequences of social mobility can often be attributed by social scientists to other factors, not only to "the facts." Moreover, evidence abounds to the effect that whatever mobility existed before the 1970s has since then been consistently eroded. Nonetheless, hoping to attain wealth appears to be a more credible and feasible goal than any other for a greater number of Americans. Thus, the propensity for wealth-seeking constitutes a much more rational form of behavior than many non-Americans consider it to be. To them this is typical American crassness, exemplified as never before by Donald Trump. But in fact it is less pervasive and needs to be more historically and culturally contextualized than many would have it.

The meritocratic and social mobility explanations must also be placed in context. Today's Western European Social or Christian democratic societies are as upwardly mobile as the United States, some perhaps more so. This was certainly not the case at the end of the nineteenth century or through the first half of the twentieth. Long and Ferrie, two contemporary economists, using longitudinal data for the nineteenth century in the United States and Britain, find that the former indeed had more intergenerational mobility than Britain.[39] Despite the enormous social gains by the industrial working class in Germany, France,

Britain, and the Scandinavian countries before World War I, and then again after World War II, scarcity of labor in the United States and the possibility of opening and shutting the immigration spigot almost at will allowed wages to rise more rapidly. Equally important, it rendered viable the exit from the working class; "becoming" something else was imaginable: rich, among other dreams. Social mobility was a foundational myth in the United States. Like all effective ideological beliefs, it required a relative degree of substance and confirmation for it to function.

Figure 1.2 illustrates the notable comparison. In 1940, more than 90 percent of Americans at 30 or 40 years of age earned more than their parents at the same age;[40] by 1985 only 50 percent did. The number dropped considerably by the seventies and even more in recent times.[41] According to one study, "men in their 30s today earn less than did those of their father's generation (men who were in their 30s in the 1970s)."[42] In 2004, the inflation-adjusted incomes of men in their 30s were 12 percent less, on average, than the incomes of men in their

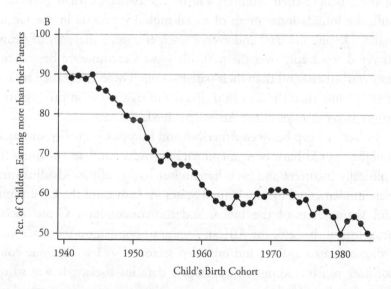

FIGURE 1.2. Social Mobility 1940–1985

Source: Chetty et al. "The Fading American Dream: Trends in Absolute Income Mobility since 1940." NBER. December 8, 2016. https://www.nber.org/papers/w22910.

father's generation at the same age.[43] The crushing obstacles millennials face today when seeking to purchase a home bears witness to this evolution. While in theory they have the same access to mortgages and consumer credit that meant so much for their parents' and grandparents' middle-class status, student loans and overall difficulties have complicated matters for them.

A similar process took place elsewhere, even though some scholars harbor doubts regarding the accuracy of international comparisons. Conclusions about trends in intergenerational mobility and comparisons across countries must be read with caution. An OECD study about the contemporary situation today found nonetheless: "A growing number of economic studies have found that the United States stands out as having less, not more, intergenerational mobility than do Canada and several European countries. American children are more likely than other children to end up in the same place on the income distribution as their parents. Moreover, there is emerging evidence that mobility is particularly low for Americans born into families at the bottom of the earnings or income distribution." Americans know this: two-thirds of them believe their children *will* not be better off than they are.[44] Still, the foundational myth of social mobility persists in the United States. Despite the data and everyday experience, a majority of people surveyed repeatedly over the past thirty years continue to believe that they *can* be better off than their parents, even if objectively they are not. It takes more than three or four decades of stagnation in this regard to trump two centuries of the American creed.

In fact, the gap between American and European equality and social mobility would have been incomparably wider until recent times if a politically incorrect and even hateful but statistically valid adjustment were implemented for the United States. At least until the Civil Rights and Voting Acts of the 1960s, and the concomitant Great Society programs of that era, the African American population remained such a discriminated against and excluded sector of society that one could consider not including it in aggregate data for society. It was so oppressed, at least until the 1950s, by acute segregation in housing, education, transportation, and elections, through federal law in some cases, or by Jim Crow measures in others, that making believe it was part of the national average seems unreal. For the first twenty-five years of its existence, Social Security was not available to most blacks in the South. Also in the South, Medicare and Medicaid were *de facto* inaccessible to many African Americans, since both assistance programs depended on states channeling federal funds to finance them. If as recently as 1992 a major scholar like Andrew Hacker continued to regret the existence of "Two Nations" in the United States, pretending that there was only one "statistical nation" before the sixties seems unreal.

The breadth of the difference in employment, incomes, educational levels, crime, and incarceration (then and now) between races is so great that any statistical amalgamation was unavoidably fallacious. It dragged down the "white averages," distorting national ones. If one compared the white middle class of the United States with the European one—at least until before the Europeans' own Great Migration from the Maghreb and Sub-Saharan Africa—American superiority in matters of equality and mobility was more notable. The reason for this was nothing to be proud of. It represented the inexorable consequence of slavery and of the realities of race relations and public policy since the Civil War. Even now, some figures are astounding, and outrageous. In Detroit, which in 1960 was one of the five richest cities in America, today one-half of the black population (in a city that elected its first black mayor in 1974 and is overwhelmingly African American) is unemployed.[45]

An obvious link exists between social mobility and inequality. The greater the inequality in a given society, the more difficult it is for someone to jump from one decile of the income scale to another. As the United States was a more equal society than most European countries until the 1960s, it was more upwardly mobile. In addition, the memory of mobility dating back to the birth of the republic led its inhabitants to retain their unbounded faith in the American dream. This fact explained part of the obsession with material well-being. As American social mobility declines, the fixation with money may also wither, if not disappear entirely. The United States may not become more spiritual, but it could move away from its traditional materialism, as one of the reasons for its emergence during the nineteenth century dissipates. What's more, among many younger Americans the very idea of accumulating personal or national wealth is incompatible with their hopes for a healthier environment, controlling climate change, and even limiting population growth.

The crassness argument must similarly be placed in a historical context. If before there was greater mobility in the United States than elsewhere, then people without the generational, educational, and cultural background one might expect in the upper reaches of society would nonetheless reach those higher echelons. In Britain, if one's parents and ancestors had all belonged to the upper deciles, and few, if any, newcomers had ever penetrated these higher social strata, it would be unusual if their children and forefathers did not possess similar manners, knowledge, and views of the world. Not always: the British in the mid-1800s celebrated the advent of the self-made man who at least in the first generation could have been referred to by aristocrats as "deplorable." The same would be true in France or Germany, and also in Mexico and Brazil, on a smaller scale. But if in the United States there were a vast number of recent entrants into the more prosperous cohorts and there were broader opportunities to escalate from one to another, the background of the newly arrived was not going to be the same as in Europe. It would inevitably resemble, for the first and perhaps second generation, the circumstances of the previously occupied cohort. Many readers may not have ever heard of James Dean today, but of the three films he made before his tragic and premature death, one of them—*Giant*—marvelously expressed this myth in American culture. His screen figure, Jett Rinks, behaved the way he did, despite all his millions (in 1950s prices), because his parents were who they were. There were no Jett Rinks in Belgium, so they were unlikely to show up at a party drunk, loud-mouthed, and uncouth. At least to foreigners, Rinks appeared as the most visible—and obnoxious—of Americans, leading them to believe that all were like him.

Which society is better depends on where each person would prefer to live. Some might fancy a more middle-class, rough-around-the-edges, and *nouveau-riche* one, where many of the new members of that rustic middle class are sons and daughters of sharecroppers, industrial workers, first-generation immigrants, or even grandchildren of the enslaved (in the mid-1900s). Other may desire a society where mobility is reduced, but whose more distasteful features are not as visible. This is in the end a personal choice. If today, as more and more economists accept the notion—often referred to as the Great Gatsby curve—whereby greater inequality leads to less intergenerational mobility, then the

United States is headed in the direction of Europe just after World War II or before the Depression.

In sum, the United States became a middle-class society long before any other nation, even including excluded minorities, let alone excepting them. This vast middle class, with low levels of inequality and high levels of social mobility, made a traditional welfare state, along Western European lines, essentially unnecessary. But after the mid-seventies, this equilibrium came tumbling down. Inequality increased, social mobility decreased, and the safety net other societies had woven did not exist. This is where America finds itself today: no longer an overwhelmingly middle-class society, but devoid of the full-fledged welfare state the other rich countries possess.

2

How exceptional is American exceptionalism?

AFTER UNIFORMITY AND THE obsession with money, a third defining trait of the United States lies in the notion of American "exceptionalism." Most frequently assigned by foreign observers as an unmistakable and irritating feature, exceptionalism is mostly self-designated. Thinkers, politicians, and poets attribute it to themselves and to the republic. Tocqueville, Bryce, and many others did underscore the exceptions which made the American Union different—better or worse than other, analogous nations. As the French writer phrased it: "The position of the Americans is therefore quite exceptional, and it may be believed that no other democratic people will ever be placed in a similar one."[1]

But this is fundamentally a home-baked peculiarity, and it is largely self-deluding, though no doubt immensely self-gratifying. It is not the key to American success, but rather a fictional product of that success. Instead of exceptionalism, which was either false or highly partial during the first 150 years of independence the proper terms might be power and success. The outstanding fact of the American saga, the basis for thinking in those terms, at least in the twentieth and twenty-first centuries, has been its exceptional success.

Although the *concept* of American exceptionalism dates back to the very foundation of the republic, the *term* was apparently first used only in the 1920s; although associated with "manifest destiny" it can be traced to one John O'Sullivan in 1845.[2] According to some historians, the words "American exceptionalism" were originally coined by the

American Communist Party (CP) while translating Stalin's condemnation of CP member Jay Lovestone. He was excommunicated for his heretical belief that the United States could consider itself invulnerable to Marxist laws of history "thanks to its natural resources, industrial capacity, and absence of rigid class distinctions." There was no such thing as American exceptionalism, Stalin decreed. Anecdotes notwithstanding, exceptionalism is as American a notion as the prairies and Disneyland. It is a homegrown description, especially complex and difficult to unravel. It is also an especially disconcerting one, as English-American historian Tony Judt warned: "The illusion of American exceptionalism is one of the more dangerous myths in which this country has wallowed, separating itself in its own eyes from everyone else."[3] The "exceptions" that constitute the basis for sustaining it, whether nearly two centuries ago or simply in decades past, may no longer be valid today. Similarly, new, contemporary "exceptions" that may justify "exceptionalism" seem less than fully warranted.

The idea of American exception springs from independence, the country's establishment as a republic; the emergence of a representative democracy including individual freedoms, particularly of expression; the rule of law; immigration as a bottomless source of labor, renewal, and diversity; the religious notion of a chosen people; and the infinite supply of land, at least for the first century of nationhood. The initial version soon acquired a narrative. It lasted for the first hundred or so years of the nation's existence. The narrative consisted in an inward-looking society; a state devoid in principle of foreign "entanglements"; a free-spirited, unfettered market economy generating untold wealth and prosperity; individual freedoms gradually extended to all citizens; and a desire to be an example upheld to, but not imposed upon, the world.

The exception subsequently underwent an update, as the country became one of four big powers after World War I, and one of just two super-powers after World War II. The story then posited the United States as a more successful, powerful, freer, and more ethical nation than any other in dealing with the world, although perhaps that overall success as a nation only began after the Civil War. It perceived itself as more altruistic than those peers in its treatment of weaker, poorer, or less favored countries. It was imbued by its creation and destiny with the mission of extending its model across the world. Finally, as America simultaneously won the Cold War and lost its need to fulfill its self-appointed mission abroad, exceptionalism produced a new chronicle. It exhibited the United States as a more perfectible, responsible, and responsive model, of greater attraction to the rest of the world than others, no longer only through its military might alone, but also thanks to its so-called soft power, that is, language, culture, mores, ideas, technology, and a "creed"— whatever that precisely meant. We will return to the notion of the creed later.

I only witnessed close-up the two final stages of this narrative, although I became distantly familiar with the previous stages, intellectually and academically. College in the United States was one prism through which I viewed the American claim of exceptionalism; a typical Washington, DC, think tank was another. But power up close is different. I must confess that in dealings with US officials between the late '70s and the mid-2000s, American exceptionalism was never an issue. My father, with whom I worked closely at the time he was foreign minister, dealt with four secretaries of state between 1979 and 1982: Cyrus Vance, Edmund Muskie, Alexander Haig, and George Schultz. When I was foreign minister, I coincided only with Colin Powell, between 2001 and 2003, though Condoleezza Rice, with whom I dealt extensively as national security advisor, later became secretary. I do not recall any of them ever justifying, explaining, or rejecting an American foreign policy stance on issues as varied as Cuba, Nicaragua, El Salvador, Argentina, Venezuela, or Iraq, let alone Mexico, on the basis of American exceptionalism. Everything rested on the interests of the United States, occasionally on American interpretation of other countries' best interests, and rarely on their government's sheer power. Powell was especially gracious and noble in these matters, always seeking to be as respectful of Mexico and its officials as I was of him and his government. I recall our two years working together with great fondness and gratitude. Did other US foreign policy makers before or after invoke exceptionalism in their day-to-day dealings with colleagues? I doubt it. I take away both from my up-close and indirect experience a sense of "*pour la gallerie*." American exceptionalism is for academics, public opinion formation, and grand-standing, not for conducting the business of government. At least not at the higher echelons of government, though I admit that at lower and technical levels this might not necessarily be the same. A self-serving conclusion? Maybe, but one I am fully convinced of, at least until the Trump years.

Like all classifications by time-lines, the four stages described above can be challenged, endowed with greater sophistication, or broken down into a larger number of phases. They nonetheless serve our purposes. Through them, I can sift through various historical examples. They seek to show how much is true and how much is ideologically fabricated—i.e. factually false, but believed to be accurate—as the United States hurtled toward its truly exceptional status: a civilization in its own right. A number of the following discussions are age-old. In others, the contrast between the abstract belief in exceptionalism and the concrete reality on the ground may be less familiar to Americans, though not necessarily to non-Americans or to disenfranchised Americans who lived or suffered through it.

The founding and birth pains

The greatest rebuttal to American exceptionalism as defined in the foundational documents and world-view at the moment of the republic's creation was slavery (I will delve into its enduring impact in Chapter 8). During the eighteenth century, three times as many slaves as whites entered the thirteen colonies and the newly independent nation.[4] It is difficult to underestimate the importance of slavery to cotton or of cotton to the United States' economy and to the first Industrial Revolution in England. Slavery was ontologically crucial to American capitalism over its first three-quarters of a century. By 1820, as Britain's Industrial Revolution was well underway, cotton represented 32 percent of all US exports. Until 1890, it remained the number one export.[5] Thirty years after the Civil War, the United States still produced half the world's cotton.

As Marx insightfully noted at that time: "The cultivation of Southern export crops, i.e. cotton, tobacco, sugar, etc., by slaves is only profitable as long as it is conducted on a mass scale by large gangs of slaves and in wide areas of naturally fertile soil requiring only simple labor."[6] In addition, by 1861, when he wrote this, just after the bombing of Fort Sumner, states like Maryland, Virginia, and South Carolina had

become *slave-raising* states, that badly needed markets to sell their
"wares." In a dispatch from London in October of 1861, Marx quotes a
certain Senator Toombs from a state in the newly born Confederacy as
"strikingly formulating the economic law that necessitates the constant
expansion of the slave territory: In fifteen years more, without a great
increase in slave territory, either the slaves must be permitted to flee
from the whites, or the whites must flee from the slaves."[7]

This entailed a fundamental clash between the alleged exceptionalism
of the founding of the republic and an economic system which for
the first seventy-five years of that republic's existence congenitally
depended on a flagrant and widespread violation of that foundation's
very tenets. It was not only the South that depended on slavery; the
North's industrialization, its imports from Britain, the British textile
industry, even the destruction of Indian looms, all derived from the
slavery-driven cotton boom in the South. We will return to the proverbial "original sin" argument; for now suffice it to say if there was
any American exceptionalism among the North Atlantic nations at
that time, it consisted in the prevalence of an economy—North and
South—based on slavery. The violation was not limited to the initial
group of slave states—eight of the thirteen colonies—but extended to
the number of new slave states incorporated later into the Union and
to the economic expansion of the non-slave states.

This was not a secondary contradiction with the spirit of the
Constitution or the Bill of Rights. It lay at the very heart of the legal
and political scaffolding that held up the entire republican edifice.
Which is why people like Marx clearly understood that the arrangement of the 1787 Constitution was doomed from the start; the only
question was when, with time being the only variable. Fortunately the
blueprint and intentions of the Founders were not destroyed by the first
seventy-five years. The argument can be made that the Constitution's
true and valid consequences were not slavery and cotton, but what
came after: Emancipation and industrial capitalism. Absent Lincoln
and the Civil War, a modern economy may not have replaced slavery,
but that is what happened. The standard "exceptionalist" account of the
Founding is inadequate, but there is an element of truth to it.

The exclusion of women, Native Americans, Chinese immigrants,
and Mexican dwellers of conquered territories from most of the rights

afforded to white males also represented a basic flaw in the entire scheme
of things, and a new vulnerability in the optimistic view of American
exceptionalism at birth. They were not citizens, they did not have the
right to vote, often they could not own property. It did not represent,
however, an intrinsic cog in the economic system, once the land occupied by the original inhabitants had been confiscated. But the principle
of these exclusions was equally outrageous in the case of blacks. Nearly
two-thirds of the inhabitants of the territories comprising the new republic were denied the basic rights enshrined in the Declaration of
Independence, the Constitution, and the Bill of Rights. That this was
typical in other nations is true, though slavery was abolished by the
French Revolution in 1794, and in Britain by 1833. Either way, one of
the main rights these American majority-composing minorities were
deprived of was the right to vote.

Limiting suffrage to white males was part and parcel of the
restrictions applied to universal suffrage. As noted, the decision to establish conditions for voting was remanded to the states, and although
some accepted quasi-universal suffrage, many did not. Property-owning
and tax-paying conditions were imposed in many states, including
Massachusetts, Georgia, New Hampshire, New Jersey, and New York
where in 1790 less than 60 percent of white males had the right to vote.
According to the 1790 Census (the closest numbers available for the
1796 presidential election), 3.9 million people inhabited the country
at that time.[8] Estimates for 1796 reach 4.6 million. Of these, approximately seven hundred thousand were slaves, almost all of them in the
South. Somewhere near 1 million white males were eligible to vote. The
two contenders, John Adams and Thomas Jefferson together obtained
66,000 votes, approximately 7 percent of eligible voters.

This tiny turnout, however, amounted to an even smaller proportion of the total population of white males over 21: nearly 1.5 million.
Costa Rica today, for example, also has a population of roughly
5 million inhabitants; in its last presidential election, more than 2 million
voted.[9] American universal suffrage, often noted as a founding feature of American exceptionalism, was simply non-existent at the time.
Whether one accepts the most drastic estimates—i.e. the franchise
was limited to around 60 percent of white adult males—or the most
lenient—80 percent—the abyss with regard to universal suffrage was

enormous. John Adams, the first American president emanating from a contested election, was voted in by a minuscule minority of individuals residing in the former thirteen colonies and two new states. He received 35,000 votes. This was undoubtedly better than a monarchy, an emperor, or even a parliament elected through explicitly restricted suffrage, but a model of democracy, it was not.

Some political scientists argue that the presidential system designed by the Founders contains the true loadstone of American exceptionalism. They are right, undoubtedly, in that the institutional framework devised in 1783–7 was the first presidential system in the world. But very quickly, by the 1820s at the latest, all of the newly independent nations of Latin America, with the exception of Brazil, followed the American example. Today, the discussion over the comparative merits and disadvantages of presidential and parliamentary regimes continues, but it is perhaps exaggerated to buttress the entire notion of exceptionalism on a single institutional contrast, as important as it may have been originally.

The initial hundred years

In the narrative regarding the first century of American independent life, several further complications emerge. No foreign entanglements and an inward-looking republic consolidating its independence and gradually expanding to the west by extending its rule over the various, dispersed, Native Americans territories were perhaps not very noble quests, but did constitute an understandable ambition. Unfortunately, even this hardly corresponded to the facts. The young nation began its first war in 1801, against the so-called Barbary pirates in the Mediterranean. It declared war on the British in 1812 (not the other way around), and in 1823 expounded the Monroe Doctrine, which asserted that non-continental great powers should remove themselves from or cease their incursions into the Americas. Even after World War II, when the United Nations' Convention on Genocide was adopted in 1948, the United States entered an "understanding" with regard to the second article's reference to the "intent to destroy" a national, ethnical, racial, or religious group because it feared that it would apply to the Native American population, both east of the Mississippi (under Andrew Jackson) and west of it, after 1865.[10] Most significantly, during the nineteenth century, on at least four occasions the increasingly ambitious and muscular nation acquired or occupied territory, directly or not, in what we call Latin America today. It did so by force of arms, whatever justifications it claimed.

The first example lay in the Texan Secession from Mexico in 1836. It had been obvious to many Mexican observers—including those sent to Texas *ex professo* to survey the situation—that the central government in Mexico City held no authority nor was capable of exercising any control over the land now known as Texas. Similarly, every national government in Mexico at the time grasped that American settlers, led by Stephen Austin, were altering the demographics and politics of the northeastern part of what only fifteen years earlier had still been New Spain, with consequences extending to a sense of being deprived of their lands among the original Mexicans there today. In addition, as a recent study of the American empire suggests, "the decision of the Mexican government in 1829 to ban slavery altogether put a serious doubt over the whole scheme of colonization."[11] Without slavery there was no cotton cultivation; cotton was king in Texas too, which is why the Cotton Bowl is still played in Dallas. Lastly, many Mexicans then, and historians today, were convinced that President Andrew Jackson was actively encouraging the settlers, financing and arming them, hoping eventually to provoke secession, then annexation. Within ten years, both occurred.

If there existed willful intent on Washington's part or not, the fact is that by force of arms and thanks both to avoidable Mexican mistakes and inevitable weakness, the United States practically doubled its size. In 1848 Texas and California, Arizona, New Mexico, Utah and Colorado, as they are known today, were all seized from Mexico and brought into the Union. The march west, that laid the ground for the transcontinental railroad and the extension of the frontier past the Mississippi, was only possible because of the twin expansions of 1836 and 1847–8. The question is not whether this was ethically acceptable—obviously not, from a Mexican perspective—but whether these acts differed greatly from what the British, French, and Dutch were undertaking in Africa and Asia at the time. Could they be distinguished from previous colonial conquests by the same British, French, Spanish, or Portuguese? American exceptionalism emphasized the differences: annexation contrasted with conquest; self-defense against aggression should be distinguished from intentional subjugation; settlement was not the same as colonization. In the light of the facts, exceptionalism shone by its absence.

The same was true for Panama as well as for Cuba and Puerto Rico at the turn of the century. In both instances, the United States pursued highly successful and bold foreign adventures. None of the European colonial powers could have objected to or differentiated themselves from such behavior. Regarding Panama, after the French failure to build a canal, President Theodore Roosevelt, first through regular diplomacy, then by its gunboat version, arranged the secession of a group of pro-canal Colombians (Panama didn't yet exist). They promptly declared independence, received US diplomatic recognition, and signed the Hay-Bunau-Varilla Treaty granting Washington rights to build and administer the canal in perpetuity. *The New York Times* labeled the entire affair an "act of sordid conquest,"[12] which it was—but nothing that the French would not have attempted had they been able to. Again, the issue lay not in the moral or legal characteristics of the events and consequences, but whether it coincided with the tenets of American exceptionalism. It did not, unless one accepts the circular argument that America was exceptional because it believed in its manifest destiny, and it so believed . . . because it was exceptional.

Just before, it was Cuba and Puerto Rico's turn with the Philippines thrown in for good measure. Both Caribbean islands witnessed the emergence of powerful independence movements well before the end of the century. Spain would have probably disengaged sooner or later, with or without American support for the insurgents. But American support there was: "a lovely little war" as the Hearst papers labeled it. It permitted the United States to annex both territories after 1899 when the Spanish surrendered and withdrew. Scholars today harbor no doubts that the reason President McKinley involved his country was to submit Cuba to United States hegemony. Once again, there was nothing exceptional about Washington's conduct in these events.

Sufficient forces were dispatched, and different types of subterfuges were utilized ("Remember the Maine!"). Puerto Rico rapidly became a colony and later a commonwealth, which it remains today. Cuba, through the Platt Amendment, acquired the virtual status of a protectorate. The Belgians in the Congo would not have felt diminished by these actions, as far as colonization was concerned, though the treatment of the colonized was different. The *de facto* annexation of the last Spanish colonies, including the Philippines, would allow the United States with time to develop a two-ocean blue water navy. The country unabashedly set aside its quirks about relinquishing colonial prerogatives or ambitions. It behaved like a highly unexceptional great power, and arguably more than anywhere in the Philippines. The war there, which was declared over many times, dragged on. The casualties on the Filipino side have been calculated to range from 250,000 to 775,000. The continuation of the war led Mark Twain to write in 1900, "There must be two Americas, one that sets the captive free, and one that takes a once-captive's new freedom away from him, and picks a quarrel with him with nothing to found it on; then kills him to get his land."[13] The war lasted for another thirteen years. As a recent history of the "American Empire" by Daniel Immerwahr concluded, "Every one of the army's first twelve chiefs of staff, in fact, served in the Philippine War. Stretching from the outbreak of hostilities in 1899 to the end of military rule in Moroland in 1913, it is, after the war in Afghanistan, the longest war the United States has ever fought."[14]

Victor Bulmer Thomas demonstrates this eloquently and in detail. In Mexico and Central America, in Africa and the Pacific, in the Caribbean, American influence and acquisitions spread, ranging from colonies to treaty port concessions—almost exactly as occurred in European empires. He argues that British India, for example, was ruled by the privately owned East India Company until 1858, but no one can argue it was not part of the British Empire.

The most notable challenge to American exceptionalism during the second stage of the narrative—i.e. the nineteenth century—sprang, once again, from slavery. Unlike suffrage, where according to Chilton Williamson, the transition took place from "Property to Democracy," in the case of slavery it progressed from less slavery to much more.[15] By 1860, of approximately 31 million Americans, 4 million, or 13 percent, were slaves. But in the South, nearly one in three were. The increase from 1790 was sevenfold, and in some states—Alabama, Florida, Georgia, Louisiana, Mississippi, and South Carolina—the proportion of slaves to the total population hovered around 50 percent.[16] By 1860, even Texas, which only joined the Union fifteen years before, included 180,000 slaves, almost a third of its population.

In comparative terms, Brazil, the largest slave country, was home to 6 million slaves in 1888, out of a total population of 10 million. The most "exceptional" feature of the first sixty-five years of the American nineteenth century was the expansion of slavery, together with the immense cost the young nation paid to abolish its existence, albeit not its legacy: more than 600,000 Civil War dead. Many foreign observers and admirers who viewed the United States as an example for independence movements across the hemisphere or throughout the world ignored this fact. But that did not diminish its importance, even today.

The questions of suffrage and exceptionalism persisted during the nineteenth century. In 1860, Abraham Lincoln was elected with 1.8 million popular votes, 40 percent of the total: a turnout above 80 percent of the eligible electorate. But that eligible electorate remained infinitesimal, at around 4.6 million voters, in a nation of 31 million, excluding slaves and Native Americans. Despite the fact that during the first sixty years of independence, one president had increased the absolute popular vote total fiftyfold, the franchise only grew in relative terms. After Andrew Jackson and the theoretical extension of the franchise to all white males in 1825, however, property and tax-paying restrictions began to wither away.

The numbers showed a small but expanding percentage of the voting age population—excluding women, Native Americans, and blacks— actually participating in presidential elections. Turnout in percentage terms would never again be as high as in 1860, but the number of voters grew exponentially. Hence the questions: was the United States exceptional because it held elections? Undoubtedly. Were those elections free and fair? To a large extent. Was this a case of a full-fledged representative, liberal democracy, or rather an Athenian-like, elite democracy where even the privileged—white males over 21—had difficulties casting their ballots? Clearly. Thus was American exceptionalism nuanced throughout the nineteenth century.

Jumping slightly ahead, the exceptionalism of American liberal democracy today is even more arguable. Firstly, because dozens of countries all over the world are exactly that: liberal democracies. Even in regions where they represented a rarity decades ago—Latin America, Africa—today they are increasingly common and lasting. In Asia, with all its cultural obstacles, liberal democracy is as alive and well in India, Indonesia, or Japan, as it is elsewhere. Europe—Eastern and Western— despite worrisome trends, live under rules and laws at least as democratic as the United States, if not more so. How much of this the world owes—or not—to the United States can be endlessly debated, but the facts seem to be quite incontrovertible. By countries, by population, by region, so-called liberal democracy is the norm today in much of the world. China and Russia are the only significant exceptions, not America.

Finally, for the first century of independence narrative, there was the theoretically exceptional nature of the free-market, free-trade, thriving economy providing opportunity and prosperity for all. Once again, "all" was a manner of speech: for everyone brought into the fold, excluding those who were not. Certainly, the American economy grew vigorously before and after the Civil War. The US share of world manufacturing output rose from 23 percent in 1870 to 36 percent in 1913.[17] But this was not entirely a "free-market" or laissez-faire era. The Trans-Continental Railroad, completed in 1869, was a typical state-sponsored infrastructure project, not unlike the Interstate Highway system constructed nearly a century later, or the trip to the moon or the Internet, all products of the American Entrepreneurial State.[18] The railroad was built by two private companies on public lands provided by large US land grants. Construction was mostly financed by state and US government subsidy bonds.

The railroads themselves worked hand in hand with the government in encouraging immigration through advertising in Europe. Hundreds of thousands of farmers from Germany, Scandinavia, and Britain arrived in the United States this way. Between old and new immigrants (first the Irish and Germans, then those from Southern and Eastern Europe) 27.5 million people reached American shores during the period from 1865 and 1918, but the doors were not open to everyone. In 1882, the American Congress passed the Chinese Exclusion Act, which halted immigration from China. Similarly, in 1907, the Gentleman's Agreement with Japan practically eliminated immigration from that country. All of this was government-managed, government-led, government-tutored public policy. Laissez-faire exceptionalism, it was not.

The abundance of land and resources was made available to millions through the successive Homestead Acts, especially Lincoln's in 1862: this was a typically redistributive policy. The federal government issued 160-acre (65 ha) tracts virtually free to settlers. Larger numbers of newly arrived or East Coast Americans purchased lands at very low interest rates from the new railroads, which were trying to create markets. As they all went farther west, something had to be done with the people who had lived there for centuries: Native Americans. Once again, the federal government intervened. It decreed that those belonging to the various nations involved either become assimilated and remove themselves from the lands acquired by the settlers or remain on assigned reservations. Force achieved both goals.

Lastly, as far as unexceptional American *dirigisme* (i.e. heavy state involvement in all areas of the economy) was concerned, after the protectionist North defeated the free-trade South in the Civil War, the entire United States became acutely protectionist, with high tariffs throughout the period. This was also a matter of fiscal policy. Between 1790 and 1860 tariffs accounted for 90 percent of the federal tax take, part of Alexander Hamilton's legacy.

Exceptionalism did prevail in relation to other industrializing countries in social terms, thanks to the managed supply of labor. This provided a regulated source of working hands and upward pressure on wages. Real wages increased by 60 percent between 1860 and 1890, and average annual income (after inflation) of non-farm workers grew by 75 percent from 1865 to 1900.[19] But even this exceptionalism enclosed nuances. Wealth became much more unequally distributed. Again, between 1860 to 1900, the wealthiest 2 percent of American households came to own more than a third of the nation's wealth, while the top 10 percent owned roughly three-fourths of it.[20] The bottom 40 percent had no wealth at all.[21] In terms of property, the wealthiest 1 percent owned 51 percent, while the bottom 44 percent claimed 1.1 percent.[22]

French economist Thomas Piketty notes that economists during this time, such as Willford I. King, were concerned that the United States was becoming increasingly in-egalitarian to the point of resembling old Europe, and "further and further away from its original pioneering ideal."[23] Or as I would say, it was becoming unexceptional. Perhaps worse: once Reconstruction concluded, the old Confederacy States mandated racial segregation in all Southern public facilities, starting in 1896 with a "separate but equal" status for African Americans in railroad cars. Public education had essentially been segregated since its establishment in most of the South after the Civil War. Jim Crow laws proliferated. This was the "Gilded Age" in contrast to a golden one, a name coined by Mark Twain and Charles Dudley Warner in their 1873 book, *The Gilded Age: A Tale of Today*. It created for the first time a class of enormously affluent "captains of industry" or "robber barons" whose network of business, social, and family connections ruled a largely White Anglo-Saxon Protestant world with clearly defined boundaries. Whither exceptionalism?

A short century of power

The third stage of the exceptionalist narrative runs from World War I through the end of the Cold War in 1991. To a considerable extent, American exceptionalism during this short century equates with power. By 1900 the United States was already the foremost industrial nation on earth. After 1918 and the Treaty of Versailles, it also confirmed its rank as the number one financial center in the world. For the subsequent seventy years, despite the bipolar rivalry with the Soviet Union, it was the dominant military power on the planet. By winning the Cold War, it ostensibly demonstrated that its exceptionalism was not only true and real, but also mighty.

In the new, third version of the national narrative, the United States was exceptional because it was all-powerful, and it was all-powerful because it was exceptional. It was an anti-colonial hegemon, unlike the European colonial powers. It was a democracy, unlike the Nazi and Soviet dictatorships. It was a prosperous, unfettered, free-market and free-trade economy, unlike the declining, protectionist, statist systems of Western Europe and Japan. Lastly, it was a middle-class society, enjoying vast opportunities of social mobility, in contrast to the stratified and ossified societies of the Old World. Most importantly, since Woodrow Wilson, it acquired a sacred mission: spreading this exceptionalism to the rest of the globe. The intrinsic contradiction of this tenet—can exceptionalism be shared with, or imposed on, others—surfaced for Americans only during the second half of the century, in Vietnam. Otherwise, how could it go wrong?

At birth and during the first hundred years of independence, there were grounds for this presumption of exceptionalism, as well as many reasons to disbelieve it or arguments to refute it. There can be no question that the United States has been unique in the twentieth century. But the basic issue is whether that uniqueness lay in its creed, its origins, its so-called mission and specificity with regard to other nations, or in its power, together with its limits. Indeed, perhaps the most damning case against exceptionalism lay in the limits the new *Britannia* encountered as it emerged as a world power. From Pershing's incursion into Chihuahua in 1914, in his futile search for Pancho Villa, the Mexican revolutionary who led a raid into Columbus, New Mexico, to Wilson's failure to obtain Senate ratification of American membership in the League of Nations, it quickly became apparent that despite American wealth and prowess everywhere, not everything was possible.

Moreover, the ideals that Washington and New York soon began touting and exporting all over the world were rapidly belied or betrayed at home: the Red Scare and union-busting practices of the 1920s; Wilson's re-segregation efforts; mass deportation of Mexicans after World War I; Prohibition and the difficulties of giving women the vote. The clashing counter-examples were not isolated or sporadic, as many Americans preferred to think. On the contrary, they were part and parcel of the US experience. The same contradictions characterized the Europeans' postwar, pre-Depression response to the Bolshevik Revolution, to the Treaty of Versailles, to the expansion of labor rights and the advent of social democracy, and to the Depression itself. None of these features were exceptional.

Was the United States faithful to its creed and foundational axioms as a great power? Was it exceptional as a great power? Perhaps the first half of the twentieth century was the time when the gap was smallest between Americans' view of themselves, as expressed in political speeches, academic treatises, everyday journalism, and other so-called *appareils idéologiques d'Etat*, and in the view of foreigners without too much of an ax to grind. Domestically, the common response to common challenges in the United States and Europe provisionally dissipated the notion of exceptionalism. The New Deal enhanced the convergence but only in matters of internal policy. Not in foreign policy, though, where it became impossible to ignore, long before Vietnam, the distance between discourse and action. It expanded to such a degree that few, if any, continued to believe in exceptionalism, other than through its definition as an expression of overwhelming power.

In Europe, American exceptionalism was often seen most clearly as that of an empire that refuses to acknowledge its very existence as such, unlike Britain, France, or even Belgium and Holland. For many Europeans, the dilemma was not whether the United States was, at least after World War I and its transformation into the globe's creditor, an empire that utilized its power to increase and enhance its hegemony. The issue was whether there was such a thing as an exceptional American use of exceptional power. Or, in fact, whether the peculiarity of the United States' experience as a world hegemon resided chiefly in the negation of its own existence. For a time, toward the end of World War II, the somewhat smug European curiosity over the strange conduct of those in charge of the American empire became more resentful. Roosevelt's anti-colonial push with the British and the French gave apparent American altruism a heavy dose of legitimacy on the ground. But it did not outlive FDR, coming to an end with the Cold War and the American intervention in Korea. Europeans could not easily distinguish between their own colonial wars—the French more than the British, but these too, in Malaysia and Kenya—and McArthur at Inchon.

The Afro-Asians struggling for independence actually viewed the United States as an exceptional power. They did so not because of America's insistence on coating its actions in a creed of equality, freedom, democracy, and development, but because Washington occasionally aided their struggles, if only to displace the British, the French, and later the Soviets. Perhaps the best example of that type of exceptionalism lay in Eisenhower's unwillingness to rescue the French at Dien Bien Phu in 1954. Another exceptional moment consisted in his ultimatum to Anthony Eden and Guy Mollet in 1956: accept Nasser's nationalization of the Suez Canal and refrain from invading Egypt. The Africans and Asians could not fail to see a modicum of hypocrisy in Ike's stance, but nonetheless in these specific cases a point could be made, for a brief interval, that this empire was different. Had they been familiar with how Britain contributed to many independence movements against Spain in the Americas at the beginning of the nineteenth century, they might have been a bit more sanguine with regard to US behavior during the decolonization period. In any case, this supposed benevolence was rather quickly nipped in the bud a few years later, in the Belgian Congo and mainly in Vietnam.

The Latin Americans hosted a different perspective. American twentieth-century exceptionalism had already encountered many counter-factual exercises in the region, including brief to lasting occupations of Haiti, Dominican Republic, Honduras, Nicaragua, Cuba, Granada, Panama, and even Veracruz in Mexico during 1914. But the United States transformed itself into a flagrantly unexceptional hegemon in the region only once the Cold War was fully underway. From the late forties through the beginning of the 1990s, American policy toward Latin America was undistinguishable from that of traditional empires' links with their colonies, leaving aside the formality of military occupation and legal subordination. One can argue endlessly as to whether local provocations or Washington's hostility came first. The same discussion can be held regarding the nature of US involvement in countless episodes of intervention: was it complementary to local conditions, or the detonating factor in the collapse or ostracism of various regimes?

Nonetheless the most unexceptional American behavior did not occur at critical junctures: the overthrow of the Arbenz regime in Guatemala in 1954; the Bay of Pigs; the invasion of the Dominican Republic in 1965; the CIA plots against Salvador Allende in Chile; the support for the Contras in Central America in the 1980s; the invasion of Panama in 1989. It was the non-eventful, business-as-usual routine engagement in practically every Latin American nation—even the larger ones, like Brazil or Mexico—that made the US experience in the region unexceptional. Americans may have thought, sincerely and with the best of intentions, that the roles their government and corporations played in Latin America were far different from those of the British and the French in Africa and Asia. In the context of the Cold War, many may have honestly believed they were fighting the good fight for truth and justice against communism and the Soviet Union, especially close to home. In most cases—except for Cuba, at a terrible cost to its people—they may have been largely successful in most of their endeavors. No matter: there was scant exceptionalism embedded in the US experience in Latin America until the final decade of the last century. For several years I jointly taught a graduate course at NYU and Columbia with John Coatsworth, my highly distinguished colleague. It was devoted to US policy in Latin America. Each year, at the beginning of the term, Coatsworth handed out a fact sheet entitled "Selected US Interventions, 1898–2004," with two sub-headings: Direct Interventions that changed governments and US Indirect Interventions in which America was decisive. He counted eighteen in the first category, and twenty-three in the second.[24] Not bad for a non-empire. Carlos Fuentes, though, detects a whisper of exceptionalism even in this conduct: "The United States has been the bearer of a nationalism as aggressive and self-celebratory as any European imperial power. But until now (the 1990s) American nationalism, as aggressive as it may be beyond its borders, has maintained a democratic system within them."[25] The Mexican novelist was perhaps attempting to establish too fine a distinction between American behavior and the Soviet Union's role in Eastern Europe and Afghanistan, but if the comparison was made with other empires from the mid-nineteenth century onward, most of them were quite democratic domestically: France, Britain, Belgium, Holland, and perhaps even Austro-Hungary.

Whatever exceptionalism there may have been in Henry Luce's American century can be summed up in two words: power and success. Between the outbreak of World War I in 1914 and the disappearance of the Soviet Union in 1991, the United States, despite its participation in two world wars, in regional strife on four occasions, and innumerable skirmishes, remained the unquestionably overwhelming power on the globe. The signers of the Treaty of Versailles came and went. Nazi Germany and Imperial Japan were destroyed. The Soviet Union, more an ideological rival than an economic or military one, imploded. China barely became ascendant as it entered the World Trade Organization in 2001. Since the Roman Empire, no nation had achieved this type of hegemony for such a prolonged period of time. Not the British for part of the nineteenth century, or the Dutch in the seventeenth century, not the Ottomans or the Moguls in Asia.

The proportion of world patents, missiles, submarines, Nobel Prizes, technological advances, tanks, first-class universities, consumer goods, consumption of electricity, nuclear devices, and records, movies, or television shows corresponding to the United States was immensely superior to its share of the world's population. Whenever a mini-crisis of confidence erupted in academia or the business community as a result of highly exaggerated extrapolations of brief trends in other countries' performance—the USSR, Japan, the European Union, China—it was rapidly dispelled by the passage of time. The projections failed, and American advances soon recovered their privileged rank. Whatever use the United States made of this exceptional power, as well as whatever consequences emerged from this asymmetric balance of forces of all shapes and sizes, is a different issue. This was the most salient expression of American exceptionalism in the twentieth century. Jeffrey Sachs has argued that this form of conceptualizing it in the twenty-first century is "especially misguided," and he is undoubtedly right.[26] But the equation remains valid, even if it may seem immoral or doomed in the long term.

The foundation of this success lay, as I have already noted, in the rise and consolidation of the American middle class, at least until 1980. It is not necessary to plow through the numbers once again, other than to say that for most of the twentieth century, the standard of living of a broad majority of the inhabitants of the United States—citizens or not, with or without papers—was infinitely higher than that of Europe, Japan, the socialist bloc, not to mention Africa, the rest of Asia, and Latin America. Every argument about French *art de vivre*, Japanese social capital, or even Scandinavian equality was rebutted by this asymmetry. After 1980 the trends began to revert, as the American middle class either shrank or saw its living standards stagnate, while that of many other First World countries expanded, and the curves eventually crossed. For much of the last century, however, the American consumer, worker, student, farmer, clerk, or housewife was the envy of the world.

Whether hard or soft, American power was unmatched in the world between 1946 and the end of the Cold War and the downfall of the socialist bloc. Hollywood movies, network television shows, American athletes' performances in the Olympic Games, as well as prodigious military might, even with regard to the USSR, left little room to argue. In spite of the Soviet acquisition of the atomic and hydrogen bombs in the late forties and early fifties, JFK's false missile gap in the 1960 presidential campaign as well as the panic over the Cuban Missile Crisis in 1962, and the hysteria over Russian SS-19 missiles in the western Soviet Union aimed at Europe in the mid-1980s, nuclear parity between the two nuclear powers never existed. It became an even greater figment of the imagination after the Sino-Soviet split in the early sixties. The USSR was, military and space industrial hardware aside, a Third World nation for this entire period. So, the United States had no rival except for those it chose to elevate to such a rank, needlessly and recklessly: Cuba in the early sixties, Vietnam just after.

Thus, American exceptionalism: an incredible difference in power, through all of its manifestations, rather than a distinction forged from ideas, customs, and traditions or foundational myths. All of these factors *contributed* to American power but were not the *essence* of America power. Victory in the Cold War did not spring from American ideals— capitalism, representative democracy, and individual freedoms—but from unequaled, drastically asymmetrical power. Had victory stemmed from ideals, absent the United States, the Western European nations, all subscribers to the same ones, would have also triumphed. We know this would not have occurred, for reasons ranging from low levels of military spending to the presence of influential communist parties, and including societies averse—perhaps wisely—to imposing their will on others, given their long and painful colonial past. Devoid of the American notions generally associated with exceptionalism, maybe American power would have been minor, different, or even nonexistent, although this seems difficult to believe. But any set of ideas, were they to be firmly planted in the soil and location of this immense continental country, would have led to power, as awesome as the power we know today and began to understand a century ago.

If exceptionalism was power, it was also *success*. Over this "short" century, the United States fought two world wars, five regional ones (Korea, Vietnam, Iraq twice, and Afghanistan), and came out winning four, losing one, and stalemating another two. It also launched multiple pinprick interventions in Latin America, Africa, the Middle

East, and East Asia. Most, though evidently not all, were eventually "successful" in that they achieved most of the objectives originally planned. American interests were defended, unfriendly governments were overthrown, allies were reassured, and foes were forewarned. This may not be the most altruistic or noble parameters of success, and the long-term consequences may have been contrary to initial aims, but for American interests, it was certainly preferable to failure, however defined.

Success was not only military. It was political, cultural, and ideological. The United States might have conceivably become the world's richest, most powerful, and admired nation since early in the twentieth century without necessarily conquering the hearts and minds of people everywhere. It could have been unlucky, as other great powers were at certain times. Unavoidable hubris could have led it down a path of recurrent over-ambitious attempts at domination or imposition, giving way to equally recurrent failures. The exceptionalism lies in success, and possibly in the overall conditions—material and otherwise—that made it possible.

Power and success, however, did not imply that the American century would last forever. After the fall of the Berlin Wall and the disappearance of the Soviet Union, the United States entered a new stage. It was neither one of slow collapse—Roman-Empire style—nor of unfettered extension of the previous phase. These last thirty years have reflected a double trend in the American saga: becoming a civilization, in the strongest meaning of the word, and being forced to acknowledge that not everything is possible, even for the United States.

The Last Hurrah

If we pursue the arguments developed by Régis Debray, the French thinker and writer, what its proponents call American exceptionalism has now consolidated itself by its metamorphosis into an American civilization. In view of the domestic and foreign limits on the use of American military might, of the decreasing weight of the United States in the world economy (trade, GDP, manufacturing), of the growing relevance and magnitude of American soft power, as well as the absence of anybody else's, the United States today dominates as only a civilization can. It was not always seen in this light. Oscar Wilde, during his stay in America in 1882, famously quipped that it was "the only country that went from barbarism to decadence without civilization in between."[27] Its ideas, technology, culture, habits, and mores are present everywhere in the world. At the same time, its capability of readily influencing outcomes in various crisis scenarios over the past three decades have drastically shrunk.

Syria, North Korea, and Venezuela, as well as the ongoing tensions with Iran, are perhaps the best examples in recent times of the limits of US military power in the post–Cold War world. Obama wanted to stop the carnage in Syria. He drew red lines, sought out allies to lead the effort, and also engaged in a protracted negotiating process. But once he ruled out "boots on the ground" it was just a matter of time before Putin's Russia and Bashar-al Assad would out-last him. They did. Special operations and high technology notwith-standing, without the French and the United Kingdom as in Libya, Washington was doomed to accept both a human rights and hu-manitarian disaster. This ensured the indefinite survival of a regime whose replacement the United States had sought and declared nec-essary. While this was neither the first nor the only occasion when American impotence surfaced so blatantly, the logic of victory in the Cold War should have implied a different outcome. It didn't. There was no Soviet Union backing Fidel Castro and Ho Chi Minh—only a weakened Russia propping up an unpopular regime domestically—but regardless, Obama was unable to unseat el-Assad or to stop the bloodshed, exercising some form of what has come to be known as the Responsibility to Protect or R2P.

Nor were he or his predecessors able or willing to restrain the downspin of one of Latin America's wealthiest and oldest democracies into economic chaos, authoritarian rule, and regional diplomatic mis-chief. Hugo Chávez was elected president in late 1998. Before he died in 2013, he thwarted three American chief executives, who in different ways sought to contain him or contribute to his ouster. His successor, Nicolás Maduro, has so far proved equally successful in resisting pres-sure from two presidents in Washington. This, in a country that sells only oil, and most of it to the United States; that possessed a strongly pro-American business elite and middle class; and that has received foreign military backing only from Cuba—an economic and military backwater.

How did this occur? Partly, because Venezuela's neighbors for years proved unwilling to follow the US path of relative ostracism and moderate hostility. When they did, it was too late. Additionally, Washington was unable to "persuade" them to do so at the right time. Lastly, high oil prices enabled Chávez, and, until 2014, Maduro, to deliver the goods to some of the Venezuelan people, some of the time. Those same high oil prices allowed Caracas to purchase intelligence and security from the Cubans at an acceptable price, and on those two counts, Havana *is* a world power. But the chief reason the Venezuelan regime has survived is because Presidents Clinton, Bush, Obama, and Trump mostly decided they did not care. No overriding American interest was involved in Venezuela, and the diplomatic cost of militarily overthrowing Chávez or Maduro was superior to any conceivable benefit; when a coup attempt took place in 2002, the United States backed it only rhetorically. Economic sanctions from Trump have weakened Maduro, but, at this writing, have not brought him down. This type of indifference constitutes a conclusion that previous civilizations, such as the Romans, would have shared: beyond the *limes*, nothing really matters.

Inside the *limes*, however, is a different story. Given its history—i.e. the Korean War—and its neighbor to the south, North Korea should fall within the boundaries of American civilization. But given the impossibility of going to war barely fifty miles from Seoul (that has massive, heavy artillery and possibly nuclear weapons targeted at it from the north), and North Korea's border with China, the United States has been stymied by the Kim dynasty since World War II. This impotence is all the more dangerous and frustrating in view of the geography and the personalities involved. Four American heads of state have drawn lines in the sand: Pyongyang cannot possess a nuclear capability. It does. They have repeatedly stated that they would not allow North Korea to acquire delivery capacity that would threaten Japan, Hawaii, or the continental United States. It has. Everyone, including, at least in principle, China and Russia, accepts the notion that these two capabilities combined are inadmissible. Washington has been straight-jacketed into three highly undesirable options: hoping North Korea can never fit a nuclear warhead on an intercontinental missile that withstands re-entry; containment, along with acceptance of Kim Jong Un as a nuclear player; or, as a former US Ambassador to Mexico and the Ukraine phrased it, war. This last option is a non-starter, even for Donald Trump. The first one is quasi-religious. That only leaves negotiation and containment, doubtfully with denuclearization. Trump's tribulation in his summits with Kim have not altered the equation.

These examples can be rebutted or nit-picked to death, but they illustrate our point. In the post–Cold War era, even a super-hegemon like the United States can no longer achieve some of its aims—whether decisive, indifferent, or morally unquestionable. In many aspects, here lies the most modern and perhaps lasting manifestation of American exceptionalism: a "hyper-power" as a French foreign minister described it at the beginning of the century, that cannot have its way all the time in geopolitical and military terms. Nor in economic ones . . . .

That the United States has a $500 billion yearly trade deficit with China is not in itself a national security issue. The world's factory exports manufactured goods everywhere, and understandably, it runs trade surpluses with many countries. The dilemma consists in the billions of dollars of American financial instruments that the Chinese purchase every year. That is how Washington finances its trade deficit, and that is how China addresses its high savings rate and low consumption levels. Logically, this holds ample security implications for the United States. Beijing can theoretically unload those securities (although their value would plummet, and its remaining holdings would also fall through the floor). It would have to find other placements, however, and there are not many today. Nonetheless, the drop in the US share of world GDP, from 27 percent in 1950 to 25 percent in 1960, and 15 percent in 2019, along with corresponding reductions in world manufacturing (from 45 percent in 1945 to 23 percent in 1982 to 16 percent in 2016), and world trade (which has not changed a great deal over the past half century, declining from 13 percent in 1970 to 10 percent in 2018), necessarily entails a weakened hegemony in purely economic terms.[28]

The United States can no longer systematically get its way in G-20 meetings, or lower or raise the value of its currency as before. Trump's economic nationalism reflects many contradictions and experiences, but a new economic balance of forces in the world figures prominently among them. The military-economic contrast between the first Gulf

War and the second one is enlightening. In 1991, George H. W. Bush imposed the financial cost of the conflict on his allies; twelve years later, his son did not even attempt to do so, among other reasons because of the far greater controversy surrounding the second war. American exceptionalism in international economic terms between the Treaty of Versailles and the last years of last century has ceased to exist. But a much more significant and lasting American exceptionalism has emerged from this twilight of traditional US hegemony. It is American civilization.

3

The blessings of American culture and the road to American civilization

BY CIVILIZATION, I DO NOT mean Western civilization in British historian Niall Ferguson's broad and useful definition. The reference here is to a specifically American civilization even if it encompasses many facets of what is generally understood by the traditional, Eurocentric concept. Yes, it includes representative democracy, a free-market economy, individual rights, and reverential respect for private property, but it is not limited to this. A civilization is a language, yet more than that. One need not speak English to be influenced in multiple ways by American civilization, from music (in translation) to jeans (which need no translation). It includes intent and desire.

Civilizations possess their own instruments of economic expansion and success. They tend to coin a currency that everyone else accepts and uses, even long after its economic foundation has weakened or withered. A civilization comprises a religion, or more specifically a certain approach to faith: a relative separation of Church and State, an ecumenical tolerance of other religions, and a non-existential definition of faith; a belief, not a way of life. A civilization is space and time: as Debray states, "Islam stretches from Dakar to Djakarta, Rome lasted a thousand years and China is entering its third millennium."[1]

Civilization is not "just" art, according to Ferguson's appropriate criticism of Kenneth Clark's classic approach, but it is "also" art, architecture, buildings, music, popular and otherwise, literature, and today, television and cinema. It is food and drink, as well as military might and diplomatic muscle. Civilization, like "culture," implies habits, customs, and traditions, with an inward-looking perspective. But it is bundled together with the will and capacity to project them: to make "others" become like "us." No civilization can avoid a certain degree of confrontation or at least explicit contrast with its peers: today with Islam, tomorrow with China. And it also entails a modicum of resistance: to deter others from changing "us."

I was studying in Paris when the first two McDonald's outlets opened on the Champs Elysées and the Boulevard Saint-Michel, opposite the central buildings of the Sorbonne. This was roughly in 1974, when there was still a powerful student movement in the French capital, and a united left was beginning its drive to power, eventually winning the presidential election in 1981. Since I lived in a small studio in the French quarter and was coursing my Ph.D. at the Sorbonne, I would often, maybe twice a week, purchase a Big Mac and fries and take them home—never to school. A major debate emerged in France over McDonald's, but to some of my Mexican friends in Paris and me, their discussion was a moot one. We all loved Mexican food, but there was none there then (or now for that matter). Even today there is only third-rate Tex-Mex fare in the French capital. We had all learned to eat hamburgers in Mexico in the sixties, when there were no McDonald's but hundreds of Denny's, Wendy's, Burger Boys, and Sanborns. At that time, hamburgers were for upper-middle-class consumers. Only McDonald's, twenty years later, would make them available to everyday Mexicans.

The French debate involved cuisine, visual pollution, history, and logically enough American imperialism. For us, in our exchanges with French philosophy students, fluent in structuralism, it also included, or even boiled down to, dollars and cents (or francs and centimes). McDonald's was cheaper, more filling, faster, and just as French (through fries). As petulant as Rive Gauche students could be in the 1970s, we never took our exchanges to the level of the nature or existence of American civilization. But that is what we were really arguing about. I perhaps should have realized back then—nearly half a century ago—that if anybody was a product or part and parcel of that American civilization, it was me. Then and now, as I have mentioned, I was not an American citizen; but I spent many of my childhood, adolescent, and adult years in the United States, like millions of other Mexicans. I spoke English and another two languages, like tens of millions of Asians, Europeans, Africans, and Latin Americans. I ate hamburgers and tacos, listened to Mexican music and to Dylan, and I believed that much of what occurred in the world was decided in Washington, for better or for worse. I was not exceptional, just simply part of the reigning civilization.

This is perhaps the true crux of contemporary American exceptionalism, after two long centuries of successive metamorphoses. The other civilizations surviving today are older (Islam, China), fading (Europe), or barely re-emerging after long stages of sublimation through oppression and colonization: Africa. The United States no longer enjoys the singularity of economic hegemony or prosperity for all its inhabitants. Despite its immense military superiority, it cannot consistently exercise that prominence because its social configuration and consensus no longer countenance it. But it does not really require brute force to project its views, interests, and presence, though the threat of force is often indispensable. The essence of that civilization, which will enable the United States to claim that the twenty-first century will also be an American one, is its middle-class nature, regardless of the fact that its social foundation is no longer what it was. The heart of American civilization is the equality of all, whether it be before the law, before the silver screen and the rock band or hip-hop, before fashion and language, before sexual mores and drugs, before automobiles and the cell phone. At least as far as access to all of the above is concerned, everyone is equal.

Europeans enjoy the best public transportation systems in the world, but they continue to worship their cars, which they all own. Latin Americans adore their music, from *reggaeton* to *bossa nova* to tangos, but they flock to rock concerts with American, British, or Irish bands. The middle-class vocation of American civilization is hardly recognized by those who embrace it. No self-respecting Italian would ever acknowledge that his or her love affair with *la machina* is US-inspired. No Mexican swaying to Juan Gabriel's pink, modern mariachi—according to his obituary in *The Economist*, at any given minute, on a radio somewhere in Latin America one of his songs would be playing—would ever admit that the very notion of an open-air, massively attended, relatively accessible concert is an American construct.[2] He or she probably suspects that this is a typically Mexican, or Spanish, or pre-Columbian notion.

A useful path for exploring the notion of American civilization lies in revisiting one of the more obnoxious and widely held views of the United States in other societies. The idea of a reigning American civilization provides a transition toward the theme of American culture. This has been the foremost, traditional flank of attack for myriad French, Mexican, Argentine, German, and many other observers. They simply cannot stand nor understand that the cultural capitals of the world today are all in the United States. Even a great admirer of the United States like Mario Vargas Llosa has his own doubts about American culture: "The United States is the least conservative land in the world, the one that changes most rapidly, replacing without nostalgia all institutions, ideas, behavior and convictions . . . and has in economic, political and social terms—culture is the exception that confirms the rule—set the tone for humanity's evolution."[3]

With the possible exception of up-scale fashion, where Paris and Milan still rule, and theater, where London holds its ground, New York, Los Angeles, and a half dozen other US metropoles reign supreme in publishing (highbrow and low-grade), the film industry, classical and contemporary music composition and performance, philosophy (together with the French), economics and dance, the arts in general, and every other conceivable definition of culture. These pages hope to show that American culture, in the broadest definition of the word, is the most sophisticated, imaginative, open-minded, and sponge-like in the world—even if so many despise it. So, what explains this omnipresent *mépris*? Even as sophisticated an "America-watcher" as Mexican philosopher, writer, and revered education minister in the 1920s José Vasconcelos could not disguise his disdain. Recalling his schoolground quarrels in Eagle Pass, Texas, when his American counterparts "dissed" him for being uncivilized, he would respond, according to his recollections forty years later: "In my home, it was always stated, to the contrary, that the Yankees were the cultural newcomers. I would stand up in class and repeat: 'We had the printing press before you.'"[4] Why has American culture been unable to push back on its own terms against these age-old dismissals and criticisms?

Before responding, a brief clarification is in order. For our purposes, it is unimportant to choose between the broadest, most "multicultural" definition of culture, including everything from Native American dried meat to hamburgers, and the narrowest, Eurocentric, elitist meaning. The points I will attempt to make are valid, for any and all expressions, origins, and ramifications of the word "culture." Similarly, the fully valid debate whether American culture today is the product of a nearly two-hundred-fifty-year-old crucible of influences and inputs, or the result of the same two-and-a-half centuries of one culture oppressing others, or the result of the tension between insider and outsider within American society is somewhat irrelevant in this context. The arguments that follow are hopefully valid in all three hypotheses. I tend to subscribe to the first one, but the second or third options do not invalidate the line of reasoning.

Foreigners both scorn and devour American culture; they admire its innovation—technological, literary, or musical—and disdain its supposedly vulgar, violent, simplistic, and "mass" nature. Even the most perceptive and empathetic, like Simone de Beauvoir, whose *America Day by Day* is by no means an anti-American tirade, found it difficult to resist this proclivity. Referring to the American literary industry, she wrote in 1954: "America is hard on intellectuals. Publishers and editors size up your mind in a critical and distasteful way, like an impresario asking a dancer to show her legs . . . . in France it is still accepted that certain values have meaning and that the public is capable of recognizing them. Here (in the US), it's a question of concealing from stupid readers the foolishness of the pages they're offered."[5] On the other hand, many Americans dismiss "foreign" culture as intellectualized, arrogant, inaccessible, and irrelevant, overlooking the fact that many of their greatest writers, painters, musicians, and movie directors lived abroad or emigrated from abroad. The disconnect is awesome.

Culture for the masses

Why have so many foreign cultural talents worked in the United States, and why have so many of the greatest American creators labored outside their country? The key lies in acknowledging what countless foreigners and Americans have always sensed: the United States is the first country to have produced a "mass" culture. How did this happen? While over the centuries, European, Latin American, and Asian nations constructed literature, philosophy, art, architecture, and music for the very few, the United States lacked the authoritarian history, centralized religion, and monarchical institutions that favored elitist culture. Instead, with the emergence of the world's first middle-class society in the early twentieth century, cultural products were generated for these new consumers in the same way as cars, homes, and iceboxes.

Over time, more traditional societies developed their own middle classes, which in turn welcomed and copied American-style culture. In fact, the United States always provided highbrow culture to its wealthy and enlightened elite, but also popular and lowbrow cultural feed for the rest of society. Instead of showing pride in their ability to develop "mass" culture and complement it with excellent "elite" culture, quite unnecessarily Americans often exhibit a kind of "cultural inferiority complex," not least in relation to "old" Europe. Perhaps the first time—and one of the few times—the United States went head to head with the Europeans on matters of cultural supremacy was the Chicago Columbian Fair of 1893, celebrating the four hundredth anniversary of Columbus's voyage, which set out to outdo the Paris World Fair of 1889, best known for the Eiffel Tower.

The initial answer to these paradoxes lies in the mass nature of American culture, from the get-go. If one compares the Enlightenment in France in the eighteenth century, the British philosophers and theater writers from Shakespeare to Locke and Hume, or the Spanish poets and playwrights of the *Siglo de Oro*, let alone the German poets, composers, and philosophers of the late eighteenth and early nineteenth centuries, with American cultural fare at the dawn of the twentieth century, there is . . . no comparison. A sprinkling of political thinkers—some of them exceptionally talented—gathered around the drafting of the Declaration of Independence, the Constitution, and the Bill of Rights (together with the Federalist Papers). The word American culture, however, can hardly be applied to the artistic, literary, musical, and philosophical production of the time. The reason is equally obvious: the United States was barely becoming a nation, the European nations pre-existed their states—Germany—or their states created them as nations: France, Russia, Spain, Britain. The United States was not a cultural producer in the eighteenth century because it didn't exist. It scarcely became one in the early to mid-nineteenth century as it evolved into a unified nation thirty or forty years before the Civil War and then later.

The first well-known, widely published and occasionally translated American authors as such emerged only in the 1820s and 1830s. After Fenimore Cooper—whose 1826 first printing of the *The Last of the Mohicans* was 5000 copies[6]—and Washington Irving, it was only by mid-century that writers such as Edgar Allan Poe (who died in 1849), Nathaniel Hawthorne (whose 1850 *Scarlet Letter*, in contrast to Cooper, sold 2500 in the first ten days),[7] Henry David Thoreau, and Herman Melville (published in 1851, but widely read only decades later) began to create a truly American literature. Indeed, Jorge Luis Borges claimed with some literary authority that: "detective fiction was invented about one hundred years ago by that ingenious North American inventor called Edgar Allan Poe."[8]

By the 1870s, with Henry James and mainly Mark Twain, truly American literature began to develop. This was in contrast to "English language writing" that happened to surface on the western side of the Atlantic. As Bryce phrased it: "So Fenimore Cooper, Hawthorne, Emerson, Longfellow, and those on whom their mantle has fallen, belong to England as well as to America; and English writers, as they more and more realize the vastness of the American public they address, will more and more feel themselves to be American as well as English, and will often find in America not only a larger but a more responsive audience."[9]

The Europeans looked down on "American culture" during the initial years of the republic, not so much from snobbishness or arrogant superiority, but rather as a by-product of being older. The disdain in other countries would grow exponentially and transform itself when, toward 1870, for reasons of urbanization, transportation, the end of the Civil War and the economic boom stemming from industrialization, the United States would become an extraordinary cultural producer and consumer. Bryce—again—quotes a man from Carl Sandberg's city late in the century: "Chicago has no time for culture yet, but when she does take hold, she will make it hum."[10] In fact, America was already making poetry hum, according to Borges: "Undeniably, all that is specifically modern in contemporary poetry comes from two North

Americans of genius: Edgar Allan Poe and Walt Whitman."[11] Not all of his foreign contemporaries shared Bryce's optimism; German sociologist Max Weber detested the place, when he visited the stockyards in 1904: "Chicago is disgusting, the ugliest city I have ever seen."[12]

If Americans were born equal, then American culture was born late, but of a mass nature. Or as Carlos Fuentes thought, it was modern at birth.[13] Conversely, José Ortega y Gasset, the Spanish philosopher, thought the United States was practically unborn (at least until the 1930s): "To be young is not to be yet. And this, in other words, is what I am trying to suggest with respect to America. America is not yet."[14] It was, once again, a middle-class culture, for the middle class, by the middle class. Herein lies the deeper meaning of Hemingway's famous acclamation of Mark Twain in *The Green Hills of Africa*: "All modern American literature comes from one book by Mark Twain called *Huckleberry Finn* . . . . All American writing comes from that. There was nothing before. There has been nothing as good since." Or we can note Jorge Luis Borges, the Latin American writer most familiar with the literature of the United States—he translated *Leaves of Grass* and *The Wild Palms*—: "The first novel I ever read through was Hukleberry Finn."[15]

Finn was published in 1884. It sold more than 50,000 copies in the first few months after publication, and by its seventy-fifth anniversary, more than 10 million.[16] Twain was truly American, and truly mass consumed, from publication until today. But even a British author like Robert Louis Stevenson sold far more in the United States than in his native Britain: a quarter of a million copies over the first ten years of publication, in the United States.[17]

Perhaps American literature was born modern, versatile, diverse, and in constant churning because there were no previously existing literary institutions to frame it. One might even paraphrase the comment attributed to Franz Boas, the German founder (at Columbia University) of modern anthropology: it was the absence of centuries-old institutions in the United States that made this possible. Or as a Chinese anthropologist put it in 1943: "A young culture, like a young person, has no taboos."[18]

Perhaps the first floor in this cultural scaffolding, whose construction was well underway by 1870, despite having been dramatically interrupted by the Civil War, was literacy. By 1870, 88 percent[19] of the white population of the United States knew how to read, thanks largely to near universal elementary education; this statistic shows the relevance of the notion suggested a few pages back about separating the numbers for the excluded and included sectors of society.

The high white literacy was partly the result of the first immigrant wave's characteristics: Irish and German, who tended to be especially insular and introspective. The best way to bring them into the fold lay in extracting the children from their traditional milieu, and the best option for that was universal education. The only way to build a national culture when no previous one existed was through universal education, meaning, as we already stated, all white males, and subsequently white women. Then and now, the figures must be adjusted by race—only 20 percent of the black population was literate; probably by gender, though in a much smaller proportion; and by the bias of self-identification. These were Americans who claimed they could read; an independently tested truth would most likely have thrown up different results.

The number of periodicals, newspapers, and books Americans perused during the last quarter of the nineteenth century grew rapidly, and surpassed the Western European equivalent, even in per capita terms. In the case of the press, as early as 1829, according to one study, the ratio of newspapers printed by inhabitant was nine times higher in Pennsylvania[20] than in the entire British Isles. In France, where newspaper reading was much more widespread than in Britain, in 1870, for example, 1 million newspapers[21] were printed every day; American circulation was several times greater.[22] An Italian chronicler of his year in Washington, DC, in the mid-nineties grasped perfectly the American propensity to consume newsprint: "The idea of starting the day without a paper is inconceivable to the universal middle class that peoples the United States."[23] That same year, the American white literacy rate was significantly higher than the British one (77 percent), let alone the French (70 percent), German (68 percent),[24] and Spanish (25 percent in 1860).[25] If there was a growing demand for reading materials, there was bound to be a matching supply. By the turn of the century, 2200 new fiction books were published yearly in the United States.[26]

Many were bought individually, but also by the 1700 free, public libraries throughout the country in 1900.[27] In 1908, Holland, in comparison, boasted . . . six public libraries. Public libraries contributed mightily both to American homogeneity (inside the system) and diversity, conserving the icons of each social sector's specificity. I can still remember when a library card was a form of identification in the United States. Fifteen American novels sold more than 100,000 copies in 1901, an astounding figure for a nation of 76 million people.[28] Hence Bryce's lapidary conclusion: "A famous writer . . . is known by name to a far greater number of persons in America than would know a similar person in any European country."[29] The explanation for these remarkable figures lies certainly in public education. By the beginning of the century, thirty-one states had compulsory public elementary education, and 85 percent of children between 8 and 14 years of age were in school. The Massachusetts Legislature in 1836 passed the first legislation in United States making education compulsory.[30] In Italy, for example, a similar percentage was reached only thirty years later. Even today, the market is what it is: Michelle Obama sold over a million copies of her memoir during its first week in print. No other country can match these figures, or those—fascinating—for Thomas Mann's four-volume *Doctor Faustus* in 1947, thanks to the Book of the Month Club: 250,000 for a work whose reading required heavy lifting, and before Oprah's recommendations.[31] Today, Americans read an average of 12 books per year; the figure for Britain is 10, for Brazil 1.8, for Argentina 4.[32]

A second mass market for culture lay in the film industry, which literally exploded at the onset of the new century. Several thousand-seat movie theaters opened in the main cities of America. The first large theater to open in France, in 1899, seated 205 spectators; in Berlin, the first hall seating more than one thousand opened in 1912. Soon after World War I, weekly movie attendance reached 40 million; according to one calculation, every person in the urban United States went to the movies at least once a week.[33] In the 1920s and '30s, over eight hundred films were released every year, roughly 50 percent more than today's number.[34]

By comparison, the French movie industry—the first and initially the largest in the world—released fewer than two hundred films every year after the First World War. Attendance, though high, never reached

American levels. The same was true for Germany, Britain, and Spain. If Hollywood became falsely synonymous in the world with lowbrow American culture, it also brilliantly demonstrated the *mass* nature of culture in the United States from the very outset of the movie industry. The attendance figures for Griffith's 1915 *The Birth of a Nation*, blatantly racist and all, dwarfed all other numbers in the world. More than 1 million tickets were sold rapidly in New York City. All told, over 3 million viewers flocked to theaters to see it;[35] the most widely viewed films where movies began, i.e. France—*Fantomas* or *Les Vampires*, for example—never reached 1 million viewers during the entire First World War. The American film industry rapidly crisscrossed the globe. As early as 1929, a Japanese literary critic regretted that "Japan has also become a vassal state of Hollywood. Even in the provinces, every movie theatre shows at least one American film on its programs, and in our cities, some theatres show only Western movies—usually from America . . . . From rural youths to urban schoolgirls, from company employees to middle-school language teachers there is hardly anyone who does not know the names Ronald Coleman, Lillian Gish, Harold Lloyd, and Clara Bow."[36]

Another example of the congenitally mass nature of American culture is music. The phonograph was indispensable, but not the entire story. Arriving on the market in 1900, by 1920 half of American households owned phonographs;[37] if we correct for Southern and rural America, the actual proportion was far higher. Thus, nearly everyone—except for people of color, mainly in the South and partly in the West and Texas—who wished to listen to music at home, could. Opera singers and piano players became celebrities. But the key device was radio. By 1930, half of all American households—roughly 15 million—included a radio, whether hooked up to electricity or with batteries.[38] In France, the corresponding figure was 1.3 million; for Germany, 4.5 million; in Mexico, the number was barely 50,000.[39] The destruction of the European economies together with the demographic catastrophe engendered by World War I probably explain partially this discrepancy. In 1926, network radio was born, with the National Broadcasting Company (NBC). While not all of the fare offered on radio like news, comedy, or advertising could be considered "cultural," a great deal was. For music in general, and classical music in particular, radio became a remarkable instrument of mass distribution. In 1937, Arturo Toscanini was hired to create the NBC Symphony Orchestra, which continued to broadcast until 1954.

Nothing of this magnitude and speed occurred in Europe or Japan, let alone Latin America. In America, whoever could conduct an orchestra, compose a symphony, sing the blues, or dance in a Broadway musical counted on a potential audience of millions. On occasion, the stream of offerings generated for this incredible demand catered to the lowest common denominator in quality, sophistication, originality, and imagination. Sometimes, it targeted the highest standard. The point is, a mass audience existed and simply needed to be supplied with cultural products of varying diversity. It was. The cultural products it consumed quickly spread across the world, including for the first time, the extraordinary cultural offering generated by African Americans in literature, but mainly in jazz and blues.

This mass nature has often confused foreign commentators and visitors, because it amalgamates genres and styles that many preferred to separate. But cultural producers, that is, people involved in creating the supply of cultural products for the nearly infinite demand located in the United States, grasped the logic behind the peculiar, mass nature of American culture. Therein lies part of a second, fascinating explanation of the American cultural experience. It lay in the open arms with which the United States received artists from abroad, and their enthusiasm for seeking out American shores to write, paint, sing, compose, and make films was subsequently enjoyed across the world.

Give me your huddled . . . artists

Like the mass nature of American culture, this characteristic was present at the creation and has persisted until today. The fact that mainstream American culture was possibly far less welcoming to domestic, minority expressions—African American, Mexican, Native American—is a different discussion. As is the reverse path chosen by countless American artists, who decided to live or dance in Europe, Russia, or several countries of Latin America. This is the other side of the universalization of American culture. It neither neutralizes nor contradicts the wave of extraneous creative genius to reach United States shores.

The obvious examples of the outward wave are well known, beginning with the generation of American novelists who settled in Paris during the 1920s: Hemingway, Fitzgerald, Stein, Dos Passos, Ford Madox Ford, and others, like Pound in Italy. Edith Wharton and Gertrude Stein arrived earlier. A few of the more intriguing cases of semi-exile are previous to this period—James Whistler in Paris, Ambrose Bierce in Mexico in the nineteenth century, John Reed in Mexico and Russia/ the USSR. Others are partly political—Paul Robeson in England— or a product of racial discrimination in the United States: the African American generation of James Baldwin, Richard Wright, Chester Himes, and Langston Hughes. The list is long, though nowhere as broad as that of those who made the opposite journey.

The most famous case on this regard occurring in the twentieth century was that of a child movie actor who arrived in 1910 in New York from London: Charlie Chaplin. He undertook his first US tour between 1910 and 1912 and settled in Hollywood in 1913. Absurdly, Chaplin was fiercely criticized in Britain for not returning to fight in the war; his films gave the troops on leave a welcome distraction from the horrors of the Western front. He would spend the following forty years filming in the United States, before he was driven out by McCarthyism. Two of Mexico's three great muralists, Diego Rivera and José Clemente Orozco (and to a lesser extent David Alfaro Siqueiros), spent long periods in the United States. According to the curator of a Whitney Museum exhibition that opened in 2020, "their influence would prove profound on American artists searching for alternatives to the art-for-art's-sake ethos of European modernism . . . . Mexican artists were a "more creative influence in American painting than the modernist French masters . . . ."[40]

Their work in Detroit, Pomona, New York City, San Francisco, and Dartmouth College testifies to the attraction and support they encountered in the United States (in the case of Rivera, often in the company of Frida Kahlo, who also painted in the US), despite their political inclinations. Except when the latter caught up with them, as when the Rockefeller family decided to destroy Rivera's mural in Rockefeller Center, for depicting an alcoholic patron and an idealized Trotsky. Jackson Pollock would call Orozco's Pomona College *Prometheus* "the greatest painting done in modern times." Rivera's MoMa exhibition, which opened in late 1931, was only the museum's second one-person show and "broke all attendance records."[41]

These renowned Mexicans were nonetheless not the only ones to spend part of their time, and produce much of their work, on American soil. Octavio Paz and Carlos Fuentes spent many years teaching, writing, lecturing, and simply rearing a family at many of the most prestigious American universities. Mexico's greatest musician of recent times, the modern *mariachi* singer and composer Juan Gabriel, spent his last years between Miami and Los Angeles, feeling at home in both cities, and in the country at large. One of the greatest salsa and Latin jazz composers and singers, Panamanian Rubén Blades, has lived in the United States—New York and Los Angeles—for most of his forty-four-year career.

The motivations inspiring foreign artists to settle in the United States were multiple. Many proceeded for reasons of asylum, i.e. people fleeing from the successive catastrophes that befell Europe, Latin America, or Asia during the twentieth century. Vladimir Nabokov arrived in Manhattan in 1940 and taught at American universities for thirty years, before spending the rest of his life in Montreux. Thomas Mann separated himself from his native Germany in 1938 and resided for fifteen years in California and New Jersey. Romain Gary, as French consul in Los Angeles, became the quintessential bi-cultural author, although unlike Nabokov, he never wrote in English and never sought or needed asylum. Isabel Allende, the best-selling Chilean novelist, who did, acquired US citizenship in 1993 and has spent much or her adult life in California. Her compatriot, Ariel Dorfman, teaches at Duke University. The trend continues today, including contemporary writers such as Afghan Khaled Hosseini and Mexican Valeria Luiselli.

It is useful to distinguish here between immigrant authors, that is, those who arrived in the United States as children or in any case that began their work in the United States, and established writers who for different reasons decided to reside for long periods in the United States. The first category exemplifies one more tale in the saga of immigration to America. The second is the peculiarly American attraction for consecrated authors from the world over to pursue their work in the United States. Many writers, like the aforementioned Mexicans, and Mario Vargas Llosa today—whose mother became a naturalized US citizen—spent time in the United States for various periods.[42] They felt the need to establish a certain distance from their home countries to reinvent themselves, or make a better living, or be surrounded by a more diverse environment. What strikes the foreign observer is how well received they all were, even in the harshest of times—the McCarthy era, or the Reagan and Trump epochs—and how most of these creative figures thrived in the United States. From Einstein to Jakobson to Malinowski to André Breton, they all enjoyed shorter or longer expressions of American hospitality.

The same can be partly said about Paris in the 1920s, undoubtedly, although the brief length of the experience impeded it from becoming a tradition. Moreover, the numbers are not equivalent, and the institutional support—universities, foundations, research institutes—was missing in Paris (and still is).

Not every European artist or intellectual who settled in the United States, mainly in exile, can be said to have found their host country endearing. Bertolt Brecht simply hated Hollywood and America in general. According to one of his biographers, he saw the United States initially as a source of fresh vitality, in contrast to a Europe exhausted by war. He subsequently viewed it as the epitome of the inevitable self-destruction of capitalism. Hollywood was that in spades. For Brecht, Hollywood contained all the reasons why the United States was bound for destruction. As Stephen Parker, his biographer, phrased it: "Brecht had devoted his life to combating capitalism as the source of planned scarcity. The US solution was, by contrast, more capitalism."[43]

Brecht's whole aesthetic position was opposed to everything Hollywood represented. Despite his love of the cinema, Brecht had never developed any real creative affinity with the industry. That could not change in Hollywood where Brecht lived on the breadline for much of the time. His contempt for the film industry pours out as he responds to the movie men's taunt in the poem "Deliver the Goods": "When I see their rotting faces / My hunger goes away." As Lyon observes, "Brecht came (to the United States) out of necessity and stayed only as necessary."[44]

The exodus to American included plastic artists, musicians, architects like I. M. Pei, dancers, and, of course, film-makers. Many of the greatest twentieth-century American painters, like Willem de Kooning, are . . . not originally American. Others, like David Hockney, came and went from their native England to the West Coast. A few, such as Mark Rothko, arrived as the children of immigrants and belong more to that category. Others, like Mondrian, only spent the last years of their life in New York, dying before they could truly develop an American inspiration for their work. While some landed in the United States earlier in their lives than others, they inserted themselves into a cultural context and milieu that allowed them to flourish and simultaneously to maintain their originality. Marcel Duchamp is one such example.

In a very broad sense, American culture has reproduced, nearly always without coercion, a unique form of syncretism, not unlike what the Spanish conquerors did in New Spain and to a lesser extent in the territories of what today we call Latin America. Guillermo del Toro, the director of *The Shape of Water*, who won an Oscar in 2018 for his pathbreaking film, phrased it best, perhaps unconsciously. When asked how he balanced "the darkness and terror in his often monster-filled films" with "the joyful and loving person" that he is, Del Toro's response was simple: "I'm Mexican." That is, quintessentially synchretic, blending all his roots and environment together, in a synchretic milieu, in a synchretic country. He won his Oscar for best director not for a foreign film, but for an American one (*The Shape of Water*), as his colleagues did.

The movie industry is possibly the most illustrative demonstration of the welcoming nature of American culture, or of this syncretism, if we can call it so. Curiously, though, the best-known example is food. Every American knows this, intuitively, but does not necessarily connect the dots. Nearly all fast food originated in Europe, traveled to the United States, was transformed there, and was re-exported to the rest of the world: hamburgers, hot dogs or frankfurters, sandwiches, pizza, increasingly today, tacos, and coffee, thanks to Starbucks. America's capacity for regurgitating foreign cultures and making them "American" is proverbial and of course extends far beyond *cuisine*.

More substantively, the list of European and now Mexican directors who emigrated to Hollywood for varying periods of time is almost endless. Many household names in American cinematography began their careers elsewhere, from Billy Wilder to Alfonso Cuarón (*Gravity* and *Roma*), from Alfred Hitchcock to Alejandro González Iñarritu

(*Birdman*), from Otto Preminger and Ernest Lubitsch to Roman Polanski, from cinematographers like Gabriel Figueroa and Emmanuel Lubezki. Others of equal or greater fame include Ang Lee, Michael Curtiz, Joseph von Sternberg, William Wyler, David Lean and Milos Forman. It bears noting how many European Jews belong to a more exhaustive list, which this is not. Some arrived after the Nazis took power, or began their persecution, but many disembarked before that. "Chain migration" was at work then as now, but like today, there had to be an existing willingness to welcome them that did not prevail elsewhere.

A similar argument can be formulated regarding musicians: composers, conductors, and virtuosos. Once again, there is a distinction between those who arrived as children of immigrants in the US and those who already had launched their careers or were established figures when they started performing in the United States. From this perspective it matters little whether they emigrated permanently or temporarily, or if their primary motivation was fleeing persecution. Many fell in the latter category, from Mstislav Rostropovich and Igor Stravinsky, to Bruno Walter, Rudolph Serkin, Claudio Arrau (originally Chilean), and today, Venezuelan conductor Gustavo Dudamel. Other musical titans simply chose to work in the United States throughout the twentieth century, without any political undertones.

As already emphasized, there were many reasons that explained this constant flow of major cultural figures to the United States. It mattered a great deal to be in a country free of wars, and most of the time, of repression, censorship, and discrimination against foreigners. The affluence and generosity of benefactors was an unquestionable factor. Diego Rivera and Orozco were extremely well compensated for their work, by the Ford and Rockefeller families, or by the universities that commissioned their murals. The transformation of Hollywood into the movie-making capital of the world was another factor, not just for actors and directors, but also for screenwriters.

American universities, nearly always wealthier than their European, Japanese, or Latin American counterparts, were a natural destination for writers, philosophers, anthropologists, historians, and academics in general. The pre-existing presence of colleagues inevitably played a role. One professor invites another, who accepts because the first one is already there. But the openness of American society and culture,

the initially virgin nature of the cultural landscape, and the hospitality afforded to foreign visitors or immigrants in this specific field
was decisive. Michel Foucault, who spent years teaching and lecturing
at American universities and throughout the United States, and became somewhat of a cult figure in America, explained his attachment
the following way, in a conversation with an American academic: "If
I had been younger, I would have emigrated to the United States . . . .
I see many possibilities there. You do not have a homogeneous intellectual and cultural life. No one pressures me. There are many great
universities that all have different interests. On the other hand, the
University could have fired me in the most undignified way."[45]

Has this notable hospitality been duly appreciated by its beneficiaries?
Mostly yes, in terms of gratitude, but not always in acknowledging that
the vitality of American culture, its mass nature, as well as its sophistication and originality, are the product of this exchange with the rest
of the world. That culture's capacity for absorption and transformation
of inputs from abroad explains why foreigners have sought American
shores. The constant reinvention of American culture is partly a consequence of adopting, assimilating, and retro-fitting those inputs. And
perhaps also possessing the resources to acquire them, as structuralist
anthropologist Claude Lévi-Strauss concluded, after his five-year stay
in New York: "The immense resources which the local plutocracy
had to satisfy its whims, made it seem as if examples of the whole of
humanity's artistic legacy were present in New York."[46]

How does this jibe with the stiff-nosed attitude of many of the
visitors' friends and colleagues in their own countries who continued to
look down on American culture and the United States over the years?
Not well, and strangely. Perhaps the most extreme cases have surfaced in
the Arab world over the decades. Even the most sophisticated thinkers
were unable to avoid this smuggishness. Witness Egyptian writer, ed-
ucator, and activist, Sayyid Qutb, who lived in the United States from
1948 to 1950, on his country's government tab. He would later join
the Islamic Brotherhood, spending many years in jail and was subsequently hanged by Nasser's regime in 1966. His views on the American
cultural scene are especially revealing: "Americans used their wealth to
buy culture from abroad, but did not understand or value what they
imported . . . . American museums had very few works by American

artists because American works are primitive and plain to the point of being laughable next to those (imported) splendid worldly treasures."[47]

It is equally senseless for part of the French intellectual elite to peer down on the cultural output of a nation where many of its most distinguished thinkers and artists, from Louis Malle to Michel Foucault, and including Jacques Derrida and Claude Lévi-Strauss, lived, wrote, lectured, and filmed, with enormous success. Mexicans understandably enough possess a long-standing chip on the shoulder with regard to Americans in general, but having writers and painters dismiss American culture for its coarseness is in their case particularly paradoxical. The back-and-forth movement between the two cultures has immensely enriched both. Perhaps the roots of this paradox can be found in a third characteristic of American culture, which is a direct outgrowth of the first two: a universal nature, which has hugely contributed to its upgrade from a culture to a civilization.

From the idiot box to Netflix

The great absence from the previous, brief description of American culture is television, together with its unavoidable corollary: advertising and mass consumption. The first TV advertisement in history, for Bulova wristwatches, ran in 1941 on a New York station, almost exactly the same date that commercial television began to broadcast.[48] Despite every American administration's efforts since the beginning of the Cold War to propagate other facets of the nation's cultural production, few of its artifacts have permeated other countries as much as television. Coca-Cola might be one exception.

American culture has universalist aspirations like no other, and consumers of cultural products the world over have welcomed it with open arms. This is not a recent phenomenon; thanks to films, the extension beyond US borders of the American cultural experience began in the 1930s. Similarly, popular music from the United States was carried across the oceans by US troops during World War II. Thanks to its extraordinary novelty and reach, by the mid-fifties it had spread throughout much of the world. But it was television that truly universalized the main features of American culture from the 1960s onward, as the rest of the earth moved into the television age. In consequence, what most people received of American culture consisted in what television broadcast. It was not then the most refined American cultural export, although in the era of peak-TV, that might be changing.

In 1953, one of the first productions of the *Ed Sullivan Show* drew an audience of more than 50 million.[49] By 1955, two-thirds of American households—i.e., 48 million homes—owned television sets; in 1960 the number approached 90 percent, or more than 70 million households.[50] Although live television actually began in Germany in 1936 with the transmission of the Berlin Olympics, by 1957 the total of viewers in what was then West Germany had barely reached 1 million.[51] The figures for France were much smaller: in 1950, there were three thousand sets in the entire country.[52] They totaled 1 million in 1958,[53] when Britain already had almost 10 million.[54] US figures dwarfed all of Western Europe's.

The figures in other parts of the world are more disparate. In Mexico, there were 20,000 sets in 1952 and only 1.2 million in 1965, when the country hosted a population of 35 million inhabitants. In Brazil, with roughly double the population of Mexico, there were 120,000 sets in 1953, and 1.2 million in 1960.[55] The distance with India was enormous: 400,000 televisions in 1960 (for a population of 400 million); 1 million in 1965, and as late as 1970, with 600 million inhabitants, only 25 million sets.[56] Finally, even Japan was far behind, including when reconstruction had practically come to an end: 8,000 sets in 1953, 1.5 million in 1958, and 22 million in 1970, when the country's population reached 100 million.[57] For a rich country, this shows the contrast with the United States: in 1960, 90 percent of American homes owned TVs; in Japan there were 6 million sets.[58] No surprise, then, that television programs the world over were initially, and subsequently, American. The disparity in these figure stems from various sources: World War II, for the rich countries; the size of the American market; the price of television sets for the poor countries; the discovery of advertising as a way to make television profitable.

American programming began appearing on television screens in much of Europe, Latin America, and parts of Asia in the late fifties and early sixties, dubbed in the local language, but clearly presented as American. While other aspects of US culture had made their presence felt previously, television transformed it into a mass affair. Since the best portion of US television—news programs and interviews, music and comedy shows—was not easily exportable, foreign viewers were offered the choice of Walt Disney cartoons, which they already knew from movie theaters, *The Lone Ranger, Bonanza, Elliott Ness*, or *Superman* and *Batman*. Spanish TVE began broadcasting a dubbed version of *The Untouchables* in 1964.[59] Japanese public intellectual and writer Motoyuki Shibata has acknowledged that he first "learned about America from the TV dramas I watched as a kid. Father Knows Best, The Donna Reed Show, and I Love Lucy: a world of opulence where every family owns a big house, a family car, a refrigerator, and a vacuum cleaner; largely mythical commodities in Japan back then (the early 1960s)."[60] The first dubbed show in Brazil, the *Ford Television Theatre*, was broadcast in 1958; in France, *Alfred Hitchcock Presents*; in Argentina, *Highway Patrol* in 1956.

As television became a mass consumption product outside the United States, it emerged as an international vehicle for the least interesting, rewarding, or enlightening chapters of American culture, despite the talent of many of the people writing for the networks. Neither rock 'n' roll nor Hollywood could truly compete. Even the somewhat ridiculous role of women on American television of the fifties and sixties was exported. Countless soap operas showed US housewives in the suburbs patiently awaiting their husbands' return from work while they utilized one appliance after another to make life easier. Quality American television—news shows, talk shows, theater, interviews—was not exportable in those years and wasn't exported.

Simultaneously, though, the universalization of the very *best* of American culture in general was also taking hold. The Latin American literary boom of the sixties, for example, generally referred to as magical realism, was, according to its heroes, deeply indebted to the great American authors of the preceding decades, especially Dos Passos and Faulkner. García Márquez, Fuentes, Cortázar, and many others frequently recognized and expressed their gratefulness for the inspiration stemming from these colleagues in relation to time, memory, and punctuation. As Mario Vargas Llosa, the Peruvian Nobel Literature prize winner marveled forty years ago: "Faulkner's works were immediately and unanimously celebrated in Latin America. The reason was not only the magic of the turbulent lives of Yoknapatawpha County, not the former prowess of fiction constructed as a beehive. It was rather that, in the turbulent and complex world that Faulkner invented, we Latin American readers discovered our own reality in a different form and learned that like Bayard Sartoris and Jenny du Prés, backwardness and the periphery also contain beauty and virtues that so called civilization destroys. Faulkner wrote in English, but he was one of ours."[61]

Yet the worldwide translation of their works and of their debt to American literature, as well as the three Nobel Prizes for Literature that these authors received (though poet Octavio Paz was not a magical realist, nor were Chilean poets Gabriela Mistral and Pablo Neruda, or Guatemalan novelist Miguel Angel Asturias) could not compensate for the reach and impact of the American networks' shoddy wares across the globe. Only after 1990, through CNN, did quality US television penetrate abroad into homes, hotels, and airports.

A similar phenomenon arose with other universal expressions of American culture, sometimes summarized as "pop culture." Everything was exportable: Broadway musicals, certain forms of fashion, advertising uniformity—the same Marlboro cowboy everywhere, the same Coca-Cola jingles—even the use of Anglicisms in the purest of romance languages, Russian, or Hindi. The everyday presence of things American for hundreds of millions of people, given American civilization's mass characteristics and universality, was often reduced to the lowest common denominator. As British writer G. K. Chesterton put it, apropos his visits to the United States in the early twenties and early thirties: "The qualities of America that reach us across the seas are the things least worthy of boasting."[62] The passage from culture to civilization inevitably entails the exposure of the entire globe to every feature of that civilization, not just the best and brightest ones. Rome did not only export its legal code, political institutions, military innovations, aqueducts, and highways. The peoples it conquered or neighbored also suffered violence, slavery, and corruption.

American civilization is as inseparable from American culture as Coke and McDonald's are from Stephen Spielberg and Spike Lee, as Levi's jeans are from Phillip Roth, as English is from hip-hop and rap, as Jimi Hendrix is from Yo Yo Ma. Foreigners consume all of the above, but intellectually dismiss the lowbrow pop culture while revering the museums, publishing houses, concert halls, and rock concerts.

Americans are frustrated with the Latin American, European, or Indian view of smug superiority and hypocritical cherry-picking: Jonathan Franzen yes, the American version of *House of Cards*, no. All are right and wrong, simultaneously.

There are few aspects of American life that puzzle, provoke, and marvel foreigners as much as the vast, multi-faceted, two-hundred-year-old culture of the United States. It is receptive, ubiquitous, mass produced and mass consumed, as well as multicultural, domineering, often amalgamated with other aspects of US "soft power," and always irritating. It gave the world jazz, blues, and rock 'n' roll, but also Mickey Mouse and Donald Duck. The former first appeared in movie theaters in Mexico in 1933, and on television in 1968. In part for these reasons, the United States neither possesses a Ministry of Culture, like most governments do today, nor cultural attachés in most of its embassies across the globe. It does not need them. As Jean Baudrillard has remarked, "there is no cultural discourse here. No ministry, no commissions, no subsidies, no cultural promotion."[63] America's cultural representatives abroad, and its cultural apparatus at home, are different, partly, of course, because they had to make money. Civilizations do not have cultural attachés. They offer something else.

A clear example of this lies in Casa Grande e Senzala, the classic work by Gilberto Freyre, the renowned and controversial Brazilian sociologist who created the myth of his country's "racial democracy." He lived for many years in the United States, doing his undergraduate work at Baylor University in Waco, Texas and his graduate studies under Frank Boas at Columbia—and constantly noted the similarities between Northeastern Brazil and the southern United States, but also contrast between the mythical racial democracy of Brazil and flagrant, outrageous, murderous racism in the southern United States. As a scholar who worked on Freyre's views of America noted: "(In his diary), Freyre relates an occasion where, on a return from a school trip in Dallas, he stops in Waxahachie, a small town between Dallas and Waco. He smells an intense odor and is quickly informed that it is the scent of burned flesh of a black man. Freyre is shocked by his informant's candor and the possibility of such a hideous act in a "civilized" country. "I never thought that such horror was possible in today's United States. But it is. Here still people lynch, kill and burn blacks. It's not an isolated occurrence. It happens fairly often," Freyre writes. His experience with segregation and lynching would later express itself in Casa grande e senzala in the idea that race relations are more harmonious in Brazil in contrast to the general atmosphere of hostility towards blacks in the United States."[64]

American civilization has also bequeathed the modern musical comedy to the world. Although it enjoys multiple birthrights—European opera, minstrels in the South, and Gilbert and Sullivan British operettas—by the 1920s, it had become the epitome of American popular culture. The Ziegfeld Follies were perhaps the first amalgamation of music, dance, acting, production, and lyrics in a major show, but from the 1920s onward the genre consolidated itself as a uniquely American creation. The names are American household words: Cole Porter, Rodgers and Hammerstein, George Gershwin, Irving Berlin. *Oklahoma* in 1943 was the first fully polished musical, combining star actors—mainly female vocalists—composers, choreographers, stage production, orchestra, and style. Over the years the genre evolved, and the British in particular contributed greatly to its success in London and on Broadway. The world-wide popularity was such that today, one can attend a Broadway musical at any given time in practically any city in the world. The subsequent generations kept the tradition alive, with growing success: from Andrew Lloyd Weber and Bob Fosse to Lin-Manuel Miranda. It is the epitome today of everything we have described in terms of openness, receptivity, and paradox. Where would the grandson of Spanish-speaking Puerto Ricans compose a musical in English about an undocumented immigrant from the West Indies who became Secretary of the Treasury and earned billions on Broadway?

The musical embraces three marvelous American cultural virtues. First, boundless optimism: there are few American musical tragedies, except *West Side Story*. Most have happy endings. The second is unequaled professionalism: everybody does everything perfectly—acting, singing, dancing, costumes, production, advertisement, national and international tours. And thirdly: resources, organization, and project management at the service of joy and happiness. It is difficult to imagine anything more American, or anyone but Americans producing anything like musicals. Anyone who looks down on them knows not what they are missing, whether one likes a particular work or another.

Along with a certain type of organization of economic and political life, American culture is the most important component of American civilization today. The passage from culture to civilization involves every feature of that culture; without it, there would be no such thing, despite the overpowering nature of the market and the vote, and its occasionally questionable association with the United States. It will survive the president in American history most opposed to any type of cultural policy, if not to culture itself. Its resiliency has triumphed over racism, foreign adventures, violence, and rejection by broad swathes of the world's population on grounds of religious beliefs and practices. But even Islam has a multi-layered approach: millions of Muslims in the United States, North Africa, Europe, the Middle East, Iran, and Indonesia consume American cultural goods, tailored to their convictions and customs. Perhaps long after the other salient features of American civilization have passed from the scene, American culture, often and unjustly the least admired, will endure.

4

Dysfunctional democracy and its discontents

BECAUSE THE UNITED STATES has for two centuries presented itself to the world as a model of freedom and democracy, outsiders like me were raised to believe that its system of government worked well. But in recent decades, its shortcomings have been accentuated to the point that its uniqueness is no longer self-evident. For Latin Americans, who with the exception of the Brazilian monarchy, copied verbatim the US Constitution and political system immediately after Independence in the early nineteenth century, that admirable system's contemporary paralysis is dismaying. Its inherent contradictions were always visible, but its effectiveness was always deemed exemplary.

For Europeans, accustomed to dealing with the peculiarities of American democracy for longer than the Latin Americans, the current troubles facing the nearly two-and-a-half-century-old political system are even more confounding. Their relationship with Washington is based far more than others on the web of alliances, international organizations, and multilateral commitments that had functioned acceptably since World War II and is now questioned by the political system that gave them birth. Moreover, the Europeans are more flabbergasted than ever at the nature of elections and campaign financing in the United States. As one of the more recent, and critical, foreign books on America laments in regard to presidential campaigns: "Money has taken such a place, the sums are so enormous, that funders demand to be heard . . . . This is one of the great myths of American democracy: that each citizen counts, that with his donation of tens or hundreds of dollars, he or she contributes to the proper working of democracy."[1]

America's adversaries are probably more confused than anyone else. China is relieved by Washington's withdrawal from the anti-Chinese Trans-Pacific Partnership, only to find itself immersed in a trade war that is the only subject of consensus between Trump and his Democratic rivals in Congress. Iran in turn negotiated a nuclear disarmament agreement approved by one American administration, only to see it rejected by the following one. Russia thought it had contributed to a friend's election to the presidency, and an end to American sanctions; it ended up more conflicted with Trump than it probably would have been with Hillary Clinton. And the entire world, as we shall describe in the last chapter of this book, remains astounded by recurrent mass shootings in the United States, and the political system's excruciating inability to do anything about it.

For myriad foreign observers, these perplexing events are not the product of foreign policy mistakes or aberrations. They are the symptoms of a political system's deeper malfunctioning. The fault lies not with the foreign policy of the United States, but rather with a political system that appears ineffective, incapable of adapting to domestic and international change, and that has aged poorly. What follows is one foreign observer's exploration of what's not working, why it isn't, and the reasons explaining the difficulty of change.

American democracy will no doubt survive. But how it rides out its current storm will inevitably shape its future. Whether this entails a more or less painful process depends on two factors in particular. First, the incomplete or unfinished political transformations of recent decades must bear fruit. Second, further changes to the political system will be necessary in the near future. That democracy will live a longer and better life if and when the country addresses the fundamental challenges that have surfaced since the 1980s: the deep metamorphosis of American society, coupled with the immobility of a political system designed and built for an entirely different social alignment.

There is much more to liberal democracy than elections, but elections matter. Many of the other components of representative democracy are derived from electoral rules and regulations. This point has been eloquently stressed by multiple scholars and commentators over the past quarter century.[2] In most cases, however, the argument centers on one fundamental aspect of the conundrum: the (in)compatibility of the American political system with the re-emergence of inequality in the United States, with the down-sizing of the middle class, as well as with the stagnation of wages and wealth in the middle deciles of the income distribution scale since 1980. And indeed, these are all factors that have contributed to the dysfunctional nature of numerous American institutions.

Others point to the extreme polarization within and among political parties that has emerged in recent years as a fundamental cause of this dysfunctionality. According to these views, with ample evidence to support them, polarization reached its initial peak in the early 1900s, then receded from 1940 to 1980. It has now returned to its highest levels ever in 2010–20.[3]

There is, however, an additional and different point, that does not rest on statistics or knowledge, but is nonetheless crucial. It is that the changes in American society go deeper than the shrinking middle class. The political ineffectiveness of countless institutions emerged before the rebirth of inequality in American society. Viewed from afar, even before the advent of inequality, the American model displayed serious failings.

Over the years I have interacted intensely with many mainstays of the executive branch in the United States. But my contacts with the rest of the political establishment—Congress, governors, mayors—have been more sporadic, but nonetheless sufficient to shape an idea of its merits and drawbacks. In testimony before various congressional hearings in Washington, DC, since the early nineties, in countless lobbying efforts, and at lunches, dinners, seminars, and retreats, I have managed to forge my own idea of the *modus operandi* of the legislators, staffers, local officials, and the people who work with them.

I can recall the portly graciousness of a conservative, racist, and on occasion xenophobic Jesse Helms. I witnessed in the flesh both the insolent boorishness and extreme solidarity of an Edward Kennedy, the unending loyalty and decency of an Ernest Hollings, the statesman-like liberalism of Republicans like Chuck Hagel and Richard Lugar, and the unceasing intellectual curiosity of a Jerry Brown. I engaged for years with staffers in the Senate and House, who worked relentlessly for the right causes, from human rights to stopping the wars in Central America, from defending democracy and combating arms sales to striving for immigration reform against all possible odds. They are among the treasures of the American political system. All of them give the lie to the cliché about the insularity, ignorance, or indifference of the American political elite regarding the rest of the world. Both the principals and the staffers I came into contact with were undoubtedly exceptions, but I also learned that the bench is deeper than it is often purported to be. My colleagues from many countries, including my own, share my convictions, or opinions. Everyone admires our American governmental interlocutors; few respect today the system they work for.

This is why I am more convinced than ever of the inadequacy of the American political system. Its dysfunctional nature today is all the more surprising given the quality of its members and by the depth of the educational and informational institutions that produce them. The challenge lies not in the people; they are mostly exceptional. It springs from the system itself. The best and the brightest—and many of them are exactly that—cannot turn this system around easily, or at all. Its defects stem from the disconnect between its contours and content, and the society it is meant to serve. As it stands today, that system will continue to demolish, neutralize, flip, or even corrupt the most well-trained, honest, and devoted public servants, at least in the areas referred to here. Americans deserve the notable political establishment they have built over the past two-and-a-half centuries, but they deserve a far more effective, modern, and well-suited political system than the one they are today condemned to suffer.

From few who are all alike to many who are all different

The American political system transited from a constantly homogeneous membership to a heterogeneous one. There were always vast segments of American society that remained outside the political system, but those inside it were homogeneous—from property-owning white males to the successive, gradual, and partial additions. The homogeneity prevailed in a country far less perfect than today's: more excluded minorities and other sectors of society, more discrimination, more oppression. The United States is a far better country now than before woman's suffrage, the New Deal, or the civil rights movement. But its present electoral configuration is partially incompatible with the political system that rested upon the previous homogeneity. It has come to resemble the "elite democracies" that emerged in a few Latin American nations toward the end of the nineteenth century: free and fair elections for those who voted (a tiny minority), and a relative separation of powers coupled with a great deal of corruption.

Homogeneity here does not have a political or ideological connotation. It is of course in the eyes that behold it. A society viewed by insiders will see all its variety and complexity, while that same society viewed by an outsider may easily display sameness. In casual conversation, I may generalize about "the French" or "the Indians" or "the Australians" because I know that my interlocutor, not being French, Indian, or Australian, will immediately grasp my meaning. Yet if I am told that "the Mexicans" are this or that, my response will inevitably be, "which Mexicans?" True, in Mexico's case, there is a high degree of ethnic homogeneity since the vast majority of the population carries both pre-Columbian indigenous blood and European blood, with those of purely European, African, or Asian extraction constituting a tiny minority.

That has served to create a Mexican identity, but not a Mexican character. From Chiapas to Chihuahua (and now well into the United States), people may *feel* Mexican, but how they define this differs dramatically. Thus, in my lifetime, during which Mexico's population has quadrupled, the notion of *being* Mexican has changed little. Where the Mexican experience contrasts sharply with that of the United States is that past American homogeneity—the American middle-class dream— has now been transformed not only by economic change but perhaps even more so by immigration. But the political system has not.

In the American context, homogeneity is not an antonym of pluralism (although in logic it arguably is). Homogeneity, and its contrary, heterogeneity, in this context reflect a factual situation. Pluralism is an indispensable component of any type of democracy, because at the end of the day, any society divided into classes inevitably transposes those divisions ideologically and politically. But democracy can exist and thrive in different societies, homogeneous or not: religiously, ethnically, racially, or linguistically. This does not make them more or less democratic. They can be notably heterogeneous like India or like Austria or Finland, homogeneous societies *par excellence*. The American political system's challenge today does not derive from its pluralism; indeed, one could argue that it is less ideologically pluralistic than before. The issue is the shift from an exclusionary *homogeneous* system, to an inclusive *heterogeneous* one.

An initial reflection in this regard springs from the changing composition of the American *electorate*, as a reflection of the changing nature of American *society*. As many have stated, the American system was partly Athenian, in that everyone who participated in it was roughly equal to everyone else, but a great many did not participate. The most transparent—and outrageous—example of this process, after Emancipation, consisted in the Chinese Exclusion Act of 1882. Not only did it bar further immigration from China, as I mentioned before, but it permanently excluded from citizenship Chinese individuals already in the United States. At that time, people of Chinese origin made up nearly one out of every ten inhabitants of California.[4] By determining that the Fourteenth Amendment, which granted citizenship to former slaves, did not apply to people of Chinese descent, the Act condemned them to permanent alien status. It was not repealed until 1943, due to Roosevelt's alliance with China in World War II. Now, Asian-Americans have a higher median household income than white Americans. The irony is flagrant: in today's highly unequal electorate, as Dutch author Geert Mak points out, "an American of Asian origin in New Jersey lives an average of twenty-six years longer than a Native American and is eleven times as likely to have been to university."[5] Given that both individuals he mentions actually participate in the traditional political system, for a European such a degree of inequality makes that system dysfunctional.

This gradual incorporation generated myriad consequences, some highly negative and others partly conducive to peaceful and restricted democratic governance. The latter depended on one premise in particular: the *sine qua non* continuing homogeneity of the existing, gradually expanding, electorate. The Senate's case was the most flagrant. Its members were elected by state assemblymen until 1913, very much like in Europe, and even in France today. That "electorate" was by definition male, white, tending toward middle age, and originating in the middle class. The *presidential* voters were almost identical to those for the House of Representatives, and equally homogeneous. In 1912, 6 million Americans elected Woodrow Wilson president; mostly white and all male.[6] Black turnout in the South that year, where a large majority of African Americans still lived (the Great Migration began in 1916), was almost nil: 2%.[7] In 1932, 23 million voters sent Franklin Roosevelt to the White House; that electorate included women, but still only one out of every five actual voters. Of those, an overwhelming majority were white and of European descent.[8]

This was due to the well-known fact that the initial impulse to expand African American suffrage under Reconstruction vanished rapidly. In the 1868 presidential elections, half a million freedmen and northern blacks voted for Ulysses S. Grant; by the end of the 1870s, African American registration in the South practically disappeared.[9] Only after the civil and voting rights reforms of the sixties would black turnout rise significantly, at least in the South.

As the electorate began to diversify, something happened. African Americans and Latinos, as well as Asians somewhat later, contributed to the *heterogeneity* of the sum of all voters, but they themselves voted *homogeneously* in astonishing proportions. Nearly 80 percent of black voters cast their ballots for Harry Truman in 1948 and may have given him his surprise victory over Thomas Dewey. In one of the first polls taken within the so-called Democratic Coalition, in 1952, three-fourths of "Black non-Hispanic" Americans identified with Democrats or were "leaners," although they only made up a slight part of the Democratic coalition.[10] The Democratic share of the black vote oscillated around that level for the next half century, with a low of 59 percent in 1960, and a high of 94 percent in 1964.[11] Between 1936 and 2016, it averaged more than 80 percent.[12] Exit polls only included Hispanics after 1966, when more than eight out of every ten Latinos interviewed considered themselves Democrats.[13] The figures stayed around that level until after the 2012 election, when they descended to around 60–65 percent, where they remain.[14]

For many years, the absolute number of minority voters remained small, so their nearly uniform voting habits rarely affected outcomes.

Foreigners were often puzzled by the fact that decades after Emancipation, blacks did not vote. They rarely understood that, in fact, they were not allowed to do so, thanks to a series of electoral shenanigans. Some foreign observers, particularly the more politically sophisticated, reached dramatic and largely accurate conclusions. Max Weber, fifteen years after his 1904 visit to the United States, including the South, was categorical: "In the South, democracy has never actually existed, and still does not to this day."[15] In 1964, only 5.5 million blacks voted, largely for Lyndon Johnson. They represented approximately 7 percent of all voters.[16] African American and Hispanic minorities accounted for barely 10 percent of actual voters in 1976; 13 percent by 1988. In 2000, minorities accounted for 19 percent of the vote, including, for the first time, 2 percent of Asian descent. In 2012, Obama's second election, the total jumped to 28 percent. In Donald Trump's election, 30 percent of all *actual* voters belonged to minority groups; a similar figure emerged from the 2018 midterm vote.[17]

This increasingly heterogeneous electorate, however, did not divide up or break evenly, like the originally white, male voting population of European descent. From the very first exit polls taken in the United States, African American voters have cast their ballots overwhelmingly for Democrats, attaining the astounding figure of 92 percent for Barack Obama in 2012. The same is true for Latinos, at slightly lower levels. If one separates the chiefly Republican Cuban-American vote in Florida and New Jersey from the overall Latino percentage, the Democratic share rises, reaching approximately three-quarters of all Hispanic voters. I deliberately mention the Cuban-American electorate in order to clarify a key point. In this text, the words Latino, Hispanic, Mexican-American, Cuban-American, and other hyphenated terms are considered synonyms; the same is true for the newer LatinX. They possess an essentially legal and ethnic origin: people of Hispanic-American origin, with American citizenship. The vibrant, often acrimonious debates that take place within this very broad community are fascinating but different from the issues addressed here. That is a strictly intra-American discussion; from a foreign perspective, considering the above-mentioned terms as synonyms is the logical course.

Conversely, the white electorate is growing increasingly Republican, and particularly in its male, non-college-educated, over-50 segment.

In sum, minorities have become a major part of the electorate, and they tend to vote homogeneously for Democrats. The white, over-50, shrinking majority tilts heavily Republican. If everything continues this way, the writing on the wall is as clear as its consequences. The existing political system was not built for this equation.

Almost for the first two hundred years, the American electorate was composed of basically identical voters (white women of European descent, for many years voted like their male counterparts), who cast their ballots for either of two parties that, with a few exceptions—Roosevelt, Reagan—were also highly similar. From progressive intellectuals to Fidel Castro, countless foreigners expounded on the parallel between Republicans and Democrats on the one hand, and Pepsi and Coke on the other. They were not entirely mistaken, but they misunderstood the reasons for their insight: understandably enough, a homogeneous electorate elected a homogeneous political elite.

The Congressional representation of these voters was also comparable, in terms of race, gender, ethnicity, age, and political inclination. None of this remains true today. There is not only a greater polarization of the electorate itself, but the distance and distinction between an administration elected by one set of voters and the following or previous one is also widening. Furthermore, there are fewer opportunities for this situation to change, thanks to another mutation: the growing homogeneity of districts, in the context of the growing heterogeneity of the electorate as a whole.

Whose vote remains excluded and distorted, and what difference would they make?

The rise of voter suppression in the past twenty years, and the intensification of the struggle against it, reflect the disconnect between a political system built for a homogeneous electorate and the latter's increasingly heterogeneous nature. Voter suppression, especially in the South, is the equivalent of attempting to revert to homogeneity. It began with the end of Reconstruction and the establishment of Jim Crow voter restrictions and requirements, and continues to this day in states like Georgia or Mississippi, where if enough blacks and Latinos voted, most elected officials would belong to one or the other minorities. As late as

1940, only 3 percent of black citizens in Florida were registered to vote.[18] Since literacy, property-owning, or other egregious stratagems became illegal after the Voting Rights Act, new and imaginative schemes have replaced them. So-called motor-voter requirements (a driver's license); street addresses where there are no streets; proof of residence; previous, long-term registration; ex-felon disenfranchisement; and voter-fraud fake scandals or scares all form part of this trend.

The felon and ex-felon question is both symptomatic and substantial. As American History Professor Allan Lichtman from American University points out, the United States is one of the few democratic nations that prevents former felons who have completed their sentences from voting. Out of forty-five countries surveyed, "only three others had similarly stringent disenfranchisement laws: Armenia, Belgium and Chile. Twenty-one nations imposed no restrictions on felon voting even while in prison, fourteen imposed selective bans on prisoners and only ten banned prison voting. In America forty-eight states prohibit voting by imprisoned felons; only Maine and Vermont impose no suffrage penalties on felons."[19] Again, the discrepancy with the behavior of other democracies startles foreign observers; the reasons for the discrepancy are less obvious, unless one explores the details of voter suppression and whose votes are suppressed.

In 2016 more than 6 million felons or ex-felons had lost their voting rights temporarily or permanently, nearly four times as many as fifty years before. There is a clear bias against the African American and Hispanic population, since they are incarcerated at much higher rates than whites. Some states, such as Florida, combine draconian restrictions on felons' rights, a large black electorate, and a swing-state status. There, felon and ex-felon disenfranchisement can make all the difference between winning and losing. This explains why in 2018, through a crucial ballot initiative, voters approved a measure restoring voting rights to 1.4 million disenfranchised citizens.[20] Anti-felon restrictions are the broadest expression of voter suppression, which in turn is a reloaded attempt to restore electoral homogeneity. It is important to place this phenomenon in a historical context: it dates back to Reconstruction.

In its own fashion, voter suppression confirms the undeniable anomaly of the present paradox. The system cannot function normally with a heterogeneous electorate; it was designed and built to operate with a homogeneous one. A solution to this monkey wrench in the works lies in making the system itself as homogeneous as possible again, as part of "making America great again." The fact that so many Democrats and minorities have sued state electoral authorities over these and many other "dirty tricks" demonstrates the issue's relevance. It also proves that nothing is over until it's over, and the fight for inclusion in the United States, like elsewhere, never ends.

With the exception of Obama, at a presidential level, or in a sprinkling of congressional districts, each ethnic group of voters is more and more inclined to vote for "its own." Similarly, aside from Obama, most non-white politicians refrain from reaching out to white electorates, perversely strengthening the worst vices of the system. All of this can be the product of deliberate gerrymandering or of unconscious, unwitting "self-gerrymandering." It occurs through housing, schools, property taxes, or other factors. Thus, Latino voters, for example, are concentrated in a few Latino states, in a small cluster of Latino districts, and in a handful of Latino cities. If more Latinos register and turn out to vote, the result is somewhat irrelevant as far as how many members of Congress are Latino is concerned. Those voters are still today largely concentrated in the same districts, states, or cities. The equivalent is true of blacks, in the South quite definitively, but equally in many other areas of the country.

This is often referred to as "inefficient/wasted" voting or "packing": drawing districts to make them as black or Latino or Asian as possible. In this fashion, those districts always go to the leading minority, concentrated in that district. What Nate Cohn of *The New York Times* calls "inefficient" minority voting involves districts where African Americans or Hispanics or Asians can run up broad margins of victory for the Democratic Party, but the result is still only one seat, whether won 80 percent to 20 percent, or 51 percent to 49 percent.

The best-known result of this phenomenon consists in the overwhelming importance primaries have acquired, and the ensuing radicalization of those who participate in them. If a given district's final outcome is a by-gone conclusion in party terms, because of this hyper-homogeneity, or "packing," or self-gerrymandering, then the only real contest is within each party. Contests are decided in primaries, but only the most militant, politicized, and intensity-driven voters participate. Generally that implies that a radical candidate—Democratic or Republican—will tend to win the primary in what is the *de facto* election.

But this is not the only consequence. The starkest example of inefficient voting is California, whose absolute results hardly matter in a presidential election—the state has voted repeatedly for a Democrat in presidential elections since 1992. In 2016, Hillary Clinton obtained 62 percent of the vote, a 4.3 million vote advantage over Donald Trump.[21] In 2018, Democrats conquered 45 of the 53 House seats (as well as every seat in New England).

Nonetheless, California has seen its Electoral College representation rise only from forty-five votes in 1988 to fifty-five as late as 2016. Of these, forty come from districts where Latinos, blacks, and Asian-Americans, in one combination or another, make up more than half of the population: the so-called majority-minority districts. Twenty-one of those districts send Latino, African American, or Asian-descent representatives to Washington today, instead of eight back in 1988, roughly the same increase as in the electorate and the population as a whole.[22] The four traditionally Republican, highly conservative seats in Orange County captured by Democrats in 2018 were all majority-minority: Latinos and Asian-Americans. In a couple of these districts, the white population declined from 75 percent of the total in 1980 to 30 percent in 2017.[23]

But *every* minority congressperson from California comes from a majority-minority district; conversely, the most diverse state in the Union has still not yet elected a minority Senator.[24] People of color cannot get elected in white majority districts. I use the expression people of color because it elegantly groups together discriminated cohorts of American society who are largely discriminated against because of the color of their skin. But as we shall see in the chapter on race, and later on mass incarceration, this is a useful political, and rhetorical, euphemism, but a euphemism all the same. Most of the time, the exclusion, discrimination, injustice, and horror involving minorities are directed at the African American population, and this is true of voting rights, elected officials, and everything linked to these matters.

The vast increase in minority *voters* in California over the past few decades has brought a change in the number of minority *congressional members*. But this has not transpired in non-minority districts, nor in a large transformation of the electorate, and has brought only a negligible impact on California's weight in the presidential election. In 1990, two years after the last time the state voted for a Republican presidential candidate, it had a population of 29 million, of which a quarter, or less than 10 million, were minorities.[25] Today 39 million Californians, of which half are minorities, inhabit the state. But their influence at a national scale, or even within their state, does not reflect this change. The percentage of tax income devoted to education in California, for example, has been reduced nearly by half over the past fifty years, even though it favors growing minorities. The state today spends more on prisons—filled with Latinos and African Americans—than on higher education, which is a reflection of the white population's priorities.[26]

Contrariwise, in the country at large, white, lower middle-class, over-50 districts are the same as always, with perhaps slightly fewer *inhabitants* but more *voters*, insofar as their turnout tends to be higher than the rest. Similarly, "those who show up at the polls are disproportionately wealthy: while nearly 80 percent of high-income citizens vote, barely 50 percent of low income citizens do."[27] More importantly, the states where they reside, again, in a persistently homogeneous fashion, have essentially the same number of votes in the Electoral College. Hence the well-known paradox: since 1992, Democratic candidates have won the national popular vote in every election but one (Bush in 2004), yet they have occupied the White House only during sixteen of those now twenty-eight years.

"Packing" or gerrymandering is not such a simple maneuver. It requires a state legislature majority (they change often), Department of Justice clearance that Supreme Court standards are met, and improving technology to fine-tune as much as possible. All of this means that many districts are not that easy to shift or flip, so to speak. An additional factor, if confirmed, would be the Trump administration's ultimately failed attempt to include a citizenship question in the 2020 Census. Districts are apportioned on the basis of all people residing there; if a distinction is drawn between citizens and non-citizens, and many non-citizens refuse to answer, more radical redistricting becomes more feasible.

What do all these numbers mean politically?

The political implications of this sorry state of affairs are somber. Black, Latino, and Asian-American voters, as well as the somewhat younger, college-educated white groups on the two coasts, and in a few urban "islands" in the middle of the country (Chicago, Houston), can rarely produce legislative or popular vote majorities on national issues. Hence they often resort, inevitably and logically, to so-called identity politics, where only significant, focused, and concentrated legislative, local, or even public opinion minorities are often sufficient. Some foreign scholars, who have known the United States well, trace the emergence of identity politics back to the sixties, as British historian Tony Judt did in one of his last books: "The politics of the 60s thus devolved into an aggregation of individual claims upon society and the state. 'Identity' began to colonize public discourse: private identity, sexual identity, cultural identity."[28] Poor whites, on the other side of the political spectrum, adopted this attitude years before. V. S. Naipaul caught it well in the 1980s: "A lawyer I met said that, to understand, it was necessary to remember that 120 years or so ago there had been slavery. For poor white people race was their identity. Someone well off could walk away from that issue, could find another cause for self-esteem; but it wasn't that easy for the man with little money or education; without race he would lose his idea of who he was."[29] Minorities feel, rightly, that their possibilities of achieving significant, overall, national change are scarce, or nil. On identity issues, the chances are higher: change is within reach. The other America, still a majority but a shrinking one, the white, non-college-educated, over-50 America, is familiar with identity politics but prefers to continue to center its attention on broader ideological issues—abortion, taxes, immigration, same-sex marriage, health care—among other reasons because it is still a majority. It opposes all of the above and bases its identity partly on this opposition, although its main pillar remains simply being white. Indeed, some believe—in my view wrongly—that this opposition is driving the movement toward the extremes by parts of this sector of the electorate and society. Niall Ferguson, no friend of identity politics, senses that "Over the past three decades, self-styled progressives have insisted with fanatical zeal on the primacy of racial and sexual identities. Meanwhile, the so-called 'alt-right' has responded with increasingly overt appeals to 'white nationalism.' "[30]

Occasionally, a liberally oriented Supreme Court will rule in favor of changes espoused by the progressive side of identity politics (*Roe v. Wade*, same-sex marriage) or broader liberal causes. But mostly, either conservative verdicts will be handed down by the judicial system or these causes will lose in Congress. This was the case with immigration reform since the early 2000s, or even health care reform under Clinton—when it sank—and Obama, when it barely survived. The Affordable Care Act may have been the best available option at the time, but it was limited and watered down by various compromises.

Unavoidably, this is leading the United States toward a political system incapable of addressing the major challenges facing the country—inequality, race, education, immigration, health care, a new welfare state, climate change, gun control. But nor can it settle once and for all the other, narrower issues, that are constantly re-litigated in the courts, the universities, the media, and the entire nation. More than forty years after the Supreme Court ruling on abortion, and almost a half century since most European nations legalized it under varying circumstances, the United States is embarked in the 2020s on a new debate to revisit the question and perhaps overturn a decades-old decision. Simultaneously, in a rapidly changing world of migrations and a country with constantly replenished cohorts of immigrants, the last immigration law reform took place in 1986. This was Ronald Reagan's Immigration Reform and Control Act (IRCA). Similar conclusions can be reached regarding other major challenges such as taxation and the welfare state, gun control, violence, and mass incarceration—along with powerfully emotional issues affecting only specific groups, for example, LGBT rights or marijuana legalization.

The tax question illustrates best the American political system's dysfunctional dilemma. The United States taxpayer pays less in taxes than practically any of his or her equals in the OECD, the so-called rich countries' club. The overall tax take is inferior, and the correction in inequality, produced by taxes and transfers and measured by the Gini coefficient, is lower than in any other wealthy nation. The percentage of federal, state, and local taxes—and excluding social security and Medicare—measured against GDP in the United States in 2016 was 26 percent; the corresponding figures for the United Kingdom was 33 percent, for France 45 percent, for Germany 38 percent, for Spain 33 percent. The OECD average was 34 percent. The American Gini coefficient *after* taxes and transfers amounted to 0.39; the Canadian number was 0.30, the German and French, 0.29.[31] The pre-tax totals were roughly equal. This is a relatively new phenomenon. As mentioned before, the equivalent figures in the 1950s and 1960s were the other way around. As late as 1978, before the Reagan inversion, the US Gini coefficient after taxes was lower than France's and very similar to Canada's.

By another measure of inequality, in 1910, the share of total income corresponding to the top 1 percent of the population in the United States was approximately 18 percent. The equivalent figure for the UK was 22 percent, for Japan around 19 percent, and France 20 percent.[32] Over the next seventy years—the golden age of the American middle class— the US amount dropped systematically, reaching its lowest point in 1980 at 11 percent, higher than the other English-speaking rich countries, but only slightly above France and Japan, for example. Today, of all countries in the World Top Incomes Database, the United States has the highest shares of national income for the top 1 percent, top 0.1 percent, and top 0.01 percent of earners—only South Africa and Argentina come close.[33]

As Figure 4.1 indicates, inequality trends in the United States have displayed a U-shape curve since the booming 1920s, decreasing during

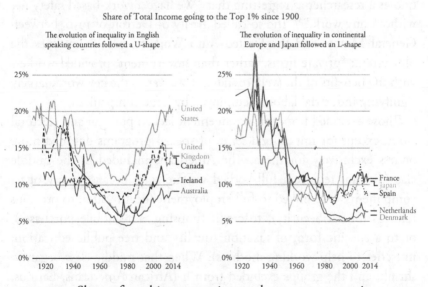

FIGURE 4.1. Share of total income going to the top 1 percent since 1900
Source: World Wealth and Income Database (2018)

the Depression and post-Depression years until the 1970s, and starting to increase again thereafter. Inequality continued to grow in the early 1980s. The figure also shows how the European, Japanese, and Canadian welfare states consolidated themselves even in hard times, adapting to new economic circumstances, with L-shaped curves for the same time period. By 2014, the US proportion of income corresponding to the top 1 percent had skyrocketed to 21 percent, far superior to the English-speaking rich countries, and twice or more as in France, Japan, Spain, Holland, and Denmark.

One can argue the case either way. Americans paid lower taxes than others because they didn't possess or desire a full-fledged, cradle-to-grave welfare state, or they rejected this social construct because they refused to pay sufficient taxes to finance it. As long as the great, white, Anglo, male, industrial, partly college-educated American middle class reigned supreme in the land, that welfare state was not indispensable. The safety net was directly linked to employment, which was abundant. Health care, unemployment insurance, Social Security, all indirectly were based on the jobs people had. As those jobs began to wither away, and were replaced by work without long-term contracts, fringe benefits, and stability, a plain vanilla welfare state became necessary. Geert Mak quotes a researcher as regretting that "We have a work-based safety net without any work."[34] The so-called Treaty of Detroit of 1950, between General Motors and the United Auto Workers, best exemplifies the old system: "private firms, rather than government, provided workers with the benefits of the welfare state."[35] *Workers* is the key word, largely signifying industrial laborers employed by large companies.

Those excluded from this arrangement lacked political and electoral clout, except for imposing a series of special programs destined more or less exclusively for them. The Americans included in the middle class did not require a full-bodied welfare state because many of its components were linked to full employment (health care), to previous reforms (Social Security), to credit (housing, automobile purchases), or to a specific form of taxation (quality and free public education, nurseries to help working mothers). When that middle class began to shrink, and the groups excluded from it (African Americans, Latinos, women, other minorities) garnered sufficient power to enact legislation addressing their needs, the entire edifice creaked.

It required a broader, more permanent welfare state. The problem is that retaining an enormous military establishment, expanding the welfare system, and vastly upgrading the country's infrastructure carry a huge price ticket. That implies more taxes: something the American electorate refuses. What's more, the only significant tax *reforms* at a federal level in years have been tax *cuts*: Bush in 2001, and Trump in 2017, although Obama slightly raised taxes on the wealthy in 2009, and Obamacare implied a large transfer of resources from the rich to the poor.

In a functional political system, enough potential beneficiaries of a broader welfare state, be they minority groups or those hurt most by the stagnant or declining status of the white middle class, vote for leaders supportive of tax increases to finance it. This is how Europe built its astronomically high, initially regressive, and tremendously efficient national Value Added Tax; the United States still lacks one. Minorities' turnout would be high, these issues would be paramount, and the resistance on the other side could be defeated through sheer numbers. At a *municipal* level, white, affluent, elderly residents, either no longer with school-age children or enrolling them in private schools, may well *refuse* to pay higher property taxes to provide minority students with better public education.

This was exemplified by Proposition 13 in California in the 1980s. Authors and travelers James and Deborah Fallows offer a splendid example of this paradox, in Holland, Michigan: "By 2005, Holland was in the familiar situation of having a mainly non-white public school population in a mainly white small town."[36] However, voters at the *state* level can *amend* this situation, as Governor Jerry Brown did in 2016 through a ballot initiative. But other than this case and a few other exceptions, the national and federal trend is exactly the opposite. Those who do not receive direct benefits from higher taxes refuse to pay them, while those who would benefit are not enough, or are unorganized, or lack the resources to mount effective campaigns. Tony Judt's reflection on taxation in the rich countries was mostly applicable to the United States: "Most taxation goes toward paying off past debt or investing in future expenditures. Accordingly, there is an implicit relationship of trust and mutuality between past taxpayers and present beneficiaries— and of course future taxpayers—who will cover the cost of our outlays today . . . . If we raise taxes or put up a bond to pay for a school in our home district, the chances are that other people's children will be the chief beneficiaries."[37]

Worse still, whoever started identity politics, its spread on the coasts and in certain circles of the Democratic Party, the natural allies of a tax-based greater welfare state, i.e. the white, over 50, non-college-educated males who have lost their jobs or seen them downgraded in wages and benefits are reluctant or adamantly opposed to joining any coalition of this nature.[38] They reject the notion that they should join blacks, Latinos, women activists, students, gay activists, or liberal Democrats to build a decent social safety net for everyone, including themselves. They have been persuaded that this is "socialism." They may not constitute a block majority, and their power may spring from their coalition with other conservatives, but their reluctance or refusal to join the liberal/minority coalition condemns it to frequent failure.

An additional paradox of American democracy stems precisely from the growth of identity politics. Its emergence as a viable alternative to the tardy and incomplete inclusion of the excluded groups of the past is understandable and laudable. It has contributed, however, to the paralysis of American society on matters ranging far beyond the issues involving identity politics, or in the reaction to identity politics by the dwindling conservative majority. A second reflection regarding American democracy's challenges derives from this paralysis. It endangers or impedes the country's international engagement as befits a world hegemon with colossal responsibilities and a history of engagement abroad.

Being a world hegemon costs money and requires political will

As Gunnar Myrdal put it nearly eighty years ago: "American nationalism is permeated by the American Creed, and therefore becomes international in its essence."[39] But that essence has not always been respected. Episodes in the past have demonstrated a recurrent and incomprehensible (to the rest of the world) American aversion to involving itself in matters and areas of the world's agenda that only the United States can influence, as recently as the Trans-Pacific Partnership and the Paris Climate Change Agreements. There are plenty of much earlier examples. They range from the Senate's rejection of the Versailles Treaty and entry to the League of Nations, in 1921; the obstacles Roosevelt encountered between September 1939 and December of 1941 in backing Britain against the Nazi threat to its very existence; Washington's constant bickering over its United Nations participation and financial obligations; and the need for the Bush (41) administration to finance its first Gulf War through donations from oil-rich monarchies or dictatorships. There are other examples from a more recent past.

The point of departure is the end of conscription in 1973. The reason is well known. Richard Nixon convinced himself, quite rightly, that he could take the wind from the sails of the anti-Vietnam War student movement by eliminating the draft. Hundreds of thousands of young Americans from all walks of life would no longer be sent to fight and die in the middle of nowhere. A volunteer army would eventually ensure as strong a military as conscription, without the political and social consequences of the draft. It was a skillful tactical move by a wily politician, but a dramatic mistake from a long-term strategic perspective with regard to equality and international engagement by the United States in the world.

The American conscripted military had been one of the nation's main instruments of de-segregation and equalization, at least since World War II. It also served as a tool for engaging the country as a whole in foreign involvements, for or against. The executive and Congress could decide to pursue a war, or a limited military intervention, knowing that they would have to drum up broad support for their undertaking, but that if they succeeded in doing so, the country would back them all the way. There would be scant domestic political consequences. The examples range from the multiple interventions in Central America already cited, to World Wars I and II and the Korean War. On the other hand, if the endeavor turned out to be fruitless, failed, or unpopular, as in the case of Vietnam, society would reject it because it had profound, direct, and immediate implications for everyone. The end of the draft implied the dilution of war's impact on American society. It also changed the United States' role in the world.

A simple number, quoted by Geert Mak, reflects the monumental difference provoked by the end of the draft. In World War II, one in ten American men experienced some type of combat role;[40] by the time of Iraq and Afghanistan, the figure was one in two hundred. The ethnic, racial, or social composition of the armed forces also no longer mirrors that of American society at large. Among enlisted recruits, 43 percent of men and *56 percent of women* are Hispanic or a racial minority. The figures for the entire US population was 37 percent.[41] In the Army, there are nearly as many black women as white women, while in the overall population, the figure is three times as high in favor of white women. For military African Americans of both genders, the peak year was 2000: 29 percent of all enlisted individuals that year were black, when the equivalent figure for the population at large reached 13 percent. In 2016, the Hispanic military contingent had not yet attained the same proportion as in the overall population but had nonetheless jumped from 9 percent to 16 percent. Measured by neighborhood affluence, the US military is still chiefly—though barely—middle class. But the trend is drifting toward a "proletarization" of the armed forces.

A volunteer military costs more. It obliges "the military-industrial complex" to economize on people and concentrate on weapons. It encounters serious domestic obstacles for participating in "principled" actions—Libya, Syria, and long before, in Bosnia and Rwanda—and even greater ones involving cases where the justification for those actions seem weak. A volunteer army should in theory allow a nation to proceed without excessive attention placed on "the hearts and minds" of its citizenry, but this has not been entirely true after 1973. Some of the cynical benefits of the absence of draftees occasionally manifest themselves, such as the feeble opposition to the Iraq invasion, but more frequently the disadvantages outweigh them.

Since the draft was abolished, the metamorphoses of the American electorate have made it impossible to reinstate conscription. The omnipresence of homogeneous districts impedes the building of any hypothetical coalition for this purpose. A center-left/center-right alliance in a homogeneous electorate devoid of gerrymandering and identity politics might conceivably have reinstated conscription if everyone paid the cost of an inevitably unpopular measure. A heterogeneous electorate, speckled with myriad homogeneous districts, makes this impossible. There will always be too many members of the House, outside the broad center, and perhaps even the Senate, refusing to risk the blame or to act against their constituents' interests or their own convictions. The center will not hold, as the saying goes.

In an ideal world, one could have it both ways. On the one hand, the United States would no longer be able to invade anybody or carry out regime changes; its military superiority would simply fade away, regardless of the nature of its armed forces. On the other, Washington might still realize its capacity and mission, as the bulwark of international governance. In such unlikely circumstances, America would more than ever satisfy its financial commitments to international organizations, regardless of their stances on Israel. Its participation in all international covenants, from the Paris Agreement on Climate Change to the Geneva Conventions, and including the International Criminal Court and the Trans-Pacific Partnership, would endure and be expanded. Whenever the "responsibility to protect (R2P)" emerged, the United States could be counted on to step into the breach and carry more than its fair share. Its contribution to addressing international issues with significant domestic connotations—immigration, drugs, climate change, human trafficking, corruption, etc.—would be ever more meaningful and decisive. Its allies in tow, its adversaries cowed, an entire world would finally witness the fruits of the full consonance of the American creed with American practice.

Unfortunately, none of this is possible. In the real world, the two sides of the same coin go together. Without American military prowess, weakened politically and socially, if not militarily, by a voluntary army, a society that doesn't tolerate an alternative, and a political system that cannot promote one, there can be no new American "internationalism." One can seriously doubt whether any form, new or old, of internationalism is viable, given the dysfunctional nature of the political system. Well beyond the example of the draft, the existing system makes almost any "internationalist" coalition impossible in the Congress and in society at large. The white, conservative, over-50, partly rural, non-college-educated electorate and its representation are traditionally isolationist, inward-looking, and wary of any sort of "foreign entanglements," principled or cynical. The younger, better-educated, minority-supported, coastal and urban electorate, and its representation, has "bigger fish to fry." It is either justifiably obsessed with domestic issues—race, education, violence, inequality—or distrusts international commitments that may go wrong. Although not opposed to trade deals, climate change covenants, further disarmament, or propagating universal values abroad—human rights, democracy, anti-corruption—it will rarely mobilize in favor of these causes, like voters everywhere.

Al Gore was able to draw people to movie theaters to watch the drama of global warming, but neither he, nor his boss Bill Clinton, nor Barack Obama, was ever able to push any major climate change agreement through Congress. They did not even try: Clinton never submitted the Kyoto Protocol to the Senate because it had zero chances of ratification; Obama crafted the Paris Agreement in order to avoid the issue of certain American congressional rejection. Any coalition of the two discordant electorates, or parts of each, seems increasingly unreachable.

A final "anti-globalist" consequence of the current political equation lies in the growing reluctance among the non-college-educated white males from old industrial states to support trade deals abroad. This unwillingness accompanies the barely grudging inclination of the liberal, identity-politics, coastal voters in favor of such arrangements. From the early nineties onward, free-trade agreements like NAFTA, the transformation of the GATT into the WTO, CAFTA-DR, and later the Trans-Pacific Partnership became the object of growing discontent and then outright rejection by voters and legislators from the so-called Rust Belt. Again, the mainly white, male, high school-educated, and aging industrial working class, which had lost jobs in the steel, automobile, and appliance industries over decades, made its anger known. This was the logic of Trump's 2016 win in Pennsylvania, Ohio, Michigan, and Wisconsin.

When China entered the WTO in 2001, and the displacement of manufacturing employment from the United States began in earnest, the occupational working class and income-related middle class cried foul. Each subsequent agreement was more difficult to approve by Congress. What had previously been possible—NAFTA, WTO, CAFTA-DR—became exceedingly difficult, if not impossible. By 2017, TPP was simply not submitted, as Donald Trump scuttled the deal, and the new NAFTA was in trouble from the very beginning. A (semi-)Free Trade Agreement with the European Union, whose negotiation Obama had undertaken during his second term, was set aside.

The Republican Party, traditionally more amenable to trade deals than the Democrats, began to split on these issues. The rural representatives remained "free-traders," given their constituents' agricultural exports. The Rust Belt legislators, governors, and activists leaned increasingly toward a form of neo-protectionism, not unlike the Democrats' labor union-based stances. .

The majority-minority districts and members of Congress, as well as the "Socialist Democrats"—like Bernie Sanders—were either indifferent, unenthusiastic backers of presidential initiatives or frankly contrarian. Either they detested presidents like Trump to such an extent that they were unwilling to vote for anything he proposed or for ideological reasons they found themselves uncomfortable on issues such as these. The fact was that along the road from difficult NAFTA approval under Clinton in 1993 to TPP abandonment under Trump in 2017, much has changed in the United States and the world. Part of the change stems from a political system no longer able to deliver the goods.

So if it's broke, why not fix it?

A last manifestation of this dysfunctional disaster derives from the system's incapacity to transform or transcend itself. No political system does so easily. By definition, the entrenched interests that benefit from a determined status quo strive to preserve it. It is especially difficult to update a political agreement that outlives its usefulness because the premises upon which it was constructed became obsolete. Those responsible for the updating . . . are also those who profit most from preserving the status quo.

It took nearly eighty years and a civil war for the young American republic to progress from the constitutional deals made between slave colonies and the others in the 1780s to a radically different scheme after 1865. No country accomplishes this well, and the United States is perhaps less prepared today than others. It amends its constitution less often than others and adapts its institutions to demographic, ethnic, and international transformations with greater difficulty than others. More defenders of the foundational compromises and pacts are present than in other countries; often they refuse to acknowledge that those transactions actually existed. Be it the Second Amendment and gun possession, the Electoral College for choosing a president, or even the role of religion in politics and the separation of Church and State, America responds slowly, fitfully, and incompletely to the need for institutional change.

A good example lies precisely in the Electoral College. As even foreigners know, twice in the last twenty years Americans elected a president who obtained fewer votes than his rival: George W. Bush in 2000, and Donald Trump in 2016. Foreigners don't necessarily know, but most Americans do, that this is due to the strange mechanism called the Electoral College, that essentially establishes an indirect presidential election. What fewer Americans are aware of is that the Electoral College was a wily, skillful, but ignoble instrument created by the writers of the Constitution to placate the inhabitants of the eight slave states that, along with five other former colonies, founded the Union.

The dilemma was quite simple. If the president were to be elected by direct, "universal" suffrage, and slaves did not vote—which of course, they didn't—the chief executive would always be a Northerner. If indirectly elected by the House of Representatives—the only chamber of Congress voted in by "universal" suffrage—that would have ended the separation of powers: a sacred trust for the drafters of the constitution. One of the more recent historians to delve into this matter, acclaimed author Jill Lepore, leaves little doubt regarding the nature of the deal, wrought, among others, by James Wilson of Virginia, one of the crafters of the Constitution.

According to Lepore, Wilson concluded that if neither the people nor the Congress could elect the president, some other body might. He suggested that an Electoral College could do the actual electing. The measure passed. The compromise demanded another compromise, though: the slave ratio. The number of delegates to the Electoral College would be determined not by states' population but by its representatives in the House: one member for every forty thousand people, and slaves counting as three-fifths of other people. She concludes: "The Electoral College was a concession to slave owners, an affair of both mathematical and political calculation."[42]

This was no minor affair at the time. Beyond the well-known anecdotes about Washington's, Jefferson's, and Madison's ambivalent stance on the question of slavery, the numbers are illustrative.

According to the same author, "The years following the end of the war (of independence) had witnessed the largest importation of African slaves to the Americas in history—a million people over a single decade."[43] The rather revolting, though perhaps inevitable setup, became partially irrelevant when the Thirteenth Amendment was adopted in 1865. After Emancipation, there was no longer a question of blacks "being worth" three-fifths of whites, since they were all free, and theoretically, enfranchised. What's more, one of the reasons for Jim Crow laws and voter suppression after 1875 and the end of Reconstruction lay in the need for the Southern captains of the Democratic Party to ensure that the fewest number of African Americans showed up at the polls. They would all vote for Lincoln's Republican Party and bestow forever upon it a lock on presidential and congressional elections.

Despite the obvious obsolescence of the Electoral College, it has survived until today. Even modest reforms such as assigning electoral votes by proportional representation have not prospered, except in Maine. Smaller states and mid-size ones have much to gain—as occurred with Pennsylvania, Michigan, and Wisconsin in 2016, when a difference of 80,000 votes in three states, out of more than 120 million nationwide, made Trump president. The twenty-two smallest states, many of them rural, possess a total of ninety-eight electoral votes, though their combined population is roughly equal to that of California, which has fifty-five. One can imagine reasons why the very large states might prefer to change this scheme. California, New York, and Texas—though not Florida—could conceivably welcome a return to the time when they made the difference, in contrast to now, when a huge margin of victory or a tiny one has no incidence on the final tally. That's why presidential candidates rarely campaign or spend money there.

The mounting criticism and call for reform of the Electoral College after 2000 and 2016, despite the obvious conflict of interest on the part of those who support and benefit from it, has made scant headway. Although some scholars have insisted that the original agreement was not a result of placating the slave states, the last attempt to abolish the Electoral College failed because of Senate Southern segregationists' opposition.

In 1966 Indiana Senator Birch Bayh introduced a constitutional amendment bill to slightly modify the Electoral College. He soon espoused the cause of a direct presidential election, which received the support of 80 percent of Americans, according to Gallup polls.[44] By late 1969, with Richard Nixon's support, the House of Representatives overwhelmingly approved the constitutional amendment. According to *New York Times* columnist Jesse Wegman: "As soon as the amendment reached the Senate, it was blocked by Southern segregationists, led by Strom Thurmond of South Carolina, who were well aware that the Electoral College had been created to appease the slaveholding states. They were also aware that it continued to warp the nation's politics in their favor, since millions of black voters throughout the South had been effectively disenfranchised by restrictive registration and voting laws, although the 1965 reforms had begun to change this. Even those who were able to vote rarely saw their preferences reflected by a single elector. A popular vote would make their voices equal and their votes matter—and would encourage them to turn out at higher rates."[45] The amendment lost in the Senate by five votes in 1970 and never was voted on again, although several Democratic hopefuls in 2019 and 2020 insisted on revisiting the issue if they were elected president. They were in tune with the voters: a survey taken in 2018 showed that two-thirds of all Americans thought presidents should be elected by popular vote.[46] The United States is no closer than decades ago to elimination of the Electoral College and its replacement with a direct election, as every presidential system in the world (parliamentary regimes are a different story). A different approach has been in the works since the beginning of this century, known as the National Popular Vote Interstate Compact or NPVIC. This is an agreement among a group of states to award all their electoral votes to whichever presidential candidate wins the overall popular vote in the fifty states, effectively eliminating the Electoral College while bypassing the constitutional amendment process. States approving it include California and New York, and it "only" requires passage by states accounting for 270 electoral votes.

Nonetheless, the existing political system's ability to reform itself is practically nil. Many Americans would reply that this was exactly what the Founders sought: the virtual impossibility of modifying a constitution that has only been tinkered with seventeen times, aside from the first ten amendments contained in the Bill of Rights. If one looks at other countries' foundational documents and the number of modifications or replacements they have experienced, there are reasons for respecting the original US authors' wisdom. But not to this extent, on a matter of deep substance, or on additional, fundamental issues such as gun control or the death penalty. The reason the existing system is unmovable resides in its current dysfunctional nature; as recently as the 1960s, some reforms were attainable. Today, none are.

With House members elected every two years, and the equality principle among states determining the composition of the Senate, a reform of the system does not appear feasible. Even "easy" issues such as the Equal Rights Amendment, initially introduced in 1923(!), which was passed by the House and Senate in 1971 and 1972, has still not been ratified by the necessary 38 state legislatures; the 38th finally passed it in 2020. The ERA does not imply any structural reforms of the political system; the last constitutional amendments that truly affected the political system were probably the 17th, that provided for the direct election of the Senate, and the 19th that gave women the vote. This first was ratified in 1913; the second in 1920.

Initiatives such as abolishing the Electoral College, or introducing rank voting, proportional representation, or facilitating independent or third-party candidates rarely get off the ground and never gain any traction.

For this to occur, the coalition of "reformists" would need to be broad and deep. The likelihood of "coastals," blacks, Latinos, Asians, and college-educated whites of all genders coming together on these matters is simply too convoluted and remote. Just thirteen small, conservative states are needed to block any constitutional change, even if they represent only a minuscule fraction of the country's population. Modifying the rules regarding constitutional amendments requires . . . a constitutional amendment, in contrast to other nations, where often this can also be achieved by referendum. The United States contemplates the latter at a state-by-state level, where they are known as ballot initiatives, but not federally.

The American polity is not split into two parties, but rather fragmented into various large, powerful, intrinsically different electoral fractions. Even the predominant one today—still, the white, middle-class semi-college-educated, heartland plurality—is barely large enough to impose its will on the White House, the Senate, or the House. The transformation of the American electorate, from lily-white, male, and middle-aged into a heterogeneous, diverse, atomized, and fractious one, is a highly welcomed change by anyone who believes in America's better angles. It brought about, however, the unforeseen and unwelcome obsolescence of a political system based on Athenian homogeneity. No solution appears on the horizon. Donald Trump is one product of this contradiction. There will be others.

One of them springs from the past. Gradually, with the passage of time, the United States is becoming a country with a history. Ortega y Gasset was not totally mistaken when he wrote, in 1930, that "the American has not yet begun his history. He is living the prehistory of himself."[47] Today, history matters, and where history matters, it will be forced to respect history, know it, and simultaneously laugh about the chapters of its history that deserve to be mocked, applying to it that most powerful of American virtues and genius: a sense of mostly self-deprecating humor.

5

Don't know much about history . . . but "If you find it hard to laugh at yourself, I would be happy to do it for you." (Groucho Marx)

IT MIGHT SEEM BIZARRE to address together two of the most salient traits of the misnamed American national character: the absence of a sense of history, and an extraordinary sense of humor. The first has been well studied, though not often well explained, particularly as time goes by and what was a young country is now drifting into middle-age. From the aphorism attributed to Henry James—"If you scrape Europe, you will find history; if you scrape the United States, you will find geography"—to historian Daniel Boorstin's quip—"Whereas Europe is a land with too much history and not enough geography, America has little history and plenty of geography"[1]—the irrelevance of history to American life has become a truism. The American self-deprecating sense of humor has also been delved into, though not nearly as much by foreigners as by citizens of the United States. Not all of them. Oscar Wilde denigrated it: "American humor is a mere travellers' tale. It has no real existence. Indeed, so far from being humorous, the male American is the most abnormally serious creature who ever existed."[2] The American sense of humor is perhaps too colloquial and parochial to be truly grasped by anyone who does not use English as the equivalent of a native tongue. It has nonetheless become proverbial in the world, from Mark Twain to *Saturday Night Live*. This chapter is devoted to these two American constants, as well as to their transformation over time.

There might be a link between the two traits. Perhaps the national lack of a long-standing solemnity originating in nation-founding roots from the Battle of Hastings to Charlemagne's coronation at Aachen in 800 AD allows Americans to see themselves in a lighter fashion. As proud of their heritage as anyone else, they take it less intensely and more detachedly than those who carry "the weight of history" on their shoulders. That distance may explain why it is so much easier for Americans to laugh at themselves, and with themselves, than others.

I first encountered this enigmatic American combination of no sense of history and a marvelous sense of self-deprecating humor when I embarked on a perilous journey, during which I understood the two traits go together. The best humorists in the United States are the off-spring of immigrants and slaves; they have histories that the official narratives silence. My first book, published in Mexico in 1978, had been a joint affair. Since then I have co-authored seven titles. The second was the toughest: it was a double effort on US–Mexican relations with a close American friend. Robert Pastor served as President Carter's National Security Council advisor on Latin America. He played a de-cisive role in negotiating Carter's devolution of the Panama Canal, as well as devising and implementing much of Carter's human rights policy in the region. Until his premature passing in 2014, we remained close. I had the privilege of delivering the keynote speech when the Mexican government posthumously awarded him the *Aguila Azteca*, the country's highest award for foreign friends of Mexico. He worked closely with Carter till his death and was one of the key founders of the Carter Center for monitoring elections.

Back in 1986, we decided we could not write common chapters on a traditionally complex and prickly relationship. We were too far apart. So we wrote twosomes: each author's point of view on the same issue, i.e. drugs, immigration, Central America, trade, the border, etc. And history . . . which prompted our first disagreement. Pastor, with a Ph.D. from Harvard in political economy, could not fully understand what he called my obsession with history. I could not comprehend his dismissal of history's significance, especially for this relationship, dating back to the Monroe Doctrine. We argued over this in Washington, Mexico City, Atlanta, New York, and Cancún (twice: Cancún is the best place to write a book). He was never able to convince me that the

American attitude of looking to the future and not worrying about the past was a model others should replicate. I never persuaded him that countries with a real history of their own evoke it constantly, on occasion excessively.

But Pastor never stopped making fun of his American prejudices, weaknesses, and contradictions. He invented a quintessential self-deprecatory quip about American unawareness; his countrymen were so ignorant about things foreign that they thought Taco Bell was the Mexican phone company. He joked unendingly about Carter, his boss and mentor Zbigniew Brzezinski, and about Ronald Reagan. His self-deprecating humor allowed me, in turn, to feel comfortable mocking my compatriots, or my friends among the Nicaraguan Sandinistas, or Pastor's late friend Omar Torrijos, the Panamanian strong man who received the Canal from Carter in 1977, and even the French in general, whom I revere and he never liked. Some might argue that a Jewish boy from New Jersey, with a modest economic background, a Ph.D. from Harvard, and a job at the NSC is not quite typically American. I would answer: As typical as any other American.

Two types of histories

The "New World" established two different types of links with history. The Spanish and Portuguese came to conquer and plunder the wealth of pre-existing civilizations, not to farm or raise sheep, as Cortés himself said. They inevitably acquired an interest in the survival of the peoples they defeated, and in the history of their previous existence. Someone had to work in the mines and the plantations, and while the enslaved people from Africa were brought to many colonial enclaves, they only survived in a few—the Caribbean, including today's Colombia, Peru, Ecuador, and Venezuela, along with Brazil. Elsewhere, the pre-existing original peoples became the forced creators of colonial Eldorados. This implied a so-called "other" conquest, meaning a spiritual, religious, and cultural domestication. It was feasible partly thanks to the sedentary, sophisticated, and structured nature of various civilizations encountered, in particular, by the Spaniards. Syncretism was only viable if two civilizations came into contact, one conquering the other, but not annihilating its victim, because there was a need to ensure its survival. The necessity sprang from labor force requirements to standing off the powers of the Crown in Spain, as the *criollo* population expanded and became more autonomous. Something of the past—religious icons, myths, food, customs, even language—was preserved or, more accurately, assimilated. This did not take place out of any respect for the predecessors by the Spanish conquerors, but only out of sheer convenience.

The two most significant icons of this assimilation were *mestizaje* and the Virgin of Guadalupe. They sprang from the clash, mix, and birth of different ethnic, racial, and cultural entities. The story began with *La Malinche* and Cortés in New Spain and their son, Martín, often referred to (falsely) as the first Mexican. It continued with the *Vírgen morena*, or dark-skinned virgin, who appeared before Juan Diego, the young Mexican peasant who handed her a bouquet of roses in 1531 and rapidly adopted her as his patron saint, and the patron saint of all Mexicans ever since.

The Spanish and Portuguese felt they possessed an evangelical mission in the Americas and soon understood, in a classic example, that constructing a church on the site or the ruins of a previous place of worship facilitated the original peoples' attendance. This complex bundle of values, historical processes, and local conditions—the mines in today's Mexico, Bolivia, and Peru were located at extreme altitudes, where efforts to employ African slave labor notoriously failed—established a link with the past. So did the fact that the conquerors and their governing successors, or viceroys, came and went constantly to and from Spain and Portugal, strengthening the nexus between colonies and colonial powers.

This was not entirely the case in what became the United States. Factors on both sides of the Atlantic explain the differences. These colonizers were nearly always settlers, not adventurers seeking fortune. Some left for religious motives, others on political grounds, others still with an economic purpose that entailed settlement. They were not obsessed, at least not initially, with retaining a local work force necessary to produce wealth. When tobacco emerged as a cash crop in Virginia toward the beginning of the seventeenth century, the landowners opted for slavery rather than the Native American inhabitants of the colonial territories. The Native Americans were not as well suited for conquest, evangelization, assimilation, syncretism, or *mestizaje* as the Aztecs, the Incas, and what had survived of the Mayas. They were more nomadic, unstructured, and isolated groups or tribes that, beyond folktales of Thanksgiving and Pocahontas, had scant contact with the English or Dutch settlers. As long as they did not constitute an obstacle to the ambitions of the newly arrived, the original peoples were tolerated. Once settlement began to push away from the ocean and inland, they were either placed on reservations or exterminated. Not unlike what other settlers did in nineteenth-century Chile and Argentina.

The New England, Mid-Atlantic, and Southern settlers were fleeing from their own past and lacked a new one to latch onto, even if superficially. Their new history then only begins upon arrival in America. But it was not a national history, since there was no nation for it to de derived from. To paraphrase Tocqueville, the United States was born late and without a history at the outset. The extreme case obviously comprised the enslaved population: blacks had their African history extirpated from them. They were forbidden to learn a new one until well past Emancipation.

An absence of history implies the erasure of memory for all of the inhabitants of the thirteen colonies. The original peoples "forgot" their past because of the tremendous shock provoked by the arrival of the newcomers. Africans "forgot" theirs, because of the pain it wrought; and the settlers themselves "forgot" their European past because they wanted to distance themselves from it as much as possible. Octavio Paz, the Mexican Nobel Prize–winning poet, phrased it eloquently: "The United States was founded on a land without a past . . . . For this reason, one of the most powerful and persistent themes in American literature, from Whitman to William Carlos Williams, and from Melville to Faulkner, has been the search for (and invention of) American roots."[3]

Mexicans have constructed many myths about the Spanish Conquest and subsequent colonization and infinite ways of contradicting them. The *mestizo* race, as it is labeled in Mexico, is presumed to be neither Spanish nor indigenous, but a new ethnic construct owing as much to one as to the other. This is less clear-cut than it seems. On the one hand, Mexicans often refer to the pre-Columbian peoples present at the time of the Conquest as "we" and to the Spanish conquerors as "they."

On the other hand, the inferred symmetry in formal *mestizaje* is some-what fictitious. The men were Spanish, the women indigenous; the former were desirous, the latter coerced or resigned. In any case, a suf-ficiently common origin emerged over the centuries for many of these nations to eventually acquire a common foundation, that is, a common history and memory. Only Argentina, Uruguay, parts of Chile, and the Sao Paulo region of Brazil experienced immigration and were thus partly exempted from this process. A continuum does appear in this world-view, even if it is partly a fictitious one. Paz, again, summarizes the point well: "Mexico City was built on the ruins of Tenochtitlan, the Aztec city that was built in the likeness of Tula, the Toltec city that was built in the likeness of Teotihuacán, the first great city on the American continent."[4]

The Europeans share a similar continuum and world-view with their former colonized victims. The Indians and Chinese possess a long history before colonization and incorporate the colonial period as a nightmare that must be remembered. They have a common, extended history. The Japanese were never colonized, nor did they really colo-nize anyone, outside of the military occupation in Asia during World War II. They have an entirely Japanese, common history to share among themselves. This perhaps explains why their observers of the Americans scene, now nearly a century ago, disdained Americans' lack of history: "In terms of history, America is almost too insignificant to take notice of. If America were excluded from world history before the twentieth century, its influence has been so negligible that is absence would hardly be noticed, except for Edison's invention of the elec-tric light . . . . Traditions and history predating (the invention of the steam engine) have some meaning for Europeans, but for Americans they are useless relics from the past."[5] One of the many components of the incessantly re-questioned and re-constructed nationhood of these societies consists in that common history, which spills over, in some areas more than others, into language, religion, and ethnicity. For the French, British, Germans, and Spaniards dwelling on the past, glorifying it, hiding its most odious passages, constantly evoking it as a source of nationhood, constitutes an instrument of national affirm-ation. History, as false as it may be (until recently, in French public schools in the Arab and Muslim projects outside of Paris and Marseille, children were taught to respect "*nos ancêtres les Gaulois*"—the Gauls, our ancestors is a recurrent theme of political, ideological, commercial, and philosophical discourse. The French and others are all obsessed with it because it exists. Like the Mexicans, Peruvians, and Bolivians, as well as to a lesser extent other Latin Americans, it exists because they are obsessed with it.

In the United States, however, there is no common foundation before Independence, because there is no common history or memory to speak of until late in the nineteenth century. This does not signify that different segments of American society did not share a common past among themselves. They simply could not share it with other people located in the United States not yet labeled Americans. Jill Lepore understands this splendidly and refers to that nineteenth-century historiography quite accurately: "one way to turn a state into a nation is to write its history. The first substantial history of the United States, George Bancroft's ten volume (work) was published between 1834 and 1874 . . . . Bancroft wrote his history in an attempt to make the United States' founding appear inevitable, its growth inexorable, and its history ancient."[6] But Bancroft also shows how narrow that attempt can be, in the passage Lepore quotes exquisitely: "The origin of the language we speak carries us to India; our religion is from Palestine; of the hymns sung in our churches, some were first heard in Italy, some in the deserts of Arabia, some on the banks of the Euphrates; our arts come from Greece; our jurisprudence from Rome."[7] He simply omitted African Americans, Native Americans, Chinese, and Mexicans, among others. Needless to say, foreigners who have visited, studied, and lived at length in the United States beg to disagree.

Hanna Arendt may have put it best, in an interview she gave in 1966: "this country is united neither by heritage, nor by memory, nor by soil, nor by language, nor by origin from the same . . . by nationality . . . there are no natives here. The natives were the Indians. Everything else are citizens, and these citizens are united only by one thing—and that is a lot. That is, you become a citizen of the United States by simple consent to the Constitution."[8]

A miracle occurred when out of a maelstrom of roots something like an American nation finally surfaced: from the original peoples, the first settlers from England and Holland, African Americans, the Hispanic-heritage communities located in the regions annexed from Mexico in 1848, the enormous flow of immigrants from Germany and Ireland in the 1850s and 1860s; to the arrival of large numbers of Chinese immigrants in California; and to the subsequent stream of Eastern and Southern Europeans (mainly from Italy, Poland, and Hungary) later in the century. Inevitably though, the United States would lack, virtually until today, one of the basic pillars of nationhood: a common beginning, a common past, and a common path from that past to the present. Reasonably enough, what individuals or societies lack, they tend to neglect, de-emphasize, or just ignore. This is what Americans do with history. Again, to quote Santayana's reflections on *Character and Opinion in the United States*: "What has existed in the past, especially in the remote past, seems to him (the American) not only not authoritative, but irrelevant, inferior, and outworn. He finds it rather a sorry waste of time to think about the past at all."[9] History is not a fountainhead, even though Americans have attempted to pretend otherwise (i.e. that their history is not irrelevant) through a reconstruction of past events that were either meaningless—TV series, hit records, sports achievements, or individual heroic exploits—or simply fake. History is almost never present in public discourse, in political rhetoric—except for the constant and often obnoxious reference to the Founders—and much less in everyday conversation, business, and entertainment. History is the Wild West, the idyllic plantations of the South, the charge up San Juan Hill, and perhaps the War for Independence, along with a Hollywood version of the Civil War and World War II, perhaps today more popular than other moments. Foundational myths are few and far between, largely because they are not, and cannot be, common to all. Moreover, one identity group's lodestone is another's humiliation, symbol of oppression, or source of fighting words. Even the Constitution, given its consecration of slavery, exclusion of Native Americans from citizenship, and consolidation of a subordinate role for women, lacks the attributes necessary for unifying a disparate constellation of memories and interests. This is not necessarily unique to the United States; other "settler colonies," i.e. Canada, New Zealand, and Australia—have lived through a similar experience.

Who cares about the lack of history?

So what's wrong with having no history or imagining it along the way? Even if the claim by countless Europeans and Latin Americans of the United States' historical orphanage were entirely true, the negative consequences are not easy to discern. Perhaps only poets, like France's Paul Valéry, understand how regrettable it is that "New countries without history will transmit to us their idea of happiness."[10]

Some of the consequences are obvious, for example in foreign policy-making. Carlos Fuentes put this well in regard to the Central American wars of the 1980s, in his Harvard commencement speech in 1983: "We shall be the custodians of your own true interests by helping you to avoid these mistakes. We have memory on our side. You suffer too much from historical amnesia."[11] Two monumental mistakes committed by the United States since World War II are iconic: Vietnam and Afghanistan; Iraq also qualifies, but I will insist on the first two. Not because people surrounding Johnson and Bush (43) suffered from a dearth of historical expertise. American universities produce and employ some of the world's greatest historians and scholars in general. The resources available to them are incomparably superior to those in any other nation, rich or poor. Many occupants of the White House have hired and depended on them (Walt Rostow and Condoleezza Rice are relevant examples).

But history's weight in decision-making by presidents and secretaries of state and defense is lighter, no matter what their specialized advisors may recommend. The lessons of history in Vietnam, from conflicts with China centuries ago to the resistance against the French from the 1920s onward, should have sufficed for Johnson—and Kennedy before him—to resist any temptation to involve themselves. The information was available, wholesale. But its pertinence was disregarded, partly because history is disregarded. Robert McNamara himself confessed, in one of his published recollections: "In every way, American ignorance of the history, language, and culture of Vietnam was immense."[12] This dismissal, in turn, proceeded from history's scant existence in the American psyche.

The same is true for Afghanistan. The list of foreign invaders subdued by the mountains, the weather, the tribal fighters, and local pride is lengthy indeed. Just the British and Soviets in modern times provide a sorry example of how questionable an idea it was to invade

Afghanistan. History proved the futility of attempting anything in that country other than chasing bin Laden and retaliating against the government that allowed him set up shop in Tora Bora and organize 9-11. Again, it is not that Bush's people at State, the National Security Council, the CIA, or the Defense Department were devoid of experts' historical advice. There were people there, or in academia, who possessed as much as knowledge and information as anybody about the perils of sinking into the Afghan morass. But they didn't carry the clout they deserved, because their expertise was not as respected as that of others.

They were merely just a bunch of historians, in a country, and most importantly, in a political elite, totally uninterested—more so than during Johnson's years—in history as a factor to incorporate in any policy decision. The Afghan war has become the longest in American history, with no victory in sight, and very little to show for the enormous expense of human and financial resources expended on it. Have other countries with a longer history, and a greater sense of history, also found themselves bogged down in interminable wars? Of course: France and Britain entangled their very soul in Vietnam, Algeria, and Afghanistan, though Britain only briefly each time in Afghanistan, and at the end of the day, the French pulled out, defeated, in both Vietnam and Algeria. Moreover, nothing demonstrates that even if endowed with a memory and a past, Washington would have avoided these and other costly mistakes. But there is a point to history and the past, and perhaps the United States has lived too long without it.

Americans sense this. On occasion they invent a history they lack, hypostasizing events or individuals and transforming them into monuments, celebrations, and remembrances that don't add up. French writer Bernard-Henri Lévy, in one of the most recent travel books on the United States and perhaps not his most remarkable work, points to this penchant somewhat sarcastically. But by evoking Nietzsche's third type of memory, he makes a philosophical point: "The third one, the memory he calls 'the antiquary's' and that is attached to 'what is small, restricted, old, about to turn into dust,' the memory which stems from 'the blind thirst for collection' and 'the untiring accumulation of all of the vestiges of the past,' is a useless memory, that instead of strengthening human beings 'damages them, whether they are men, peoples or a civilization, and ends by destroying them.' Well, this third case seems to be appropriate for the United States' generalized Halls of Fame. These museums that conserve everything, these places that mix everything and make no distinction between what is worth remembering and what is not, these rural towns and counties where everyone seems to have forgotten the liberating benefits of forgetting and where one is crushed by the nonsensical relics of any nonsense . . . these are the mark of the antiquary's history."[13] This long and winding quote none-theless makes a valid point. Instead of history, Americans have relics; theme parks; baseball, football, and basketball halls of fame; as well as countless museums where nothing worthwhile is ever kept, outside of the major cities.

Time has gone by, nonetheless. A young country deprived of a his-torical memory has today become, with the UK, the world's oldest de-mocracy, at nearly two hundred and fifty years of age. It boasts a degree of continuity in its institutions and lodestars that few others enjoy. These simple facts contribute, along with peculiar American traits, to the dawn of what many might consider history with a capital H: the emergence of political, ideological, religious, and ethnic clashes over it. Oscar Wilde was wrong when he wisecracked, "The youth of America is their oldest tradition. It has been going now for three hundred years."[14] The United States is reaching middle age.

Race and gender enter the fray, and on occasion, the entire nation struggles about the truth and meaning of its past. When the latter becomes something worth fighting over, it begins to exist meaningfully. This process commenced in the late twentieth century. During the in-itial decades of this new century, it has blossomed into open conflict. The way it should. African American historians and white American students of the history of slavery, the Civil War, Reconstruction, re-demption, racism, and the civil rights movement know well that, as Crystal Fleming has put it, "most US citizens have never seriously studied history of any kind, much less racial history. If the vast ma-jority of the population is ignorant of the racist past, how can they un-derstand the impact of that past on the present?"[15] Authors like her, and such as Henry Louis Gates Jr., Ibram X. Kendi, Eric Foner, and David Blight, along with many others, make this point repeatedly, and they should be thanked for doing so.

Is history worth fighting over?

The disputes over history range from tearing down statues of—or monuments to—Confederate so-called heroes, to re-naming institutions like the Woodrow Wilson School of Public and International Affairs at Princeton University, or the John Calhoun House at Yale. The twenty-eighth President of the United States probably accomplished more during his eight years in office than anyone before him—excepting Lincoln, or after—excepting Franklin Roosevelt. But part of the price the former president of Princeton University paid in seducing racist Southern Democrats in Congress to approve anti-trust legislation, the Federal Reserve Bank, the income tax, and much more, was the re-segregation of the American civil service and the extension of Jim Crow practices to the nation's capital.

I studied and taught at the Woodrow Wilson School and considered myself a relatively well-informed observer of the namesakes' biography, given his deep involvement in the Mexican Revolution. I had no idea of his racism's extent, or in any case, the perception and racist consequences of his policies. Therein lies my recent and initial perplexity regarding the brouhaha over the school's name, but also my ulterior appreciation of the debate's intrinsic value.

These historical controversies involve mainly the Civil War and slavery. There are more than seven hundred statues erected in honor of Confederate figures throughout the South, almost all of them after Reconstruction and as late as the 1950s. The debates apply equally however, to episodes of discrimination and racism directed at Mexican-Americans, and Japanese internment camps during World War II, for which Ronald Reagan apologized in 1985, and that Obama called one of the "darkest chapters in American history."[16] Those discussions include revisiting the lore and fantasies of the Native American communities' decimation, from the Trail of Tears to Wounded Knee, through Custer and all the way to the Keystone pipeline protests. They crisscross from the overdue—downgrading Custer from his martyr status to his ruthless, ambitious, and racist reality—to the mystifying (calls for removing Italian icon Columbus from Columbus Circle in New York, as well as Joan of Arc in New Orleans) and the convoluted: restoring the name of Mt. Denali to Mt. McKinley in Alaska, baptized as such during his presidency. The debates also comprise a series of long-delayed atonements for the Chinese Exclusion Act and include the absurd and ephemeral attempt at repealing the Fourteenth Amendment and birth-right citizenship or *jus soli*.

On occasion, women and workers are the subject of the skirmish. At other moments, different groups marginalized from American mainstream life lie at the heart of the conversation. Sometimes the vehicle chosen or utilized to bring such issues to the fore is somewhat convoluted—i.e. seeking to re-name the Washington Redskins football team—but the underlying cause is praiseworthy. Rarely, but sometimes, the battle is frankly absurd, as when in 2019 the San Francisco School Board decided to tear down Victor Arnautoff's mural *Life of Washington*, because, among other things, it lacked Native American or African American input, and did not contribute to "making kids mentally and emotionally safe at their schools . . . . Destroying them was worth it regardless of the cost [$600,000] . . . . This is reparations."[17] Arnautoff was a member of the Communist Party who created several public art works thanks to FDR's public works administration. He had worked as an assistant to Diego Rivera in Mexico.

Frequently, there is more than mere history at stake: demanding reparations for a slavery-profiting business belonging to the founder of Brown University might appear unseemly. No matter: the fundamental question is whether these debates or bouts signal the long-awaited advent of history in the American narrative or simply fireworks in the continuing discussion on political correctness. I think the former, and all for the better. It was high time.

It would be unfair to claim that other nations have acted more diligently in matters such as these. It required a courageous German chancellor like Willy Brandt to lay a wreath and break down in tears at the Warsaw Ghetto Memorial in Warsaw in 1968. France took decades to finally apologize (under President Jacques Chirac in 1995) for the French state's complicity in the deportation of 76,000 Jews during the Nazi occupation. Only later did it apologize for the French Army's direct involvement in torture during the Battle of Algiers in the late fifties (by President Emmanuel Macron in 2018). Justin Trudeau asked forgiveness only in 2018 for Canada's refusal to allow Jewish refugees on the steamship St. Louis to disembark nearly eighty years earlier, apologizing also for the well overdue nature of this gesture. But precisely because these countries—even Canada, thanks to its French heritage—boast a different sense of history than the United States, these examples show the difficulty of such steps. They make the American steps mentioned below all the more noteworthy and express the beginning of an American consciousness in recent times.

The basic quandary regarding the treatment of history is illustrative and educational: how can history be revisited without rewriting it? If the statues honoring the Confederacy were erected in the immediate aftermath of the Civil War, it is one thing. Quite another is when they were ordered and inaugurated decades later, as an explicit statement of white supremacy. What was the Civil War actually about: states' rights, or the perpetuation of slavery and the entire economic system that rested upon it? Is it possible—and desirable—to separate histor- ical fact (Lee was the commander of the secessionist military) from an unacceptable, deplorable conduct (he spearheaded a treasonous, racist, oppressive defense of an odious epoch)? Can there be a monument recalling the historical record and simultaneously reprehending it? Is it acceptable to celebrate symbols, individuals, events, and theories that ignored or whitewashed the virtual extermination of the Native American inhabitants of much of North America (including parts of today's Mexico)?

That these arguments are actually taking place, no longer on the fringes of American academia but in the mainstream of American media, politics, and culture, is enormously significant, new, and most likely a welcome and splendid turn of events. It is not a uniform trend, unfortunately. According to a 2019 article in *The New Yorker*, "history has been declining more rapidly than any other (college) major . . . . It accounts for between one and two percent of bachelor's degrees, a drop of about a third since 2011."[18] Not all is sad, though. The same piece revealed that "it's boom time for history at Yale, where it is the third most popular major, and other elite schools, including Brown, Princeton and Columbia, where it continues to figure among the top declared majors."[19] A partial explanation for this trend may lie in history's being an excellent road to law school and the upper echelons of the meritocracy.

This evolution has contributed greatly to America's gradual recogni- tion that history matters. For nearly two centuries, the usual American response to any criticism deploring the lack of historical sense has been to pivot to the future. The United States looks to the future, only "old" countries brood about the past. Now, even on foreign policy, American presidents admit that history must be reviewed. Bill Clinton apologized to the people of Guatemala in 1999 for the CIA-sponsored coup against the democratically elected government of Jacobo Árbenz in 1954. Secretary of State John Kerry did as much for Argentina, in 2016. Missing still is the case of Chile, and US participation in the coup that overthrew Salvador Allende, although Colin Powell did admit it was not something to be proud of. These and many other episodes will be the object of future apologies or admissions of guilt. They will be unavoidably accompanied, in other cases, by exaggerations, excesses, and simplifications, and the obvious postponement of new revisions during the Trump years. These constitute the price to pay for a different approach to history.

These struggles are fought out everywhere, but perhaps nowhere more than in K-12 history or social sciences textbooks. Leaving aside for the moment the fiery and century-old debate about evolution versus intelligent design, what actually occurred over the past three hundred years in what today constitutes the United States has recently become a crucial issue. Settlements, colonization, slavery, independence, conquest, expansion at the cost of others, the true role of iconic figures and memorable moments, are all the subject of endless, relatively recent discussions in school boards and textbook companies. A widespread case concerns APUSH—Advanced Placement United States History—textbooks. In some school districts—Oklahoma for example—books affirming that the Civil War was waged over slavery, and not states' rights, have been banned. Other states, such as Texas and even New Jersey, include several districts that continue to use textbooks insisting on states' rights as the origin of the 1860s' carnage.

Some foreign observers suggest that the very sense of nuance is un-American, and that no amount of history will ever change that. Simone de Beauvoir is quite guilty in this regard: "to accept nuances is to accept ambiguity of judgement, argument, and hesitation; such complex situations force you to think. They (Americans) want to lead their lives by geometry, not by wisdom. Geometry is taught, whereas wisdom is discovered."[20] This is not inevitable, as we are witnessing in regard to countless historical controversies in the United States today.

A typical controversy, involving Mexican-Americans, slavery, and foreign policy, was that surrounding the reference to the "heroic defenders" of the Alamo in 1836, in the course of a history textbook discussion in Texas during 2018. The original text comprised those words; the state textbook advisory committee suggested deleting the word "heroic," because it was "value-charged." After a lengthy and passionate debate, the term was retained: too much pushback from the governor, among others. This euphemistic and slightly anomalous controversy in fact reflected a deeper debate, regarding the fact that the Alamo defenders . . . were actually defending the right of the aspiring Texas independence fighters and Southern slave-state leaders to own slaves.

According to a recent history of that period, more than a quarter of the entire English-speaking population of Texas was enslaved; the enslaved population was growing more rapidly than the rest. As the author phrased it, the Texas secession was "also a slaveholders' rebellion against a regime hostile to slavery—or more accurately, 'a race war against a *mestizo* nation.'"[21] They were largely a group of mercenaries and responded to New Orleans slave merchants and President Andrew Jackson's "covert ops" to eventually annex the Mexican territory. The substance here is less significant than the symbolism. Nearly two hundred years after the events on the ground, a debate took place in American (conservative) circles on the importance of history. Was this the best way to undertake a re-evaluation of history's importance? In my view, the exact method—a school board argument over the meaning of the word "heroic"—is much less significant than the debate itself. This is also, clearly, the case involving reparations, which we will examine in Chapter 8.

Similarly, whether Harriet Tubman eventually replaces Andrew Jackson on the twenty-dollar bill or Donald Trump succeeds in overturning his predecessor's decision matters less than the debate enjoined over this symbolic issue. Jackson was not only a slave owner and the instigator of the Indian Removal Act and the infamous Trail of Tears of Cherokee nations. He was probably the first American treaty breaker, kicking off a long tradition. According to Simon Schama, another Englishman turned American, the eviction of five Indian nations from Georgia "was one of the most morally repugnant moments in American history, one that ought by rights to take its prime mover, the seventh president, off the currency of any self-respecting nation."[22]

The godsend of an American sense of humor

That sense of humor functions frequently as a substitute for the historical self-criticism of other nations. It also serves as an instrument for taking a certain distance from events, national peculiarities, and embarrassing features of the national character, which only lately began appearing in American mores. Broad, sweeping statements, treatises, even laws or presidential decrees regarding history are still largely absent in the United States. Acknowledging recent, or present-day, shortcomings, mistakes, and enduring sins is nobody's preferred way, and certainly not the American way. Other countries do this through history, brooding introspection, or self-flagellation, because of a national soccer team's humiliating defeat or . . . crimes against humanity committed on a wide or narrow scale, in the far-removed past or only a few years ago. Obama was not only unable to apologize for Hiroshima or criticize the fact; he proved incapable of doing so for Abu Ghraib, much closer in time and space.

But American humor can do all of that and more. It is relentless, implacable, and unforgiving in its critiques of everyday life, government policy, cultural attitudes, food, education, and health in the United States. If one wants to delve into the most negative or pessimistic psyche of Americans about themselves, it is toward the great national humorists that one should gaze. The "roast" is a typically American experience; the White House Correspondents' Dinner, where presidents since Eisenhower—until Trump: but the end of the president's presence at the dinner doesn't entail the end of humor in Washington—make fun of themselves, of their friends and adversaries, and are made fun of, is a quintessentially US phenomenon. One can hardly imagine Charles de Gaulle, Xi Xin Ping, or Vladimir Putin mocking themselves in public, let alone being mocked in public and in their presence.

Interestingly, for the purpose of this chapter, there is a tie with history, not so much with the absence of it, but with a certain relationship to it. There are humorists in other countries. The British have dozens, starting with Shakespeare. The French have always enjoyed Molière, Voltaire, and their *chansonniers*; Mexicans, Cantinflas, and *carpas*. The Italians still enact Machiavelli's satirical *La Mandragola* and have almost elected comedians to lead their country; Guatemala and Ukraine did. The English dry and acid sense of understated humor is proverbial and has extended also to television: witness the original *Monty Python* and *Yes, Minister*. But nobody quite does it like the Americans. Nothing is off-limits and hasn't been for more than a century.

Needless to say, not all foreign visitors or observers share my admiration for the American sense of humor. Some with a splendid sense of humor of their own, like Italian writer Beppe Severgnini, believe otherwise: "In any case, Americans haven't got a great sense of humor."[23] Whatever other characteristics American humor may possess, however, its self-deprecating nature stands out as something few other nations profess. Only a country blessed with the self-assurance of the United States could invent such a sense of humor, practice it incessantly, and even "import" foreigners like Trevor Noah or John Oliver to make fun of them every night. Only Americans enjoy the self-confidence to engage in it on a personal level, in everyday life and exchanges with their peers. Whether one chooses Mark Twain as the creator of American humor or reaches further back in history to lesser-known figures, the art of laughing at oneself, of not taking oneself too seriously, of sincerely being amused by one's own weaknesses is quintessentially American. Until the Marx Brothers and much later Woody Allen, it was also unexportable, partly because of language, partly as a result of the sarcasm and humility it comprises. So, in many ways, the best of America remains unknown to the rest of the world, which is one more irony of history.

The principal expression of the American sense of humor resides in comedy. I prefer to visualize the American comedian, from Chaplin (despite his English roots) and Buster Keaton or Harold Lloyd to Jon Stewart and Stephen Colbert, as only *one* manifestation of this fabled humor. All the more so since the self-deprecating originality in question is not common to *all* comedians; Colbert started off making fun of Bush (41) and Dick Cheney, not himself.

Many of the initial comedians, at least through the end of silent movies, engaged in slapstick as their specialty, with more or less grace and wit than their counterparts in Britain, France, Germany, and Spain. Conversely, great early humorists, like Ambrose Bierce, never practiced comedy: they simply wrote. Self-deprecation was by definition limited for many years to the written word; vaudeville and burlesque did not quite lend themselves to this view of life and humor. It probably began with Mark Twain's accounts of his misadventures in the West (in *Roughing It*) and in Europe and the Middle East (with *The Innocents Abroad*). His great successor, as a humorist, was Mencken, more vicious and ruthless than Twain, but equally able to stand apart from himself and smile. But it was the advent of "talkies" that truly socialized this peculiar and marvelous facet of the Americans, beginning with the Marx Brothers.

Historical, white, and Jewish humor

A few references to Twain, Will Rogers, Mencken, and Groucho Marx illustrate the self-deprecatory, irreverent, and introspective nature of this sense of humor. They apply it to themselves, to others, and to Americans at large, and as a whole. Their comments are politically incorrect, personal, and at the same time applicable to Americans in general (or whatever name the author uses to designate them). Understandably, individual self-deprecation draws the most laughs, but only sets the stage for the broader blows. When Will Rogers quips about himself that "When I die, my epitaph, or whatever you call those signs on gravestones, is going to read: 'I joked about every prominent man of my time, but I never met a man I dident [*sic*] like. I am so proud of that, I can hardly wait to die so it can be carved,"[24] he is only laying the ground for his more general musings about the American character. They reveal more, perhaps, than the many insights generated by numerous foreign visitors. He was more directly political and comical than substantive, but even in this vein his views reflect the spirit of his opinion of America: "I bet after seeing us, George Washington would sue us for calling him 'father.' . . . America is a nation that conceives many odd inventions for getting somewhere but it can think of nothing to do once it gets there."[25]

Mark Twain is both humble with regard to his own *persona* and devastating in his self-criticism of American idiosyncrasy. He meekly recounts how he fell in the far West for one of the oldest tricks in the book: "Imagination cannot conceive how disjointed I was—how internally, externally and universally I was unsettled, mixed up and ruptured. There was a sympathetic crowd around me, though. 'Stranger, you've been taken in. Everybody in this camp knows that horse. Any child, any Injun, could have told you that he'd buck; he is the very worst devil to buck on the continent of America . . . he is a simon-pure, out-and-out, genuine d—d Mexican plug . . . ."[26] His personal self-deprecation allows him the luxury or leeway of being devastatingly critical of the American character.

After acknowledging his own naiveté and ignorance, he can self-confidently plow ahead with the type of negative stereotyping of his fellow countrymen than no foreigner could get away with, and that even few Americans would ever dare to utter: "In America, we hurry—which is well; but when the day's work is done, we go on thinking of losses and gains, we plan for the morrow, we even carry our business cares to bed with us, and toss and worry over them when we ought to be restoring our racked bodies and brains with sleep. We burn up our energies with these excitements, and either die early or drop into a lean and mean old age at a time of life which they call a man's prime in Europe . . . . We bestow thoughtful care upon inanimate objects, but none upon ourselves. What a robust people, what a nation of thinkers we might be, if we would only lay ourselves on the shelf occasionally and renew our edges."[27]

H. L. Mencken was perhaps the most caustic of the great American humorists—until Comedy Central—but also the most acerbic and bitter. How much of a racist, anti-Semite, and conservative he actually became remains open to discussion, but his scathing wit, directed at everyone and everything under the sun, is undeniable, and perhaps unmatched. Again, the self-deprecating nature of his acid humor about himself allowed him to use the same viciousness against Americans (or Anglo-Saxons, as he often referred to them). His generalizations would be anathema today, and even in the 1920s and '30s were heretic, extreme, and bordering on hysterical. Nonetheless, the fact that he ventured to turn his vitriolic sarcasm against his own people underscores the pre-eminent role played by humorists in describing America.

He was often outrageous: "But here I pass them over (the good qualities of the Anglo-Saxon) without apology, for he devotes practically the whole of his literature and fully a half of his oral discourse to celebrating them himself, and there is no danger that they will ever be disregarded . . . . In this fact lies the first cause of the ridiculous figure he commonly cuts in the eyes of other people: he brags and blusters so incessantly that, if he actually had the combined virtues of Socrates, the Cid and the Twelve Apostles, he would still go beyond the facts, and so appear a mere Bombastes Furioso . . . . Civilization is at its lowest mark in the United States precisely in those areas where the Anglo-Saxon still presumes to rule . . . . What are the characters that I discern most clearly in the so-called Anglo-Saxon type of man? I may answer at once that two stick out above all others. One is his curious and apparently incurable incompetence—his congenital inability to do any difficult thing easily and well, whether it be isolating a bacillus or writing a sonata. The other is his astounding susceptibility to fear and alarms—in short, his hereditary cowardice."[28]

The fact that Mencken referred to himself as an "Anglo-Saxon of far purer blood" partly entitled him to formulate such extreme judgments. His comments regarding his own nature and shortcomings made his shocking appreciations somewhat more tolerable, though by the eve of World War II, he had outworn his welcome in the pages of many newspaper readers and publishers (with the exception of Alfred Knopf). Mencken's personal self-deprecating foundation was as robust as his colleagues'. He might, however, have been somewhat more fond of himself than they. "I never lecture, not because I am shy or a bad speaker, but simply because I detest the sort of people who go to lectures and don't want to meet them.[29] . . . All men are frauds. The only difference between them is that some admit it. I myself deny it."[30]

Groucho Marx (along with his brothers) reproduces the qualities of his predecessors, but had access to film, that is, to a much broader audience. His self-deprecating witticisms are far better known than the previous ones mentioned here. Some of them are legendary: "I don't want to belong to any club that will accept me as a member"; and, "Those are my principles, and if you don't like them . . . well, I have others." Some are, like Mencken's and even Twain's, remarkably sexist: "I did a bond tour during the Second World War . . . . We were raising money, and we played Boston and Philadelphia and most of the big cities. And we got to Minneapolis. There wasn't any big theater to play there, so we did our show in a railroad station. Then I told the audience that I knew a girl in Minneapolis. She was also known in St. Paul, she used to come over to visit me. She was known as 'The Tail Of Two Cities.' I didn't sell any more bonds, but eh . . . they didn't allow me to appear anymore." This personal self-effacement rendered his recitals of the distinctive traits of Americans at large more palatable, and more incisive: "In America you can go on the air and kid the politicians, and the politicians can go on the air and kid the people."[31]

After the initial Jewish classics, there was Woody Allen, an icon-like figure from the 1970s through the 1990s but eclipsed later by scandal and age. Like Groucho Marx, with whom he corresponded briefly in the mid-sixties, he had the advantage of the screen over his predecessors. This has made him an American export, although once again, the Jewish sarcasm, self-deprecation, and caustic wit do not translate easily. There are few things as painful as watching an Allen movie with subtitles in Spanish; he doesn't wear well outside the United States. But the French adored him (he has opened the Cannes Film Festival on three occasions), and he was often the American most foreigners love to love.

The movies, the interviews, the theater, and short stories provided an endless commentary on himself, contemporary American society, life, sex, and depression. He was both a reflection and product of much of what foreigners considered the best of the United States, before his dramatic fall from grace. Like his forebears, he juxtaposed uncommon, sarcastic, and even cynical introspection, with social criticism of his country and compatriots. He refers less often than his colleagues to "Americans" in general and is much less political than they were. Yet he explains more about the United States than many sociologists or political scientists, even with his "coastal," Jewish bias.

He may not have captured all of America, but he looked more deeply into the soul and structure of many parts of it with greater insights than scholars or even novelists. And it was his sense of humor that allowed him to do this. As a garden-variety writer, he would have been far less interesting. His versatility as a film-maker, his cosmopolitan range, and distance from the city where he grew and lived, starting out as a writer, then a stand-up comic, made Allen one of the United States' foremost social critics of his time, or in any case the one most foreigners familiar with America referred to and identified.

Some can argue—Allen himself acknowledges as much—that his humor and his films were "coastal" or college campus constructs. It can be said that the broad swathes of American life ignored him, or at best found him obnoxious and representative of everything they hate: New York, Jewish snobbishness. He certainly did not reach the broad masses through television like other humorists mentioned here, or those who tens of millions of Americans came to know through television: Jacky Gleason, Lucille Ball, Milton Berle, even Carroll O'Connor's Archie Bunker or Carol Burnett. But thanks to the Marx Brothers, to those who preceded Allen, like Danny Kaye, or those who followed him, like Jon Stewart, Jewish humor entered the mainstream of American entertainment and humor, remaining Jewish and becoming quintessentially American.

This is also partly true about the next generations of humorists: those epitomized by *Saturday Night Live*, and subsequently by *The Daily Show* and Comedy Central. Stephen Colbert, Jon Stewart, Noah Trevor, Bill Maher, and others are the new Menckens, Rogers, and Marx, but with a much more politicized content, a more devout if not necessarily broad following (ratings are not that high), and a connection with the young their predecessors perhaps never enjoyed. SNL has been a comedy powerhouse and incubator for dozens of humorists since 1975. Being an SNL alumnus—unlike Alec Baldwin the host with most appearances—is a point of pride. Alumni since 1975 include, in chronological order: Chevy Chase, Dan Ackroyd, John Belushi, Al Franken, and Bill Murray, from the seventies; Eddie Murphy, Billie Crystal, Dana Carvey, from the eighties; Chris Rock, Adam Sandler, Will Ferrell, and Jimmy Fallon, from the nineties; and this century, Tina Fey, Kate McKinnon, Amy Poehler, Maya Rudolph, Kristen Wiig, and Seth Meyers. The cast is complete. Or rather, almost complete. I must now turn to the extraordinary tradition of African American humor—not without apologizing for neglecting the case of women comedians or female humor, represented by figures ranging from Lucille Ball and Joan Rivers, to Amy Schumer and Sarah Silverman. I am too weakly familiar with them and their colleagues.

Black humor: from the plantations to TV

As numerous scholars and participants have written, it begins under slavery as a multiple-use instrument, along with spirituals, dance, and pantomime. It served as a tool for the enslaved peoples from different regions of Africa who lacked a common language, or who suffered the excruciating pain of the Middle Passage in different periods. It also enabled the enslaved on the plantations to make fun of the white owners, among themselves, or even in their presence, without fearing that they would understand they were being mocked. African American humor under slavery also functioned as a means to exchange encrypted information, so to speak. It was quintessential *double entendre*. Given the enforced illiteracy of the enslaved population, humor was inevitably oral or physical.

The minstrel show was originally developed by whites in what came to be known as "blackface," something justifiably unacceptable today but common in those times. "Daddy Rice"—a white minstrel singer named Thomas Dartmouth—created the theatrical Jim Crow this way in 1828, but after the Civil War and later in the nineteenth century, minstrel shows were increasingly performed by African Americans, themselves in "blackface." The most renowned example, a man who came to be recognized as the first black comedian, was Bert Williams. He entertained millions of Americans—black and white—from the 1880s through the twenties and might be labeled the first crossover black comedian.

Initially black comedians—all oral, until much later—played for black audiences. Traditionally, African Americans didn't perform for white audiences, unless it was a minstrel show. When they performed a stand-up routine, they tailored it so it wouldn't generate anti-bodies. This self-restraint was absent before African American crowds. One author phrased it this way: "As time progressed and society became less segregated and more accepting, this differentiation wasn't viewed as necessary."[32] The main impulse for this evolution sprang from the Great Migration: black humor moved north, and partly, at least, to white audiences.

Minstrel shows began to fade away in the early twentieth century. Blacks more frequently than not performed before white audiences. In some cases, the audiences included blacks in remote spaces. Even under slavery, humor "included self-deprecation, as the slaves themselves were often the subjects of their comic tales." Self-deprecation was a recurrent feature of black humor, especially for black audiences.[33] Presumably, those audiences enjoyed the fun being poked at them. As another author, from Clark Atlanta University suggests, though, perhaps not everyone. Although, "this was the origin of the self-deprecatory nature of black humor,"[34] it did not necessarily please all African American audiences, starting with the emerging black middle class.

Originally, when the public was mixed, the self-deprecatory characteristics rarely extended to white themes or American ones in general, devoid of racial connotations. But the self-deprecatory seed was present from the beginning. With time, through the great comedians who began to play for bi-racial audiences, it would become scathingly critical—and self-critical—of American society. When a Dick Gregory mocked the country, he was mocking whites, but also blacks and Americans as such: "This is the only country in the world where a man can grow up in a filthy ghetto, go to the worst of schools, be forced to ride in the back of the bus, then get $5,000 a week to tell about it."[35]

There was a tension in self-deprecation from the outset. Not everything had the same appeal for white and black audiences. After Gregory, Sammy Davis Jr., and Redd Foxx—the first black comedian to perform for a white audience in Las Vegas—the more explicit humorists like Richard Pryor and Eddie Murphy may have grated on white audiences. The more nuanced ones, like Bill Cosby, had an easier cross-over, long before his personal, professional, and ethical debacle. When Pryor would use his classic line—"I was a nigger for twenty-three years. I gave it up—no room for advancement"—it did not exactly ingratiate him with whites. Cosby was smoother; some said, whiter. Pryor began making fun of whites as he did blacks, and subsequently the next generation—personified by Chris Rock and Dave Chappelle—basically took on everyone and everything. They became social critics who spoke of racism but certainly did not limit their commentary to it.

They are at once irreverent, iconoclastic, and self-deprecatory. And while they are emphatically part of the African American humor tradition, they also address universal themes. Rock mocks America: "We got so much food in America we're allergic to food. Allergic to food! Hungry people ain't allergic to shit. You think anyone in Rwanda's got a fucking lactose intolerance?!"—and white Americans: "Every town has the same two malls: the one white people go to and the one white people used to go to"[36] —and blacks, along with himself: "I live in a neighborhood so bad that you can get shot while getting shot." Chappelle, who—unlike Rock, an SNL alumnus—made only a stop at *Saturday Night Live* at the beginning of his television career, took a long leave of absence from TV and stand-up, though not from films. He moved to South Africa for a few years, somewhat mysteriously. But he also retains the same strain of humor, peculiarly African American. He blasts American society as a whole, whites in particular, and his fellow blacks almost indistinctly. For whites and his own society, he is devastating: "Somebody broke into my house once, this is a good time to call the police, but mmm . . . , nope. The house was too nice. It was a real nice house, but they'd never believe I lived in it. They'd be like 'He's still here!' "[37] For whites, he seems unforgiving: "If you're black, you got to look at America a little bit different. You got to look at America like the uncle who paid for you to go to college, but who molested you." For blacks, he is withering: "Every black American is bilingual. All of them. We speak street vernacular and we speak 'job interview.' "[38] And he is, like all his predecessors, merciless in his personal mocking: "I enjoy my own thoughts sometimes."[39]

For reasons already explained and that date back to slavery, African American humor was purely oral for a considerable period. But that began to change, as early as with Web Dubois, who according to acclaimed novelist Paul Beatty, "had a sense of humor. His 1923 essay 'On Being Crazy,' while by no means hilarious, is at least an example of the great man letting his 'good' hair down to engage in a little segregation satire."[40] Then came Langston Hughes and his *Not without Laughter*.

Since then, black authors emerged repeatedly. And black humor also emerged in films, mainly, though not only, through the now classic works of Spike Lee. Perhaps the most recent and successful African American writer with humor is Beatty himself, whose novel *The Sellout* won the Man Booker Prize in 2015, even though it was turned down by eighteen publishers before Farrar, Strauss, and Giroud took it on.

Despite their "coastalness" or location in the campus archipelago of the American heartland, all of these contemporary incarnations of

American humor understand they are dealing with more than jokes. They keep the American tradition alive and in good shape. Especially among the young, in the case of the great Comedy Central stars, they are not only comedians or humorists. They provide news, carry out interviews, do roasts and highbrow events in New York and Washington, and have become a reference point for everybody. *The New York Times* posts their best lines every day; politicians of all stripes beg to go on their shows and pay attention and homage to their irony. They are, in many ways, the social critics of the day, despite their relatively restricted reach and undeniable abhorrence from much of Middle America. Trump and his followers never forgave them.

The national sense of humor does not belong to the humorists exclusively, though. Americans in general are funny. They laugh at themselves, they engage in large doses of *humor negro*, as it is called in Spanish, or gallows humor in proper English, I suppose, which is a mixture of a lampooning, irreverent, and dark-sided ability to mock everything: life, death, pleasure, illness, even the most unpleasant and obnoxious features of daily and social life. No one cracks jokes at a memorial service, a funeral, or a wake; Americans do. They make fun of themselves and of their friends, not to mention their enemies. The distinguishing characteristic is self-deprecation; it contrasts with most other nations' humor.

The American sense of humor can prove a vital tool in raising its self-awareness. Humor has a unique way of highlighting a country's— and an individual's—weaknesses. And in this case, it means recognizing the loss of the United States' across-the-board hegemony and the need to project its power toward addressing its immense internal problems. A country content "in its own skin" carries more weight in the world than one that must constantly boast its muscles. America will need its sense of humor more than ever in the coming years. Laughing about oneself when, like Muhammad Ali, "You are the greatest," is one thing. Doing so in the thick of rivalries, of cut-throat competition with others, of approaching old age, is quite another. Using humor when dealing with the British is certain to be unlike resorting to it with the Chinese, in general not known for their comicality, though certainly known for their wit. Its marvelous sense of humor will serve the United States well as it faces the coming challenges.

Similarly, the awakening of a sense of history is crucial for a nation, or a civilization, to understand where it finds itself in history and in the world. The United States is moving from the position of unquestioned economic superiority it enjoyed since World War II to one where rivals—the EU, and mainly China—no longer find themselves as far behind as before. The transition is less abrupt than some believe, as I hope to show in the next chapter. In that transition, history will become indispensable. America is finally beginning to acknowledge the importance of history for understanding itself. It will also increasingly appreciate its usefulness when dealing with age-old civilizations like China, who place an enormous accent on history and its long view in particular. In perhaps one of the greatest recent tributes to American maturity, partly thanks to Donald Trump's admiration for Andrew Jackson, Harriet Tubman's possible presence on the twenty-dollar bill is joked about on Comedy Central. So is Tubman herself, as a black Union spy. When traditional American sense of humor converges with the emerging American sense of history, things are really beginning to change. Now nothing, not even history, escapes American humor, which makes it exceptional, withering, and admirable.

If to this we add the broad window the United States will own before its economic pre-eminence is overtaken by others, one can be relatively optimistic about the future, at least in this field. We will peer through that window now, with a slightly counter-intuitive approach.

6

Apple and Wall Street

THE AMERICAN ECONOMY HAS received a series of dire warnings over the past forty years. In the eighties, it was the Japanese juggernaut and the "Fall of Great Powers" syndrome that would soon lay it low. At the turn of the century, the creation of the Euro and the reform of the German economic machine generated a new pessimism, despite the Clinton years' boom. By 2015, China's explosive growth, together with the glowing achievement of having overtaken the United States in GDP around 2012 (at least in purchasing power parity) generated unending news reports and essays about the imminent demise of American economic prowess and pre-eminence. This occurred in 2012, but in GDP per capita, the United States still surpasses China by almost four to one.[1]

Donald Trump, as doomsayer-in-chief, aggravated the last somber forecast, despite his self-contradictory, boosterish bombast. None of these predictions came true, at least in the short term, and even China's surge appears unlikely to threaten American economic superiority anytime soon (not before 2030).[2] All of which does not imply that there are not serious weaknesses in the way in which the US economy functions, nor that one day, simply as a product of demographics, India and China will not surpass American GDP in current prices. In per capita terms, however, that day is still removed. As well as in a more intangible standard, for example that of an "important role in the world." A poll taken in twenty-five nations in 2018 found that 31 percent of those interviewed said the United States played a more important role in the world than ten years before; 35 percent thought it was equally important. Only a quarter believed it played a less important role.[3]

In the case of India and China, the issue is one of large aggregate numbers. America's economy outrivals all others still in the manufacturing stage, no matter how populous or diminutive, even if they have also advanced to a service-based, technology-driven level, or have united as the European Union. The latter is in the same league as the United States—size- and population-wise—but is still not structurally homologous. There are very few exceptions (such as Airbus) where a European firm as such—not a German or French or Italian firm—competes successfully with an American one (Boeing) in a given sphere of activity. There are regions of Europe with which useful comparisons can be established, but by definition they cannot stand up to the US economy as a whole.

The fact that America no longer possesses the command over the world economy it held during much of the first half century after World War II does not mean it is not still the largest, most dynamic, and innovative economy on the globe. A relative weakening in the balance of economic forces should never be interpreted as an absolute decrease in every area of economic endeavor: productivity, technological advance, corporate size and monopolistic dominance, market share and conquest.

Similarly, if other societies prefer to divide their time working and producing in a different fashion—in a manner that many of us observers from abroad find more attractive—this preference should not should deter anyone from recognizing that the "American way" is still the most seductive "way" for millions all over the world. The Americans and the English work many more hours per year than the French or the Germans: 1780 for the United States and 1543 for the United Kingdom, versus 1408 for Norway or, not stereotypically, 1356 for Germany.[4] I personally prefer the latter option. Americans have fewer days of vacation, less leisure time, and a lower quality of life. I dislike that choice. But given their druthers, billions would select the American preference, because they can see the results in real time, everyday, in their everyday life.

Constant continuity

The fascinating question for foreigners is why nearly one hundred and fifty years after the great American invention boom of the Bells, Edisons, Wrights, and others, the United States continues to reign supreme over technological innovation. It still generates incredible advances in people's lives everywhere. Ever since the retailing breakthroughs of Sears Roebuck and Montgomery Ward, at the end of the nineteenth century, or domestic consumer goods businesses, like Isaac Singer's (arguably the founder of the world's first multinational company), let alone Ford's path-breaking steps during the first decade of the twentieth century, American capitalism never lost its stride. Today Apple, Alphabet, Amazon, Facebook, and Microsoft are the equivalents of the corporations built by the geniuses of the nineteenth and early twentieth centuries and are still American.

By revenue, five of the top ten technology companies in the world are American, the first four by huge margins; the other five are Chinese.[5] A perspective from afar focuses on what endures of American ingenuity, innovation, and educational achievement at the highest levels. The domestic viewpoint, held by many local observers of their own country's evolution, sees the glass half empty. But there is not a single area of economic, technological, military, space conquest, or artificial intelligence activity where an American entity does not occupy first place; renewable energy might be an arguable exception. Other nations may find niches or be planning for the medium-term future with greater foresight, resources, and focus. But in every field, the United States, through an individual, an institution, or a corporation, continues to be at the head of the class. Among other reasons, this is thanks to what Italian author Mariana Mazzucato, has called the Entrepreneurial State, that is, the involvement of the federal government in the economy through myriad channels and instruments.[6]

In 1925, halfway between the end of World War I and the Depression, the ten-largest companies in the world by revenues were all American. In 2018, of the top ten non-extractive corporations in the world, six were American.[7] Partly this stemmed from the destruction wrought by the Great War in Europe, but also by the sheer dimensions of the country on the other side of the Atlantic. After 1870, the Pennsylvania Railroad became the largest enterprise in the world and continued to be so until the late twenties. In 1917, US Steel was the largest steel-maker in the world, despite the far greater size of the armament manufacturers in Europe. American Telephone and Telegraph was the second largest firm in the United States, and in the world's top ten. In 1900, Rockefeller's Standard Oil Company was the number one company in the world by market capitalization. After its break-up in 1907 it remained so; in 1920, its spin-off, Standard Oil of New Jersey, remained in first place. For seventy-seven years, from 1931 to 2007, General Motors was the largest automaker in the world, and through the late forties, the largest company in the United States and the world. No business has since equaled its size in relation to America's gross national product. IBM joined the club of world leaders in the mid-fifties and dominated the computing industry in the world until 1980, when new giants began entering the competition.[8] In 1980, the top ten corporations were still American. By 2015, the number had dropped to seven, but the other three were Chinese state-owned companies.

Foreigners today who connect the dots and detect the continuity in these specific aspects marvel at the almost perpetual advantage Americans held, and still hold. They are, on occasion, mystified by the process's longevity, even if they have explained it successfully. Technological innovation is one thing; the Germans, British, and French beat the Americans in many key areas in the late nineteenth and early twentieth centuries: automobiles, cinematography, television, etc. Capitalism and business are another thing: their birthplace was Britain; their ideological nurturing took place in France. Germany generated their most sophisticated expression, creating the first military-industrial complex (along with Japan), the first welfare state, and the first long-standing alliance between capital and the state.

The United States did not reach any of these stages until far later. But it was the first and only modern economy and society to meld the two processes together: technological innovation and business; inventions and profits; engineering and economics; management (through people like Frederick Taylor) and creative imagination. Obviously not every invention transformed itself into a profitable company. Not every successful business originated in its founder's ingenuity. But the partnership, or synergy, took root in so many sectors of the economy and society that it became almost inevitable for it to dwarf anything else, when coupled with the magnitude and natural wealth of the United States. As a Chinese traveler put it in 1918: "No matter what the branch of science, once it is transmitted to the United States, Americans use their talents to imitate it, put it to practical use, and develop it."[9]

This endures today, with Steve Jobs's legendary garage, Zuckerberg's Harvard dorm and dropping out, Jeff Bezos's $250,000 from his parents to start Amazon in 1995, and Michael Dell dropping out of college at 20. Any country can produce a genius; dozens of nations have created modern, lucrative businesses. Nobody has joined both over a century and a half like the United States. There is something in the nature or DNA of American capitalism that makes this possible, unlike any other country in the world.

The breadth and pace of American technology's introduction into industry, households, investment, and consumption after World War II was astounding. It continued after the 1960s, when Western Europe and Japan had recovered from the destruction wrought by the conflagration. It persisted past the 1980s, when China's reforms began to spawn results. It took place not only much more rapidly than in any other country, but also at the same pace, or even more quickly, than in the late nineteenth or early twentieth century with the telephone, automobiles, or radio.

The contemporary examples provided by Robert Gordon, the economic historian from Northwestern University, who compares them with the American past itself, are well known. Yet they continue to provoke fascination abroad: the mainframe computer that rapidly generated spin-offs into airline reservation systems, life insurance companies, banking, with sub-spin-offs, so to speak, in credit cards, automatic teller machines, and barcode scanners and labeling; the photocopier, introduced in 1959; the electronic calculator, and, obviously, the personal computer (1981). These innovations were joined by the Internet in the early nineties, and by broadband access a few years later. According to Gordon, by 2013, 85 percent of US households owned computers and enjoyed Internet access, which by that year was almost entirely through broadband.[10]

Again, some foreigners wonder: why in the United States, and not elsewhere? China, at least until now, has proved unable to combine these two features of American capitalism. There are still no Chinese inventions girding the globe. The large-scale Chinese firms present in dozens of countries, other than the so-called state-owned companies' investments in commodities and commodity-linked infrastructure, are still few and far between. Huawei is the best-known example, partly because it is almost the only one; the ongoing rivalry or conflict with the United States over 5G and trunk lines in many countries is a good predictor of what will surely occur but has not yet happened on a broad scale. China's political and administrative structures do not seem to favor this type of combination, at least for the moment. Japan may have passed through a somewhat analogous stage in the 1980s, where something along these lines could have plausibly occurred, but it proved to be a fleeting moment. It persists in very specific cases—i.e. the automobile industry—but not as a generalized phenomenon. Indeed, the American edge has remained so powerful that it has transcended itself, as Hegel might say. The smartphone is an American construct, was developed by an American company, but is built outside the United States, and increasingly, by non-American manufacturing businesses (Samsung, LG, Huawei, etc.). Yet it is perceived as a quintessentially American product. Given that the direct and indirect jobs created by its manufacturing and the profits generated by its sales are certainly not all based in the United States, one could say that this perception is misleading. This is a decades-old discussion about whether multinational corporations have a home or nationality; I tend to continue to believe that they do.

A similar evolution took place previously, with the PC, then the laptop, then tablets. As with the sewing machine toward the end of the nineteenth century, it seems to make no difference where the final process actually takes place. What matters is that the creation, development, launching, and marketing of the product "be American." Saying that an iPhone is "Designed in America" and "Made in China" is not much different from describing a Singer sewing machine designed in Chicago and manufactured in Scotland in 1895. In 1863 Singer inaugurated a manufacturing plant in Bridgeport, England, with a daily output of 1400 machines by the beginning of the 1870s. Then, in 1885, the Kilbowie factory in Scotland opened and replaced the production of sewing machines in Bridgeport. The firm inaugurated a foundry in Germany in 1883 and opened its Russian factory in Podolsk in 1900. What is the difference with Apple?

From the 1940s onward, a distinguishing feature of American capitalism has been a perhaps praiseworthy but discomforting unique trait. It has engendered a rare mixture of terror and admiration among outsiders, sympathetic or not to the American project. Since its entry into World War II, and particularly after the Manhattan Project, the United States established a symbiosis between science, engineering, technology, and military hardware (and software, through the Internet or World Wide Web) that has begotten remarkable achievements in countless fields.

This symbiosis can be traced back to the early twentieth century, when Army doctors Walter Reed and William Gorgas essentially eradicated yellow fever in Cuba and Panama, to stem high casualty rates in the Spanish-American War and the construction of the Panama Canal. Both were military ventures. Army doctors began research experiments in Cuba with a team led by Reed, with doctors James Carroll, Aristides Agramonte, and Jesse William Lazear.[11] They successfully proved the "mosquito hypothesis": yellow fever was the first virus shown to be transmitted by mosquitoes. A broader implication of this same process has been described, again, in Mazzucato's Entrepreneurial State, through the enormous sums assigned to the National Institutes of Health since 1938 by the federal government for drug research and development.[12]

The atomic bomb was the most spectacular result of this remarkable synergy. It brought together genius, starting with Oppenheimer, but including all the Nobel Prize winners who worked in Chicago. Management, through the US military's involvement and General Leslie Groves and Oppenheimer's leadership, was mixed with financial resources, thanks to US government direction. Finally, the Project illustrated American capability to convert the prototype of Los Alamos into a terrifying arsenal in a brief period of time. This pattern of cooperation continued throughout the Cold War and until today, sometimes infamously (rocketry and missile technology with former Nazi Wernher Von Braun), sometimes admirably, with Kennedy and NASA's race to the moon. It persists today, through ongoing research in high-technology military to dehumanize wars, for example, but that can also be applied, eventually, to civilian use.

The two more recent, and less toxic, examples lay in the mainframe computer, developed by the War Department at the University of Pennsylvania and made public, under the horrifying acronym ENIAC, which stood for Electronic Numerical Integrator and Computer, in 1947; and the Internet, born from the Pentagon's Advanced Research Projects Agency, or ARPANET, in the late sixties, as well as thanks to Tim Berners-Lee, the British inventor of the World Wide Web. No country in the world has been able, or will be soon, to amalgamate all of the necessary ingredients into similar finished products that can eventually benefit a corporation, a nation, or even mankind.

The famous patent comparison is also highly illustrative. It is not a perfect equivalent of innovation, but nonetheless an appropriate proxy. In 1900, of the five main nations in the world depositing patent requests (the United States, Great Britain, France, Belgium, and Germany), American petitioners obtained slightly below 40 percent. In 1920, the figure dipped to 30 percent. By 1950 it spiked to 44 percent, chiefly because of the destruction created by World War II in the other leading countries. But the most interesting numbers spring from later dates.

In 1980, when American hegemony was beginning to decline, the United States lost its first place to the Soviet Union, to Japan in 2000, and to China in 2015, but maintained a very similar proportion of world patents granted: respectively, 34 percent, 34 percent, and down to 25 percent in 2015,[13] largely as a result of China's entry into the equation. Between 1920 and 2015, the share of US patents among the world's leaders shifted from roughly one-third of the total to one-quarter: over an entire century, a degree of continuity that seems difficult to believe.

This is not to say that American leadership will last forever, in *all* fields, and in the *same* fields as before. Once again, if only as a result of China's and India's dimensions, the United States' lead in technology, patents, innovation, and corporation size will not persist indefinitely. China's catching up will be more rapid in some areas—perhaps green tech—than others. But there is a large difference between this "natural" evolution, which has to do with demographics and development, and any decline due to the exceptional performance of others. Once various nations have mastered the manufacture of iPhones, the use of online retailing, social media diffusion, and search engines, American companies will emerge and head the pack in new areas: artificial intelligence, bio-genetics, robotics, etc., even if in specific fields—green tech, facial recognition technology—China may now and then leap forward. America appears to possess an inherent, almost built-in advantage that has allowed it to remain the front-runner over a century and a half in practically every realm of modern life. The question any foreigner asks, one more time, is self-evident: where does this edge come from?

Why? Additional explanations

The previous answer, involving the combination of individual genius and innovation with a certain type of capitalism, is valid, but partial. There are other complementary, though individually insufficient, explanations. They include size, openness to the rest of the world, social recognition and prestige for inventors—self-made men or women—a tax system that encourages this social recognition, and the special nature of an educational system unlike any other.

Size matters. The American market has been simply immense, thanks to the United States' middle-class nature since the early twentieth century. It is not only a product of demographics, territory, and immigration, but also of purchasing power, that is, the result of multiplying all these factors together. Ford could sell millions of Model Ts because there were millions of Americans able to buy them, millions of immigrants on their way to American shores, and an infinite territory for them to live in. Retailers, housing construction companies, appliance and airplane manufacturers could ply their wares on a massive scale, because of the massive scale of the domestic market. Bill Gates could install tens of millions of operating systems or Windows in as many PCs as possible because there were tens of millions of consumers who needed one. As late as 2018, despite the incredible ascent of China and India in this field at least, Apple sells more iPhones in the United States than in either of those two nations. Its American sales topped those in each of the twenty-eight countries of the European Union or Japan (roughly 50 million units in the United States, versus under 40 million for Great Britain, Japan, China, Germany, and France, in that order). Apple in 2017 sold fourteen times more devices in the United States than in India.[14]

Equally significant, the American capital market is vaster than any and than most others put together. If you invent something, transform it into a technological breakthrough, and then devise a reasonably feasible business plan, you will face far lesser and fewer obstacles than elsewhere finding the capital to produce your new gadget, service, or app in the United States. The New York Stock Exchange has a higher market capitalization value than the combined exchanges of London, Frankfurt, Tokyo, and Shanghai: 21 trillion dollars vs. 17 trillion for the four together.[15] There is more money available in America, and it is easier to obtain. US corporations may stash their profits away in Ireland, but they are quoted on Wall Street, and that is where they launch their IPOs. There are more of these every year in New York, again, than in all the other cities put together.[16] If we add Silicon Valley and venture capital funds, American dimensions in terms of capital availability dwarf anything else, still today.

The magnitude of this market was the greatest imaginable incentive for anyone wanting to invent something and transform it into a capitalist commodity, in Marx's terminology. It meant producing something, a widget or a gadget, that millions could purchase and that would make money. Despite increasing inequality, the American market has continued to expand, partly thanks to immigration, partly to the gradual inclusion of less recent arrivals, though at a slower pace than before. In its own way, that market has remained a relatively protected one. Not through tariffs or even non-tariff barriers, but through its breadth. Foreign trade represents a smaller proportion of American GDP than of any rich country, even if in absolute terms it is comparable to many. The US automobile industry does not export many vehicles to Western Europe, Japan, or China. Mercedes and BMW, let alone Toyota or Honda, export millions of cars every year to the United States. But the American automobile industry could survive even if it was condemned to manufacture only for the US market, despite the fact that German-made cars are, in the eyes of many foreigners, including this one, far superior to Buicks, Cadillacs, or Lincolns. But no manufacturer could survive without America's market.

Allowing in foreign cars is the least of it. American openness to the rest of the world, despite all the nativist, protectionist, and persecutory episodes over the past century and a half, has made an enormous

difference in terms of plowing invention into profits. This type of capitalism could barely endure if there were not myriad inventors, from
many countries, seeking their fortune in the United States. It could not
flourish without a welcoming attitude toward immigration, without
which those inventors would not have ventured far from their shores.
Had their products, services, attitudes, and experimentation not been
well received in the United States they would not have thrived.

Americans love to experiment with everything, not always successfully, but never pessimistically nor with fatalism. I remember spending
a year as a child at the home of a German friend of my parents in Fort
Lee, New Jersey, in the early sixties. He had married a modestly educated
Mexican woman from Puebla, voted for Nixon in 1960, and detested
Kennedy, and was about as conservative as anyone could be without
crossing several red lines. He also had a large machine shop in his base-
ment with what seemed to me countless lathes, drills, presses, and other
devices. He would spend his days inventing useless contraptions, but
never losing his enthusiasm and hope that one day he would hit pay-
dirt. Frank Grosseborger summed up this notion: a foreigner, married
to a foreigner, received by the United States with open arms, constantly
experimenting, never succeeding, but never despairing.

The matter is not merely personal, as American lore would have it,
nor limited to celebrities, from Alexander Graham Bell to Jan Koum, the
Ukrainian inventor of Whatsapp. Countless foreigners have invented extraordinary devices in the United States. Some died poor, others became
immensely rich, as they transformed inventions into technology, then
the latter into business goods or services. According to three scholars
who have studied this issue carefully, "The foreign-born were more prevalent among inventors active in the US than in the non-inventor population. This is consistent with entry into invention being relatively open
compared to occupations such doctors and lawyers that required some
degree of cultural assimilation or formal qualification."[17]

Every child in the United States knows the saga and repeats the
narrative of the heroes of invention. For the record, here is a short
list: Nicholas Tesla, alternative current, Serbia; Charles Feltman,
hotdogs, Germany; Ralph Baer, videogames, Germany; Levi Strauss,
jeans and denim, Germany; James Kraft, processed cheese, Canada;
Sergey Brin, Google, Russia; Elon Musk, everything, South Africa;

Andrew Grove, microprocessor chips and Intel, Hungary; Enrico Fermi, the first controlled nuclear chain reaction, leading to the atomic bomb, Italy; Carl Djerassi, contraceptive pill, Germany; Jan Koum, Whatsapp, Ukraine. I already mentioned Bell.

The American patenting system, along with the tax code, also contributed mightily to the process of turning inventions into dollars. The patent system was designed from early on to be different from Europe: faster, cheaper, simpler, more accessible. The tax system, unwittingly perhaps, made it easier for a robber baron to become respectful, by inducing or forcing him (or her) to donate large sums to foundations and philanthropy in general. The existence of inheritance or estate taxes consummated the mutation of the Carnegies, Fords, Rockefellers, and Guggenheims of the late nineteenth and early twentieth centuries from brutal exploiters of the working classes into altruistic, Medici-like patrons of the arts, universities, research, and even international peace.

Much the same thing occurred in the late twentieth and early twenty-first centuries with Buffet, Gates, Zuckerberg, Bezos, and others. If an inventor can become a tycoon, and the latter can subsequently be recognized and appreciated as a mainstay of the most noble segments of society, the circle is complete. The inventor is transformed into an idol, a hero, a great man or woman, whom others want to emulate. How many Jobs and Brins and Musks are there in Europe, and when they appear, like Richard Branson, are they not promptly "Americanized"? There is an enormous social prize and acknowledgment in the United States for being a great inventor, a great entrepreneur, and being immensely wealthy. This does not quite occur elsewhere, though there are specific cases everywhere: in China, India, Brazil, Japan, and Europe. In these countries, though, we are facing individual examples. In the United States, this is a social and historical phenomenon.

Lastly, teach your children

Our last possible explanation for this remarkable continuity of American innovation and technological pre-eminence lies in the peculiar nature of education in the United States. It is peculiar because of the simultaneous and contradictory conjunction of several well-known facts, laid out here consecutively.

First, American students systematically place less well in international educational tests than their counterparts in the other rich countries. Second, the American elite higher education system is the most successful in the world, by any standard: research, Nobel Prizes, scholarly publications, successful careers for its graduates, resources available for myriad activities. Third, while high school completion reached its peak at practically 100 percent some years ago, four-year college graduation at public universities has leveled off at around 32 percent, except for Asian-Americans and Indian-Americans.[18] The relative number of Americans obtaining a four-year college degree is stagnant and could shrink in the coming years. Fourth, the two- or three-tier system in American education, from high school to Ph.D., is becoming increasingly consolidated and rigid. The average rate of return on a two-year community college education is practically nil, although some advocates claim that it can be as high as 20 percent.[19] This is also the case for many low-tier four-year colleges. Finally, one of the additional features of American higher education that distinguishes it from European, and most Latin American, Asian, and African structures, is the college-based system, or what is sometimes called the liberal arts arrangement.

I can start with this last factor. Unlike in France, Mexico, or Japan, where high school graduates—generally 18 years of age—must immediately choose their career and enter a Department of Law, Physics, Philosophy, or Business, in the United States most schools allow a student to wait until their junior year to select a major. Even then, it is not an irrevocable choice, as in the aforementioned countries. In the United States, a young person will enter medical school, for example, at 22 or 23 years of age; in Spain, at 18. Having put children through both systems, and at the best universities both in Mexico and the United States, I can testify that the American path is far healthier and friendlier. It allows young people to postpone painful, often irreversible life decisions for two or three years, to change their minds (up to a point) and be better-rounded individuals when they understand what they wish to do in life.

The downside, however, is that often a four-year college education, outside of the top thirty schools, tends be remedial for a deficient high school preparation, and leaves graduates with a more universal, but less profound, education than their foreign counterparts. Between end-of-K–12 exams such as *vestibular*, A-levels, the *Baccalauréat* or *Abitur*, and a three- or four-year non-graduate degree, a typical European 22- or 23-year-old will be more perturbed by the choices he or she has already made than the American equivalent. But the German or Brazilian or Indian graduate will also write better, be closer to acquiring a profession, and in general possess a higher educational level than his or her American counterpart, unless the latter graduated from a high-quality private prep-school and a top thirty college. The comparison of American elite students with elite students from other parts of the world may be more difficult to carry out; impressionistically, my sense is that Americans lose out. As a Brazilian writer and professor who emigrated to the United States put it: ". . . college in the United States is meant to be the time when students explore questions of meaning. Through their general education curriculum, they are provided with the collective wisdom of human civilization. Supposedly this should help them acquire the needed tools to gaze into their souls, to ponder the shape of their lives. College in Brazil, on the other hand, was strictly utilitarian. When I was growing up, the bachelor's was a terminal degree based on career requirements rather than self-exploration. You learned a trade and proceeded to pursue it. My two bachelor's degrees—law and theology—afforded me little introspection and much professional practice."[20]

The American, however, will be more open-minded about life choices ahead, more flexible and experimental, having not yet decided on a career, or be barely in the throes of doing so. The American will be searching, probing, doubting, and, more recently, thanks to gap years, biding his or her time. This inevitably creates an atmosphere where invention and innovation, as well as bold and frequently failed ventures, abound, and in which some business models or breakthroughs succeed. The coming technological changes in modern capitalism will erupt in medicine and pharmaceuticals, in robotics and 3-D printing, big data and artificial intelligence in general, and in driverless automobiles. This higher education format will allow the United States to maintain or even widen its innovation lead. If it were the only factor, this difference might not ensure such leadership. Together with the following factors, it almost surely will, if certain obstacles do not get in the way. Student debt overhang is undoubtedly one of them. The construction of any type of American social democracy or advanced welfare state in the coming years will necessarily include a return to free, quality, higher education for all who seek it.

The next two factors go together, and in a sense represent two sides of the same coin. They also confirm the basic thesis just outlined above. In 2015, among the thirty rich or OECD countries (excluding Mexico, Chile, Turkey, and Colombia), the United States placed twenty-eighth in math, eighteenth in science, and twentieth in reading, in the on-going PISA tests among 540,000 15-year-old students throughout the world.[21] Correlating with GDP per capita, it should have been in the top five. Given the already high levels of inequality in the United States in general, in comparison to other rich countries, and in educational achievement in particular, if one removes the top percentile in the United States, the numbers would be worse. They are particularly disappointing among blacks, Latinos, and whites in poor states.

The situation continues to deteriorate as one goes up the educational ladder. Those with low or bad results at 15 (roughly tenth grade) will either not graduate (a minority), will finish high school but not pursue a college degree, or end up in a community college where they will receive some vocational or technological education. In 2010, 40 percent of all 18 million American undergraduates attended a two-year community college.[22] This proportion grew more than one-third since the 1970s. In 2017, only 14 percent of community-college enrollees graduated in two years.[23] Slightly more than 20 percent will finish in three years, and less than 30 percent will do so in four years. A few specialists question these figures, arguing that some community-college students either need more time to graduate or transfer to four-year institutions but are counted as "drop-outs." Forty percent of all students who enroll are placed at entry into at least one remedial class, and one out of every four work full time and go to school full time.[24] They will not have the tools throughout life that their peers in other OECD countries acquire and use—excepting excluded minorities there also. Nor will they enjoy the benefits of a cradle-to-grave welfare state. Furthermore, their educational foundations will make it more difficult for them, in their forties and fifties, to learn new skills, professions, or even simple trades. Some students of the community college tier or system are less pessimistic. James and Deborah Fallows, for example, visited the East Mississippi

Community College in 2014. They write: "The modern 'career technical' programs that we were beginning to see across the country, in contrast, aspire to help people avoid the minimum-wage service-or-retail trap with better-paid jobs as skilled repair technicians, in health care, in construction and design, in advanced modern factories, in law enforcement, and in other 'living wage' categories. Many of these schools naturally operate on a dispersed public-good principle. They have no way of knowing where the students they're training will end up working ten or twenty years from now."[25]

But those foundations do make our third factor feasible. It might be an exaggeration, yet also be true, that the American elite system is made possible by the existence of the other tiers. Some Americans from all walks of life—not just white aristocrats descended from the Mayflower—can attend high-quality public or private high schools, then elite colleges, and finally the top graduate or professional universities, because many more Americans do not. Every country has a least a two-tier educational system—India has the seven ITTs and then everything else, the French, their *grandes écoles*, the British have Oxbridge plus Imperial College, and LSE, Brazil its USP in Sao Paulo, etc.—but the American set-up seems much more segregated and polarized. Some 8000 students graduate every year from the Ivy League colleges[26]—many with financial aid—while hundreds of thousands attend state, community, or low-quality public university systems that cost little but that nobody wants to pay for. According to the president of La Guardia Community College in New York "(In 2016) more than 41 billion was given in charity to higher education, but a quarter of that went to just twenty institutions. Community colleges with almost half of all undergraduate students received just a small fraction."[27]

The degree of elitism is astounding, even compared with the French, British, or Indians. At the turn of the century, according to sociologist Roger Geiger, just ten schools took 20 percent of all the students in United States who scored in the top five centiles (or percentiles) on the SATs. Forty-one schools accounted for half of them.[28] The dichotomy is not necessarily public or private. The public university systems in California, Texas, Michigan, Virginia, and Wisconsin, at least, are world class. Conversely, dozens of private colleges are fly-by-night outfits out to make money and nothing more, despite their nominal non-profit nature. The chief difference lies in the financial and fiscal resources available to the elite tier, as a result of the monies unavailable to all the others. In addition to which the bottom tier becomes on occasion a low-cost feeder of the upper tier: assistant professors lacking tenure or job security, laboratory technicians, low-level semi-engineers, etc.

Could the elite system survive without the other side of the coin? It is difficult to say, but the idea that they couldn't is not far-fetched. Especially if one considers the contrast between the endowment per student at schools like Harvard or Princeton, and the meager fiscal resources available for public systems and junior colleges in most states of the Union. The rich and famous, as well as the American economic, political, and social establishment, can get away with the country paying low or no taxes to fund public higher education. Its needs—large by international standards but modest given the size of the United States—are met by the elite tier. It produces the indispensable military, political, business, diplomatic, intelligence, cultural, and administrative elite for perpetuating the establishment's station in life.

The elite system has going for it an enormous amount of resources per student or instructor which no country in the world possesses. The first contrast one notices when teaching in the United States' elite institutions instead of Mexico or France, in my case, is the incredible disparity of money and opportunities available to students in the United States (foreign or native-born), from junior years abroad to research grants, from amazing libraries to sophisticated laboratories and extraordinary students-per-instructor ratios. There is nothing comparable anywhere. Harvard dropouts like Jobs and Zuckerberg or Princeton graduates like Bezos enjoyed incomparable advantages before leaving school in regard to their elite peers in other nations. Not to mention other Americans or foreign students at run-of-the-mill institutions anywhere.

Given American size and resources overall, this implies that the pool of inventors, technological wizards or innovators, and entrepreneurs with the appropriate education is from the outset larger than elsewhere, even than China for now. It is not only the number of college and doctoral students with STEM degrees, but also the number of business school graduates, lawyers, and even medical doctors. Some nations may produce more of one or another of these categories—mainly India and

China—but no one does it all. It is not just the quantity that counts, although this is not a negligible question, but also the quality.

Between 1904 when the awards were launched, and 2018, Americans received 368 Noble prizes in all fields. France was awarded 62, Germany 107, Great Britain 132, Japan 26, China 9, all together a similar total.[29] A quarter of these winners were foreign born.[30] Granted, for every success story filmed by Hollywood, there are innumerable failures or cases of resigned passivity. In the long term, it is likely that China and India will catch up, given their demographics. Building a higher education system like the United States' and its perfect fit for American capitalism may nevertheless require a very long time. A German-American critic of the "declinist" school has pointed out that 17 percent of the world's science and engineering Ph.D.s are earned in the United States, which has 5 percent of the population. Although a large share is obtained by foreigners, most of these remain in the United States after obtaining their degree: 92 percent of Chinese candidates, 81 percent of Indian ones.[31]

There is, however, an underlying weakness in this star-system. Two-year enrollment is increasing, and state-system four-year enrollment is also, whereas elite school figures—let's say, the top thirty universities—are stagnant. By 1990, there were 5.1 million in community or junior colleges, and 8.3 million people enrolled in four-year colleges.[32] At the turn of the century, there were 6 million two-year students, and 7.2 million four-year enrollees. In 2010, the figures were 7.8 million and 10.2.[33] As a percentage of the overall population, the four-year cohort has diminished, and the two-year one has slightly grown. If one considers that part of the four-year group includes poor or weak state system institutions that should be almost properly grouped with the two-year one, the contrast with the elite tier is striking.

It has been stagnant. For some time, with a few exceptions (Cornell, UCLA, UC Berkeley, USC, University of Virginia, University of Michigan, and New York University), all the top thirty national universities have a typical undergraduate enrollment of around 6000 students, and a graduating class of between 1000 and 1500 young persons.[34] This has not changed in over half a century. Between 1970 and 2019, total enrollment at the top thirty schools was almost exactly the same. But the American population, establishment, corporate world, and public administration have all grown substantially during this half century. At some point either the second and third tier must improve dramatically or the elite tier must expand, as may be occurring in some regions. Here too, size matters.

Anyone betting on the upcoming twilight of America's technological pre-eminence, and of the United States' lead in innovation, higher education, and sheer magnitude of its entrepreneurial sector, is in for a disappointment. When foreigners see Americans regretting a golden age gone by, or leadership surrendered and threatened, or even imminent parity with China, they are often bewildered by this strange American penchant for seeing threats and decline when no one else does (remember the missile gap in 1960). Jeffrey Sachs is of course right in underlining how China's rate of patenting has nearly caught up with the United States, and that it now "produces more science and engineering PhDs than the United States."[35] China also houses nearly five times the population of the United States. Some Americans may want to make their country great again; in this field, at least, many foreigners believe that it continues to be great, for better or for worse. Where they worry is that the United States uses its technological superiority much as it continues to project its military might. Seen from abroad, what is good for America is not necessarily good for the world. The pragmatism and hypocrisy with which it addresses fundamental issues such as immigration and drugs (the subjects of the following chapter) are a reflection of this ongoing power or semi-hegemony, as well as a reminder of American ingenuity for managing problems with no solutions.

7

American pragmatism and hypocrisy: drugs and immigration

IT IS GENERALLY CONSIDERED bad taste and politically incorrect, at least in liberal circles in the United States, to group drugs and immigration together. After all, Donald Trump did exactly that when he lobbied for his wall, conjuring images of so-called "illegal" Mexicans and Central Americans pouring over the border loaded with fentanyl, heroine, and cocaine from Mexico, China, and South America. One especially obnoxious conservative Congressman used the metaphor of illegal Mexicans with "calves like cantaloupes" smuggling drugs into the United States.

Speaking about both issues in tandem simply reinforces views like Trump's, doesn't it? Similarly, referring to pragmatism and hypocrisy as two distinctive but linked American traits is tantamount to rehashing stereotypes: one—pragmatism—that has been overwrought, though many Americans and sympathetic foreigners delight in it; and another—hypocrisy—that no one likes but that is often excessively criticized. After all, there is much to praise in hypocrisy, when it works.

Nevertheless, in this chapter immigration and drugs will be addressed together, mainly because American attitudes toward them are both pragmatic and hypocritical. In addition, after trade, these are two of the most important interfaces between the United States and the rest of the world, and have been so for many years (obviously, immigration long before drugs). On the two accounts, the United States manifests a highly pragmatic approach as well as a starkly cynical stance that irritates individuals and countries around the world. It especially annoys those who must deal directly with Washington and America on these issues. Trump is more aggravating on immigration than his predecessors, as Ronald Reagan and his wife were regarding drugs, but in both cases, they are part of a pattern that stretches back for some time.

There are no two issues as intractable as drugs and immigration for Mexican leaders in their dealings with the United States. Now and then there is a trade war or negotiation; occasionally a security threat. Over the past sixty years, perhaps three or four diplomatic crises or disagreements have complicated relations between the nations. But drugs and immigration have been there as long as I can remember, or since I began studying these matters. For me, this begins with my father, who was foreign minister from 1979 to 1982; my brother who was deputy foreign minister from 1988 to 1994; and myself, as I held the same cabinet job as my father from 2000 to 2003. No matter how reasonable, friendly, and even collegial our counterparts in Washington may have been, the issues themselves outraced their sensitivity, and our patience and negotiating prowess (or lack of it). What anyone who has been involved with these items on the bilateral agenda at least since the mid-sixties knows full well is that they defy any short-term solution. They can be managed, or administered, but not solved.

Even when dealing with someone as sensitive to immigration as my colleague and friend Colin Powell—he is the son of Jamaican immigrants—the pressures upon a secretary of state on these matters are immense. When his boss is sympathetic to the cause of immigration reform—as George W. Bush was—he can attempt to resist trends in other areas of government. But only so far. If the president is fundamentally a friend of Mexico, as George H. W. Bush undoubtedly was, he is still frequently forced to listen to the cowboys in Washington: the Drug Enforcement Agency, what was then called the Immigration and Naturalization Service (INS)—or ICE-CBP later—and the extremists in the Congress.

Inevitably, interlocutors such as these, and many others, particularly when they are friendly to their Mexican colleagues, wind up resorting to the welcome tool of a two-tone discourse. They are obliged to spout an enormous amount of nonsense in public, particularly when testifying in Congress, about "illegals," drug cartels, crime, and violence. At the same time, we need not pay too much attention to these antics because they also have to negotiate myriad other matters with us. The only way to achieve this delicate and fragile balance is through pragmatism and hypocrisy. I have dealt with the Mexican mixture of both elsewhere; here I concentrate on the American blend.

Immigration: somewhat legal, somewhat tolerated

The essence of American hypocrisy on immigration can be boiled down to the famous or notorious distinction between what people in the United States, mainly on the conservative side of the ideological divide, usually label "illegal" immigration, and its legal counterpart. Liberals, foreigners, and scholars tend to use other terms: unauthorized migrants, undocumented immigrants, people without papers (somewhat of a Gallicism). The United States, at least since the 1924 National Origins Act, and perhaps reaching back to the previously cited Chinese Exclusion Act of the 1880s, has established a distinction between the two types of immigration. It insists, to the extent that there is a single agent on this matter, that Americans support and welcome "legal" immigration, that is, foreigners who arrive in the United States with proper papers and who keep them in order throughout their stay, whether a few months or forever.

They must enter properly, behave appropriately, and "follow the rules." These are the "good guys," except when they cease to be so, or when the rules change. Suddenly, certain nationalities are no longer welcome, and their rejection is crafted into law, directly or elliptically. At other times, limits are placed on certain categories (refugees, for example, or Muslims from certain countries). On other occasions, previously legal individuals are transformed into "illegal" ones (such as Dreamers or DACAs, or people under Temporary Protection Status who are subsequently deprived of it). Thus what was legal may abruptly no longer be so. José Vasconcelos, the Mexican education minister responsible for the glorious murals in Mexico's presidential palace and education ministry, recalled another time, not only when he crossed the Rio Grande every day to go to school, but when "We could travel freely, without passports or procedures. In those happy pre-World War I times, no one could limit anyone's right to freely enter any country in the world . . . . The only discomfort on crossing the dividing line (between the United States and Mexico) was the contrast between the prosperity, the freedom, the smiles on the Anglo-Saxon side, and the squalor, the resentment, the policing attitude on the Mexican one."[1]

Contrariwise, Americans oppose or abhor undocumented immigration, according to many, because the United States is a nation of laws. But laws are made by humans, not by gods, and they either change or are applied in different manners at different times. They can be drafted in such a way as to allow them to be by-passed. Thus it was not until 1929 that laws forbade entering the United States other than through legal and pre-established points of entry. Before then, Mexicans in particular would just walk across the border wherever they chose. During the entire Bracero Program, from 1942 through 1964, there was less unauthorized migration from Mexico than before or after, because it was mainly legal. Nobody had to sneak unlawfully into the United States; World War II demand for Mexican labor was insatiable. This did not mean that Mexicans, those without papers who had entered before 1942, or those whose documents expired during the program, were not expelled from the country. Hundreds of thousands were, during Operation Wetback in 1954.

Thus a first point of American pragmatism and hypocrisy with regard to immigration derives from the weak, frequently false, and never rigorous application of the Law, with a capital L. ICE agents today refrain from scheduling raids in Soho restaurants in Manhattan to round up Canadians, French, German, and Dutch millennials who have overstayed their authorized time in the United States (ninety days to six months). But they do lurk around churches and courthouses where Mexicans or Central American migrants congregate in order to round them up and deport them. The laws are the same, their application is not. When United States authorities wish to allow certain people to enter, or remain, they find a way to achieve their goal; when the goal is to keep others out, or remove them, it is also reached.

One of the most remarkable examples of American pragmatism/hypocrisy regarding immigration is the infamous Texas Proviso. In 1952, during one of the renegotiations of the Bracero Program, Congress passed the McCarran-Walter Act, deciding to penalize those who "harbored" undocumented migrants but not those who "employed" them. This was approved at the insistence of the Texan congressional delegation, hence the name. The underlying logic was that it might be illegal to be an "illegal" or to "harbor" one but not to employ one. Cheap, unskilled labor could be hired without any risk of criminal conduct.

Pragmatism and hypocrisy characterized Congress's conduct. Many states needed largely Mexican stoop labor or back-breaking, agricultural harvest work, but in the McCarthy era and new Red Scares, respect for the law and tougher immigration policies were demanded by an increasingly conservative electorate. So Congress split the difference, and President Truman acquiesced. Everyone was happy, including the roughly 250,000 Mexicans who entered the United States lawfully every year until 1964.

Whatever the scant merits and terrible drawbacks of the Bracero Program, the Texas Proviso encouraged the rise in the number of people without papers working in the United States. Many *braceros* overstayed their work permits, brought family members from back home, and faded into the twilight zone of legal/illegal labor and hiring. Once the program ended in 1964, and after nearly 5 million Mexicans arrived in the United States to work over the twenty-two years of its existence, many did not return home. And since Lyndon Johnson, a Texan, did not want to deport them, a large, undocumented underclass was born. Twenty years later, Ronald Reagan and Congressmen Peter Rodino and Romano Mazzoli, together with Senator Alan Simpson, attempted to remedy this situation. They produced another marvelous creation of pragmatism/hypocrisy to address an insoluble dilemma.

What came to be named the Immigration Reform and Control Act (IRCA) granted amnesty—directly or indirectly—to several million unauthorized migrants, and, among other things, repealed the Texas Proviso. Hiring an undocumented worker did not become a felony, but every employer was obliged to request and keep on file a copy of each employee's Social Security Card or number and Green Card (which in fact were and still are white); not doing so became a crime. But the employer was not required to verify the authenticity of said documents. So an entire cottage industry of false papers sprang up, producing fake Social Security cards and fake work-permits.

When I was teaching at the University of California, Berkeley, in 1990, and writing a column both for *The Los Angeles Times* and *Newsweek International*, I decided to submit a piece about these fake documents. I asked my teaching assistant, a Mexican-American activist from Michoacán and San José to find us a "dealer" and purchase the necessary papers for whatever the market price was. The two publications footed the bill, not before worrying that they were financing an illegal act (forgery of official papers). Both columns ran, with a brief description of the purchasing process, as well as a picture of the two documents, with my name clearly appearing in print.

All an employer was required to do, in order to comply with the new immigration rules, was to request my documents, Xerox them, and place them in his filing cabinet. If an agent from what was then INS showed up one day and asked if the Mexican-looking, Spanish-speaking employees were "legal," the boss would simply show the copies on file. If the agent decided the documents were false, or actually checked them, he might arrest the Mexican workers, but not the American employer. The former had committed a felony by entering and residing in the United States unlawfully, but the employer had not. If this is not both pragmatic and hypocritical, I don't know what is.

The recurrent expressions of hypocrisy and pragmatism all proceed from the same underlying tension. Americans need cheap labor to harvest their crops, build on their construction sites, take care of their children and gardens, wash dishes in their restaurants, and make up their hotel rooms. They expect the price of the goods and services that undocumented laborers provide to remain as low as possible. But other Americans wish to continue believing theirs is a country of laws, that unauthorized migrants depress wages and curtail labor rights, and that Mexican and Central American immigrants threaten the so-called American creed (Samuel Huntington's argument), as we sought to define the term a few pages back.

The only way to square this circle is to place a great many laws on the books, apply them selectively and sporadically, and resign oneself to the contradiction through this magical combination of pragmatism and hypocrisy.

On occasion the pragmatism wins out. Reagan's amnesty and several efforts to achieve comprehensive immigration reform under G. W. Bush and Obama are examples in point. Or the hypocrisy will gain the upper hand, as with the rise in "legal" immigration from Mexico in particular under Obama and Trump, while at the same time the former deported more Mexicans than any of his predecessors, and the latter ranted and raved about walls and rapists from Mexico. Between 2000 and 2009, the year of the Great Recession, the number of non-immigrant admissions, mainly H1B high-skill permits, and H2A and H2B categories for agricultural work and other services, rose from 440,359 to 545,387.[2] But by 2017, the number had reached 1,068,419—roughly twice as many.[3] For Mexicans, the figures increased from 68,434 in 2000, to 192,217 in 2009, to 507,071 in 2017—almost a tenfold increase in seventeen years.[4] For certain categories, there is a difference between absolute numbers, though not for relative increases. For example, H2A *admissions* went from 283,580 in 2015, to 412,820 in 2017, an increase of 50 percent. H2A *visas* issued rose from 89,274 in 2014 to 196,409 in 2018, a 100 percent increase.[5] The discrepancy stems from the fact that visas have a three-year validity. A temporary worker holding this type of visa can come and go during three years on the same visa. Thus there can be several *admissions* registered for each *visa* counted.

Similarly, the number of legal, permanent immigrants entering the United States went from 841,002 in 2000 to 1,183,818 in 2016—almost a 50 percent increase.[6] This figure includes new arrivals and change of status for people already in the United States. Slightly less than half were Latin Americans, of which 50 percent were Mexicans. Incidentally, these figures partly explain the so-called net zero thesis about undocumented Mexican immigration. Fewer "illegal" Mexicans enter the United States, because many more "legal" ones do. Since 2007, the peak year of the total undocumented Mexican population in the United States, the unlawful flow of Mexicans began to decrease, but *legal* temporary immigration rose from 235,000 to 507,000: more than twice.[7] According to one Mexican government survey, that probably undercounts unauthorized departures: between 2009 and 2014, 720,000 Mexicans emigrated; between 2009 (the year of the Great Recession in the United States) and 2014, 760,000 did.[8] Another implicit possible disavowal of the "end of Mexican migration" hypothesis resides in the evolution of remittances sent back to the home country. They have risen from 25 billion dollars in 2008, one of the peak outflow years, just before the Great Recession, to 33.5 billion in 2018. It is difficult to surmise that the same number of Mexicans— let alone fewer—are remitting one-third more dollars ten years later.[9] The need for workers in the American economy, and the persistence of the wage gap between the United States and the sending countries, almost guarantees that there will continue to be an immense flow from the latter to the former. Creeping legalization has been a pragmatic and hypocritical response to this basic equation.

What Americans want

There are myriad examples of the contradictory nature of different Americans' wishes regarding immigration. A typical one involves meat-packing plants in Iowa. Thousands of Mexicans and Laotians (for historical reasons) work in the plants, doing chores that are dangerous, unpleasant, and poorly paid by US standards. The traditional communities in the region were unaccustomed to foreigners living in their midst, especially brown-skinned, Spanish-speaking, Catholic, and soccer-playing foreigners they had truly never come across in their lives. With time, many of the racist sentiments faded, and the people in towns like Storm Lake actually get along quite well. Somewhere, somehow, the traditional white, Anglo-Saxon inhabitants understood or sensed that either Mexicans would toil at the meat-packing plants in Iowa or they would work at the same plants in Mexico, but that it was one or the other. Americans were not going to fill those jobs, but if the plants moved south, an entire community would be destroyed. Whereas if they remained in Iowa with unauthorized Mexicans at work, the benefits to the community would also remain.

Couldn't the Mexicans be regularized, or legalized, or amnestied? They have been toiling in Iowa for nearly fifteen years. In theory, they could be, but amnesty has not made it through Congress since 1986. Granting amnesty and a path to citizenship seems the logical solution, but it also means that the meatpacker employees could eventually bring nuclear family members from Mexico, register to vote, and probably elect Democrats to Congress and the White House. Republicans do not like either of these two consequences of amnesty; that is why they steadfastly reject it, ever since Reagan. So the real, pragmatic solution, not the ideal solution, is the legal and moral limbo the Mexicans of Storm Lake live in, with the ensuing hypocrisy about a nation of laws.

Incidentally, the congressional district encompassing Storm Lake, the Mexicans and Laotians, and the meat-packing plants is represented in Washington by Steve King, generally considered the most racist, strident, hateful bigot in the House of Representatives. He has been convicted of hate-speech, denounced by his peers, but re-elected by his voters. They coexist with the hypocrisy of the pestilent, dangerous plants: living side by side with Mexicans and sending someone to Congress who hates them. A similar experience can be found with Guatemalan immigrants, also in the meat-packing plants of Morgantown, North Carolina.

Allentown, the third-largest city in Pennsylvania, provides another good example. The old, Rust-Belt town, visited by James and Deborah Fallows in their beautiful "Our Towns," had practically no Latinos among its residents in 1980; they were not even counted. By the year 2000, one of every four inhabitants was Hispanic. In 2010, the percentage reached 42 percent, and in 2017, more than half the population was Latino.[10] In other words, in the space of forty years, the growth was exponential, as was the novelty, the initial fear, and the subsequent accommodation. This in a city close to Hazleton, Pennsylvania, where one of the great anti-immigrant scares of the early 2000s took place. The small coal community was the first in the country to approve municipal ordinances banning undocumented immigrants from living there, setting off protests in the town and across the region. The ordinances were eventually struck down by the courts. Today half the population is Latino. Not every sudden rush of Latinos has provoked the same reactions, even in neighboring towns; once Hispanics settle in, however, rejection, racism, and ostracism diminish significantly.

There is a specific "national character" of Latin Americans emigrating to the United States, even if the type of reactions they have occasionally unleashed is similar to Europe's. Whether it be authorized or not, nearly 60 percent of all immigrants, permanent or temporary, authorized or not, hail from south of the United States border, not from across the oceans. A large majority of the migrants settling in the rich countries of Europe come from across one single sea—the Mediterranean— as workers, refugees, or reunified families (Eastern Europe was also a factor for a time). There have been negative, hostile, and unnerving reactions to the arrival of so many, from so far, being so different, both in Europe and the United States. Canada is perhaps the only wealthy nation that has avoided an acute xenophobic, racist backlash, so far. Perhaps this is a result of its generous and ingenious refugee policy, which allows individuals or communities to sponsor them. The United States and Europe are not Canada, although there are similarities between them, with analogous responses to common challenges or new situations. But they are also profoundly different, as we shall now see.

Lucky stars

America has always been more open, welcoming, and tolerant to foreigners than Europe. A poll taken by Pew Research in 2018 proves this impression conclusively. The question Pew asked was: "In your opinion, should we allow more immigrants to move to our country, fewer immigrants, or about the same as we do now?" Twenty-seven nations were surveyed. The median for "fewer" was 45 percent. The lowest number of "anti-immigrant" responses was Japan, with 13 percent (perhaps counter-intuitively, given Japan's history and stereotype on immigration), followed by Canada with 27 percent and . . . the United States with 29 percent.[11] Despite the advent of Donald Trump, one of the reasons why this remains true today pertains to what could be labeled the sending side, as opposed to the receiving one. The millions of Latin Americans who have arrived in the United States over the past forty years as permanent, authorized immigrants, as refugees, as undocumented workers, as victims of natural disasters, or children of any of the above, experience an easier insertion in American society than the inhabitants of the Maghreb, sub-Saharan Africa, Turkey, or Syria do in Europe. Perhaps not as much as a Brazilian immigrant proclaims, but even this exaggeration is symptomatic: "When Brazilian immigrants arrive in the United States they are gladly surprised by the level of respect with which they are treated by the business community and the government authorities. They encounter a degree of civility they seldom knew back home from those in places of authority; and this despite the fact that the Brazilian immigrants may not yet be fluent in English or even citizens of this country."[12] This delicate characteristic can be easily distorted and converted into a reverse side of Huntington's coin. He believed that Latin Americans, unlike previous immigrant cohorts or waves to the United States, were more difficult to assimilate because they did not share the American creed. Others—in that reverse side of the coin—could, however, be tempted to view Hispanics as easier to assimilate than Arabs or Africans, because Americans and Latinos share many more common attributes than Europeans share with the visitors who have settled in their countries. There is an element of truth in this impression, but matters are not that simple. There are other differences between the European and American experience.

The first difference, and perhaps the most relevant one, is that Latin migration to the United States has been ongoing, at least since the end of the nineteenth century. Pre-existing communities of Mexicans—not including those from before 1847—Central Americans, Cubans, or Puerto Ricans encourage others to join them. It was the same for all previous waves, except that they practically all came to a halt after a certain period. Not from Latin America, any time soon. They thus create a permanent flow, which can grow or shrink at any moment and also make arrival and inclusion much smoother and less traumatic for everybody. The newcomers' language, food, religion, entertainment, values, and customs are already in place, readily awaiting them.

This began to be true in Europe in the mid-sixties and early seventies, but on a smaller scale and with wider gaps to bridge. If anything, a better analogy would be with the Italian, Spanish, and Portuguese guest workers who contributed greatly to the postwar European reconstruction through the late seventies, when they either returned home or settled definitively in Germany, Holland, France, Belgium, etc. Immigration was much more demand-led, more diversified, and in theory less permanent than in the United States. Algerians arrived in France; West Indians, Indians, and later Pakistanis in Britain; Turks in Germany; Indonesians and Moroccans in Holland. They were all sought out by the labor-starved receiving countries, all accompanied migrants from Southern Europe, and all were "imported" temporarily, or so it was thought. After the 1973 oil crisis and a series of debates in each one of these countries, together with the Italian economic boom and the entry of Spain and Portugal into the EEC in the eighties, it turned out otherwise. By then, the process of importing labor from elsewhere "resulted in the permanent settlement of transient labor that was increasingly non-white, non-Christian, and non-European."[13] I could add: non-temporary.

The Southern Europeans went home, but the others did not. Guest worker programs quickly became permanent, and large numbers of migrants from other Arab and African nations began to arrive. This initially sparked broad discussions, rarely devoid of racist overtones, about multiculturalism, Islam and women, and integration. A new rash of incidents, ranging from Salman Rushdie's *Satanic Verses* in Britain to headscarves in France encouraged the debate. After 9-11 and its aftermath in Western Europe, the question of terrorism surfaced in these same discussions. By 2010–11, it became clear that European leaders faced a monumental challenge. The simplest illustration were the municipal pools in French towns, as much of a fixture as the *boulangerie*. French Muslim women began to demand that special hours be set aside for them to swim; non-Muslim men and women protested. Both had reason and the law on their side; no ideal solution was available. The conundrum continues to fester.

The number of young people with what Angela Merkel labeled a "migration" background was increasing. More radical expressions of Islam were displacing traditional, moderate forms; and local "European" societies ("*les français de souche*," Nicholas Sarkozy called his countrymen) were becoming less tolerant of differences with Islam that were, in their view, no longer purely religious. "Multiculturalism has failed," Merkel declared, and most white and Christian Europeans concurred: growing Islamic radicalism in Europe, the crisis in Syria, ISIS, and terrorism were all menacing. They also increasingly believed that their liberal, Western, secular values were threatened by the multicultural societies they themselves had built. The only acceptable integration was one that imposed liberalism on everyone, like it or not. But it was equally clear that, as Rita Chin put it in her *The Crisis of Multiculturalism in Europe*, "Across the continent, country by country, Europe's population is undeniably multiethnic, and is becoming more so by the day . . . . There is no longer room to pretend that European countries will return to some imagined, idealized state of ethnic and cultural sameness."[14] Partly because of its size, partly thanks to its own history of immigration and the absence of a colonial connection with the sending countries (excepting Puerto Rico), partly because of the inexistence of an "ethnic American," unlike most of Europe, partly as a result of its pragmatism and hypocrisy, but partly also through the characteristics of multiple Hispanic immigration waves, the United States faces a much less intractable challenge.

Americans residing in regions where before the 1980s Latinos were never sighted might have been shocked to discover people so strange that instead of playing football with an ovoid, they played what they also named football with a round ball and their feet. Many, in Ohio, or central Pennsylvania, or Kansas and Nebraska, could well have initially feared they could never coexist with such an alien exercise, especially if accompanied by an incomprehensible language, inedible spicy food, and a religion that worships a brown-skinned virgin. But once past their initial fright, many may have rejoiced to find that the new arrivals shared their enthusiasm for sports, even if not the same ones. Salvadorans are as crazy about soccer as natives of Alabama are about college football.

In a similar vein, they discovered, or will do so quite soon, that while most Americans are not practicing Catholics, the religiosity of Mexicans and Central Americans is not unlike that of their hosts. It is not just a Christian issue. Latinos are highly devout, but with a very clear notion of separating their beliefs and devotion from everyday life, and consequently of Church and State. Not unlike Protestants and many other religions in the United States, though perhaps not all: Mormons, Latter-Day Evangelicals, Orthodox Jews, and other denominations conflate existential prescriptions with religious convictions. Catholics, even conservative, religiously dogmatic ones, rarely do. What Americans may not fully appreciate is how much easier it is for various religions to harmoniously coexist in one nation when they stem from a common (Christian) origin, essentially addressing similar themes of faith, i.e. in the United States. This is much simpler than when a religion functions as a way of life and must cohabit a common space with ones that do not, i.e. in Europe—a Europe, which as we shall describe in the following chapter, is more secular than ever.

Islam in many of its current expressions in Europe and in the Muslim world includes a long list of behavioral rules as respectable as any other (except for issues concerning women), but much more involved with daily life than a set of purely religious beliefs or convictions.

The separation of Church and State and of credence and daily conduct are principles powerfully enshrined in the American psyche and the country's institutions, with the caveats I will examine in the following chapter. Thus the small, vibrant, and moderate Arab-American and/ or Muslim communities located in a few localities (in Texas, Illinois, Michigan) meshes nicely with the general framework of laws and customs. For many reasons it is not seen as a threat; even geographical distance contributes to this.

There is greater diversity within Islam today than before, both between Sunni and Shia but also within these traditions. Some factions or sects are much more controlling of daily life (and women) than others. Similarly, Muslim immigrants to Europe have changed and evolved in their understanding of Islam and life in general, as they have (to varying degrees) assimilated, with lesser traditional religious controls on daily life. Nonetheless, the differences with the United States remain abysmal. The receiving structure is different in size and history; the arriving groups are larger; but most importantly, the Latinos in the United States are a better fit with the host country. Americans might not like to hear it, but they may want to thank their lucky stars on this count. In fact, they mostly do, even if they rarely acknowledge it. The new and larger wave of immigrants, at least in absolute terms, that has led to nearly 20 percent of the United States population—or 56 million people—being Hispanic or Latino, may be more difficult to include than previous waves. But it is certainly easier to integrate than those that have crossed the Mediterranean over the past half century. The great majority of immigrants in Western Europe today are Muslims, practicing mainly Sunni Islam. There are various ongoing discussions all over the world on the compatibility of sharia law, many Sunnite practices, norms, regulations, and worldviews with European liberalism. They range from an older view, developed by Huntington in his *Clash of Civilizations* (1993), to Niall Ferguson's more recent comparison of the European dilemma with the fall of the Roman Empire.[15] In 1987, French Prime Minister Jacques Chirac, a Gaullist conservative but by no means a right-wing extremist, created a "*Commission de la Nationalité*," made up of pluralistic experts in all relevant fields. Among other points, the Commission concluded, "The introduction of an Islamic element into the French national community implies an acceptance by Muslims in France of the rules and law of a republican and, above all, secular state. For Islam this represents a real upheaval. The French state cannot renege on this demand."[16] The headscarf debate in France since 1989 also illustrated the dilemma, where both sides of the issue had a point: "The foundation of the Republic is the school . . . . That is why the destruction of the school will lead to the fall of the Republic."[17] This manifesto published in 1989 in *Le Nouvel Observateur*, signed by progressive intellectuals including Régis Debray, Robert Badinter, Alain Finklekraut, and Elizabeth de Fontenay, reflects the intensity of the issue.

In an ideal world, the slow and painful modernization process of North African, sub-Saharan, and Middle Eastern nations would be replaced by a democratic, prosperous, and swift entry into modernity, changing some habits and conserving others. Similarly, in an ideal world, second- or third-generation Algerians, Turks, Moroccans, and Pakistanis, to mention only the larger and older groups, would not be discriminated against in the host countries, lacking jobs, education, security, health care, and opportunities in general. In such a case, millions of Muslim youths would not be radicalized, be they Syrians, Iraqis, Algerians, or Moroccans either in the home countries or the host ones. But such a situation seems illusory. Europe will have to co-inhabit with a religion that is much more than a religion: a way of life, a series of laws and edicts, a form of education, and a political program. Americans, for the most part, do not face this dilemma.

How do pragmatism and hypocrisy fit in with all this? Very simply. Firstly, despite all the rhetoric and odious practices of the past decade regarding deportations, border walls, and family separation, the United States continues to welcome a growing number of authorized permanent or temporary immigrants, largely from Mexico and Central America. Its economy needs them; as does a society that owes much of its quality of life to low-skilled labor from abroad, from nannies to delivery boys to low-priced fruit and vegetables. In 2017, 42 percent of all immigrant visas and of persons obtaining lawful permanent status in the United States came from Mexico, Central America, and a few South American nations.[18] There is a tilt toward these regions, not explicitly for any of the reasons mentioned above, but rather as a result of proximity, inertia, and pre-existing communities. And, additionally, in some places, perhaps, because of a certain tacit acceptance of the Christian, Western affinity mentioned above. This tilt, however, is not inscribed in stone, and Trump, by seeking to reduce or remove family reunification as a key determinant in admitting new immigrants and replacing it with a merit-based, point system, is seeking to debilitate that link.

Wages, fears, and demographics

The pragmatic approach to immigration will persist in the United States, even if moments of hysteria may suggest otherwise. I ask my freshmen students every year at New York University if they would accept a summer job in a Manhattan restaurant as a busboy or -girl at somewhere around nine dollars per hour, ten hours per day, with little or no air-conditioning in New York City scorchers. They all say no. When I pose the same question at twice or three times the wage, they seem more willing. But there is always one of them who grasps a simple fact. If the lowest paid worker's salary is doubled or tripled, some type of equivalent increase must occur for everyone else in the restaurant: the waiters, the cooks, the hostess, the *maître d'*. Dinner will become more expensive, and some customers will no longer be able to afford it; consumers won't be happy, and politicians know it. Looking the other way is an effective response. The same phenomenon holds true for all so-called non-tradables, i.e. goods or mainly services that cannot be outsourced to other countries, and that Americans do not wish to provide, at a wage which laborers without papers and from abroad accept enthusiastically.

These workers will continue to do so, with or without American hypocrisy, as long as the wage differential between their countries and the United States is as wide as it is, regardless of whether other factors intervene in their decision to migrate: crime, violence, drought, wars, family, etc. In the Mexican automobile industry, the crown jewel of the country's globalization story, the average salary for a worker in 2018 was approximately $450 each month. In non-union plants in the American South, where pay scales are lower than in the unionized Rust Belt, a non-union worker takes home $15–20 per hour, without benefits. With benefits and overtime, in the North of the country, that worker's wage can reach more than $40 per hour. A Mexican would have to be a fool not to contemplate leaving, even if locally he makes a decent living (in Mexican terms), and knows he will not end up on an assembly line in Detroit.

Many factors will enter into his or her decision, and the tide will ebb and flow, as it has for more than a century. But the disposition to emigrate will endure as long as the wage gap does not narrow. Over the past twenty-five years, despite the promises of the North American Free Trade Agreement that came into law back in 1994, it has not narrowed. And the American economy's thirst for cheap, unskilled labor from abroad remains unquenched, even in the least imaginable cases. A long article on the upstate New York dairy industry published in 2019 in *The New York Times* provides another example of the combination of demand, pragmatism, and hypocrisy. It also reveals the damage done when either hypocrisy or pragmatism are forsaken for the benefit of extremist views. One of the interviewed farmers feared that if one of his undocumented workers received a driving ticket, it could prompt an immigration audit of his entire farm. If another was detained by immigration agents in a supermarket parking lot, others may flee. And if his undocumented workforce disappears overnight, who would replace them? "It keeps me up at night," he confessed. "There are people out there who just say, 'Send them all back and build a wall.' But they would be facing empty shelves in the grocery store if that were to happen."[19] Or the price of milk would rise, making many children unhappy. Hence the hypocrisy. According to the *Times*, the dairy industry in upstate New York has been able to survive only by relying on undocumented immigrants.

There is a further dose of hypocrisy in the American attitude toward immigration past and present. Undocumented aliens do not vote; naturalized immigrants do. With the partial exception of the Cuban-American diaspora, Hispanics vote overwhelmingly for the Democratic Party and apparently will continue to do so, especially after the Trump years. If the roughly 12 million unauthorized residents of the United States had been placed on a path to citizenship thanks to any one of the failed attempts at immigration reform since 2001, many of them would be soon be voting or would have already done so. Since half of that number is Mexican, and 75 percent are Hispanic, the disadvantage for the GOP at a national level or in a significant number of states would be devastating.

Instead of stating it openly—actually, George W. Bush did so, to Mexican President Vicente Fox, in early 2001—conservatives and other Republicans prefer to express this strictly electoral fear through the "go to the back of the line" mantra, even if, for example, there is no line for refugee resettlement from Latin America in Latin America. The only way to request asylum was, until 2020, to show up at the United States border.

According to this view, people who entered the United States unlawfully should not enjoy any privileges compared to those who "followed the rules," that is, requested family reunification and waited for up to ten years before being finally admitted. The real reason is electoral. The new citizens would vote like their families or predecessors: with a low but rising turnout, and more than two-thirds for Democrats. It is true, though, that the "play by the rules" aphorism has generated anti-Mexican sentiment in many quarters, perhaps even among Hispanic-American citizens.

In the final analysis, pragmatism and hypocrisy will win out, for one fundamental reason. The United States is the only rich country—even including China—whose overall population is not aging dramatically. Had Germany maintained its stance on admitting Syrian and Afghan refugees, it might have joined the club; as it is, a million refugees were let in, partly for demographic reasons. The explanation for America's demographic uniqueness lies in immigration, twofold. First, as a result of simple entries. Between newly arrived immigrants, temporary workers, change-of-status beneficiaries, and even the unauthorized influx, the American population is increasing more than others, well above its natural growth rate. It is consequently aging more slowly.

Secondly, new immigrants, particularly but not exclusively from Latin America, but also from North Africa, have higher birth rates than the overall population and than the traditional cohorts in Europe. So they add to the growth of the number of inhabitants by bearing more children than pre-settled Americans, at least for the first generation. The median age of the United States population today is 38 years; for Japan it is 47, for Germany 47, and for Italy 45. Only China, a much poorer country, has a lower median age than America: 37.5 years, that is, barely lower—and it is rising as a result of the previous one child policy.[20] The reason: immigration. The approach: pragmatism and hypocrisy. The aging, white, non-college-educated, small-town sectors of society may not distinguish the advantages of a non-aging overall population thanks to Mexicans, Filipinos, Indians, and Central Americans. But they too are indirectly beneficiaries.

Drugs and the world

This same functional, effective, and lasting approach has also underpinned the United States' attitude and policy on drugs. As with other reflections about Americans, it must be qualified. First, drug policy in America has not always been the same, although roughly since 1971, it has varied only slightly. Secondly, not every part of the United States follows exactly the same path. California legalized marijuana for medical use in the early nineties, and many states have since followed suit, some going even further by allowing its recreational use. Thirdly, different sectors of American society hold dissimilar attitudes toward drugs and government policy, and they are rapidly changing, sometimes in opposite directions.

Essentially, the United States administers large-scale drug consumption inside its territory and pressures other countries to wage war on drugs in their territories. This double focus had been the case even before Richard Nixon's launching of the war on drugs in 1971 and the creation of the Drug Enforcement Administration (DEA) in 1973. As mostly everyone knows, that war sprang from the student, anti-Vietnam, counterculture protests of the sixties and early seventies, and the youth rebellion that shook dozens of countries, including the United States.

The first serious crisis between Mexico and the United States on drugs took place in 1969, when Washington implemented what it called Operation Intercept, basically shutting down the border between the two countries until the Mexican government of the time "did more" to contain the flow of drugs from south to north. At the time, the issue was marijuana from Mexico, and heroin from Turkey and Afghanistan through Europe. Today it is fentanyl and heroin from Mexico and China, cocaine from Peru and Colombia, and heroin still from Afghanistan. Little has changed.

The pragmatic facet of the twin approach entails administering drug consumption, or "demand," inside the United States. This task requires a considerable dose of hypocrisy; hence the other facet. Neither the federal government nor states or cities are willing or able to persecute and prosecute all drug consumers, retail dealers, and wholesale distributors. It is not just a budget issue, although this is a major concern. It would involve enormous physical space for long-term mass incarceration, far beyond the current numbers—despite the highest incarceration rate in the world, by far, driven in part by drug prosecutions. It entails over-loading the justice system and transforming low-level users into hardened criminals thanks to their years in jail. But it also implies a degree of invasion of privacy, territorial control, and surveillance as well as repression that Americans would not tolerate. Especially since the racist subtext would be undeniable, as the discrimination between the prosecution of cocaine powder possessors—whites—and crack users— blacks—clearly demonstrated until it was corrected by the courts.

In 2017, 30.5 million Americans used an illegal drug—mainly marijuana—during the *month* before they were surveyed. Roughly 50 million Americans ingest one type or another of illicit substances *at least once a year*. Approximately 40 million Americans light up for weed at least *once a year*. Some 6 million snort or shoot cocaine at least once during the same period, and a bit below 1 million consume heroin.[21] Any estimate of the value of the illicit drug market in the United States is highly questionable; according to the Office of National Drug Control Policy, it reached $100 billion in 2013.[22] If Americans were serious about drug enforcement, in addition to mounting massive educational campaigns, they would have to arrest, try, sentence, and imprison every law-breaking individual, in the ghettoes or on Wall Street, in Ivy League colleges, and hospitals in Maine and Vermont. And dismantle multiple networks: according to a 2018 survey of 130,000 people in forty countries, it takes less time to get a line of cocaine delivered than a pizza, either in the United States or Brazil, Holland, Denmark, England, Scotland, Colombia, and the Czech Republic.[23]

I ask my students every year at NYU another question. How would their parents react if the university police implemented unannounced inspections of dorms, searching and entering without warrants and arresting anyone found with drugs on their premises? Some, with conservative parents, reply that theirs would be fine with this procedure. But most feel their parents would protest and perhaps even remove them from the school. In all likelihood, one could expect the same reaction for testing without warning everywhere and anywhere: high schools, hospitals, large offices of banks, insurance companies and trading firms, shopping malls, film theaters, or concert halls. Does all of this sound absurd? Of course it does, which is why no president, governor, or mayor, not even the most hardline or ideological, has contemplated any policy of this sort over the past half century.

Moreover, if America truly expected to eliminate drug consumption at home, doing so would also necessitate a monumental effort to interdict the influx of drugs into the United States. That intent would have to be focused on points of entry to the United States, not at cultivation and processing centers across the globe. Many of those points of entry are located on the US-Mexican border, but many more are on the border with Canada, at airports, and at marine terminals. The cost of patrolling these myriad, unsupervised accesses to the United States, as well as the time wasted on doing so at border crossings and airports, is simply prohibitive. The effort to combat corruption—inside the DEA, the Coast Guard, CBP, TSA in airports—would be awesome, and highly intrusive: who inspects the inspectors? The costs in trade, federal hires and training, deploying troops along the border, and, yes, building a wall, are unacceptable for a large majority of Americans.

The most enlightening aspect of Donald Trump's insistence on constructing a wall on the US border with Mexico—sometimes to deter immigration, sometimes to interdict drugs—lies in the impossibility of funding it. In a sense, Trump was right. If Americans want to stop drugs from entering their country, they have to build a figurative and literal wall around it, which not only means spending a fortune, but also sending a different type of message to the world: keep out. Most Americans, quite rightly, reject this.

The question that emerges from these hare-brained notions is obvious. If the laws on the books cannot be applied other than selectively, sporadically, and unfairly, why not change the laws? Marijuana legalization, whether medical or recreational, state by state or at a federal level, has been on the agenda for decades. A growing body of public opinion now backs it. Gallup began polling on this issue as early as 1970. Since then, support for legalizing marijuana has grown from 12 percent to 31 percent in the year 2000 to 64 percent in 2019.[24] Three American presidents have confessed to smoking in their youth. Countless studies prove that pot is certainly not more harmful than tobacco or alcohol. Yet only a quarter of the states have modified their statutes; barely 30 percent of the population resides in states that have legalized, and the prospects for federal legalization seem bleak. This is for marijuana. The chances for cocaine, heroin, meth, and now fentanyl are even more dismal.

The reason is not difficult to ascertain. Every rich country, with a few exceptions like Sweden, has moved in the direction of *de facto* legalization or tolerance, some more explicitly—Portugal, Uruguay, Canada—than others. But *de jure* legalization of all drugs in the entire chain, from cultivation to consumption, exists in very few nations. The explanation lies in the underlying conservatism of most modern societies (and not so modern). Not only Republicans and the right wing: black communities and their representatives often oppose legalization efforts, most recently in New Jersey, due to the havoc they fear it would wreak among their constituents. The United States is not alone, except for the size of its market—by far the largest in the world—its capacity to impose policies on others, and its ability to influence other societies' cultures. Americans are nowhere near to countenancing full, federal legalization of the production, distribution, and consumption of all drugs. Thus the law cannot be adapted to reality except very lightly, and that reality cannot be transformed. So it is *managed*, thanks to pragmatism and hypocrisy, and paying lip service to conservative atavisms through mass incarceration of people of color.

Local police departments throughout the United States practice stop and frisk policies with obvious racial profiling, particularly in large cities with a vast African American or Hispanic population. By and large, however, they allow drug dealing to proceed as long as certain unwritten rules are respected. They include keeping the violence down; not selling too close to middle schools; refraining from other types of petty crimes; and, mainly, never attacking police officers. I have seen NYPD cops patrol Washington Square at night where dealers abound, and simply look the other way as long as these tacit guidelines are complied with. Needless to say, with a very few recent exceptions (Ferguson, outside St. Louis, for example) it has been decades since the National Guard or the armed forces have been sent into ghettos or slums to enforce drug laws that everyone acknowledges are unenforceable. Or into the hills of Mendocino, in northern California, where white former loggers, hipsters, businessmen, and now companies illegally cultivate marijuana, and no one ever bothers them. Indeed, it would seem that whether under Obama or Trump, more federal enforcement resources are deployed for working place raids and combatting immigration than in fighting illegal drug production of various sorts.

The mass incarceration ingredient in the pragmatism-hypocrisy duo panders to American conservatism not only for reasons involving drug enforcement. In 1980, 580,000 people were arrested on drug-related charges. In 2014, the number reached 1.6 million.[25] Mandatory sentencing as well as higher levels of poverty, unemployment, police force discrimination, and deficient education among the black and Latino communities almost inevitably imply that a far greater proportion of people of color will end up in prison than their share of the overall population. Drugs are only one part of this challenge.

Every now and then, the American right wing becomes quite agitated over the drug question. This occurred in the early 1970s in response to the revolts of the sixties and the mayhem drugs were inflicting on war veterans. It happened again, in the mid-eighties, when a series of tragic high-profile cocaine or crack overdose deaths were splashed across the media. Nancy Reagan seized on the opportunity for her "Just Say No" campaign. Donald Trump seemed to be also reacting to a new hysteria in certain American quarters regarding the "opioids epidemic," which killed more than 75,000 Americans in 2017, in heretofore unaffected regions of the country, and with demographics that differed from the previous panics. Politicians instinctively sense when a significant sector of public opinion suddenly clamors for them to "do something." Mass incarceration has been one response. Blaming others has been another, and it jibes perfectly with the pragmatism-hypocrisy twosome.

Do something . . . but nimby

Blaming others, in this context, often goes by another name. In drug policy, it usually refers to the supply side of the equation, that is, the cultivation and production of drugs *outside* the United States. At least since the 1960s, this has been a lynchpin of American drug policy, and in all likelihood will continue to be so. It is also the butt of foreign criticism, skepticism, and often extreme annoyance with American hypocrisy, trumping the admiration for pragmatism. The reasons are easy to discern.

At least since the early 1960s, Washington has pursued a vigorous drug enforcement policy abroad. It has been based on a combination of expedients that range from drug eradication programs—including health-threatening fumigation—to crop substitution schemes. It has included a military presence in many countries, with the purpose of finding and destroying fields and laboratories. It interdicts flights and maritime or land transportation of different drugs, largely from South America through Central America to Mexico and the United States. And it has pursued a king-pin strategy of going after cartel leaders, the best example of which was the execution of Pablo Escobar in Colombia in 1994. The long-lasting manhunt for Chapo Guzmán is another such example.

America has provided aid to other countries for these purposes, in exchange for imposing its policies upon them, like Plan Colombia from 1999 to 2016. It has embedded DEA, CIA, and DOD officers and agents in multiple settings, from Bolivia in the eighties and nineties, to the Manta Air Force Base in Ecuador, many staging areas in Colombia, and dozens if not hundreds of US personnel in Central America and Mexico. Where other interests are deemed more transcendent than drug enforcement, as in Afghanistan after 2001, it prefers to let poppy cultivation go more or less untouched. This has allowed that country to become one of the world's largest heroin producers, despite the presence of tens of thousands of American troops over nearly twenty years. Poppy cultivation acreage tripled in Afghanistan between 2003 and 2009, even though the most of it was in the hands of the Taliban, the ostensible enemy of the United States. Washington has also kidnapped cartel leaders in other countries and tried them in the United States. Similarly, it has imposed extradition policies on several countries, generating much greater degrees of local violence than if trials were held . . . locally.

While pretending to combat drug-originated corruption in many countries—not only in Latin America—the United States approach has often aggravated it. By supplying large sums of money and "equipment," from Blackhawk helicopters to state-of-the-art radar systems to police forces or military establishments totally unprepared for such wherewithal, these policies foster corruption. Washington has also encouraged, or obliged, security services to pursue a war on drugs that rapidly evolves into a human rights nightmare. Most of the manpower available in many of these countries' security forces is pitifully untrained with regard to respect for due process and human rights.

In a nutshell, the United States expects nations that produce drugs, or through which drugs pass on their way to the largest market on earth, to implement exactly what Americans refuse to carry out at home. Americans want governments to deploy armed forces in the mountains and coastlines but decline to deploy *their* armed forces in the inner cities, along the border on the United States side, to test everybody and to send the DEA or federal troops into states that have legalized marijuana, despite the federal prohibition, and the possibility of detecting plantations with satellite technology.

In more recent times, Washington has sought to combat its opioid and fentanyl epidemic by pressuring China and Xi Jinping into controlling shipments of fentanyl to the United States, directly or through Mexico. It has cajoled the Chinese authorities to crack down on fentanyl laboratories and to classify the drug as a controlled substance. Beijing had not been especially receptive to these demands, wondering—discretely—why Donald Trump does not deal with the opioid crisis at home: "The US should adopt a comprehensive and balanced strategy to reduce and suppress the huge demand in the country for fentanyl and other similar drugs, as soon as possible. When fewer and fewer Americans use fentanyl, there would no market for it."[26] This, according to Liu Yue Jin, deputy chief of China's National Narcotics Control Commission. He could have been quoting any one of several hundred Mexican statements made over the past fifty years.

The opioid crisis is largely homegrown, although marijuana legalization in the United States has led Mexican cartels to emphasize poppy cultivation and heroin production. Big pharma, physicians, the federal government all combined or conspired to deliver painkillers in monumental amounts to people who needed them and to many who did not. Then they restricted prescriptions for patients or individuals in pain or with anxiety who could not afford black-market prices for licit drugs, driving them toward heroin and now fentanyl.

According to one analysis, "In an effort to address opioid overprescribing, policymakers have mounted a series of supply-side interventions. These have included crackdowns on unscrupulous providers and facilities, prescription limits and guidelines, bolstering prescription monitoring systems, reformulation of some OAs to make them more difficult to misuse, and nudging (or threatening) prescribers to curtail the quantity and dosage of opioid prescriptions."[27] Some of these efforts have indeed been successful at reducing over-prescription and diminishing or controlling overdose deaths due to legal substances. They have led, however, to unintended consequences that aggravated the initial problem. As a result of the high dependency caused by such substances, consumers that lost access to legal and controlled substances turned to cheaper, more accessible, and potent black-market alternatives, primarily heroin and illicit fentanyl. But if it was a huge, well-intended mistake to create this army of addicts, it was an even bigger one to cut them off from their supply. A recent study found that 53 percent of those addicted to opioids in the United States began with prescription painkillers given to them by a friend, or family member.[28]

Why should China make a special effort to limit or impede production and shipments abroad of what is partly a licit drug according to its laws to help a country and government that have not been especially cordial over the past few years? After a meeting with the Chinese leader in Buenos Aires toward the end of 2018, Donald Trump announced that his counterpart had agreed to "stem the supply of fentanyl." Pretty much the same statement Xi had made in 2016, when Obama announced "enhanced measures" by China to block fentanyl shipments to American shores. The Chinese seem to have stolen a page from the Mexican playbook from the seventies through 2006: say yes, but don't say when, how, where, or actually do anything. So much so that Democrats in the Senate introduced legislation in early 2019 to ban fentanyl shipments from China and Mexico. Senator Schumer of New York proclaimed that Congress wanted a "signed and enforceable agreement, a solid plan or genuine commitment . . . . We must present China with a tough but fair consequence when it comes to the wave of fentanyl flowing into the United States."[29]

Beijing has recurrently reclassified various fentanyl components as controlled substances. Producers then resort to unscheduled components in order to concoct new substances, dragging out the controlling procedures. According to *The New York Times*, they thus allow "Chinese makers of illicit drugs to create new fentanyl derivatives faster than they can be controlled."[30] This is precisely how producers of all drugs across the world have been responding to American pressure since the late sixties. The Chinese are more reserved than many others, but the substance of their "go-slow" attitude is the same: why undertake the Americans' dirty work for them? In April 2019, China placed all variants of fentanyl on a list of controlled substances instead of banning new versions of the drug after they hit the streets. This prohibited the export of all fentanyl variants.[31]

The argument often wielded in response by the authorities in Washington, or in American society in general, is that these are illegal substances that inflict enormous damage on young—and increasingly elderly—Americans. One day, producer countries will become consumers. It has not occurred. The Chinese have their answer for domestic consumption: the death penalty. In other countries, different factors intervene. Family, pricing, cartels' distribution policies: these and other obstacles have ensured that practically no producing country has become a significant consumer one, which does not mean there is no consumption at all (Afghanistan may be a recent exception).

Most importantly, though, producer or transit nations respond that the cost for them of carrying America's water is also exorbitant. Since Mexico's war on drugs began in 2006, more than 250,000 Mexicans have died, 40,000 are missing, the country's image in the world has been destroyed, and all for nothing. Many Mexicans ask, cynically and cold-heartedly perhaps, but rather logically also: why should we worry about African American youngsters in Newark or aging whites in Vermont?

Furthermore, as the recent course of events in the United States and elsewhere demonstrates, the definition of "legal" is not only dynamic but also relative. Marijuana was illegal; it isn't anymore in many countries and states. Oxycontin with a prescription is legal; without one, it is not. Heroin production is tolerated by American troops in Afghanistan; in the sierras of Guerrero and Sinaloa, it is forbidden and attacked.

Many designer drugs are produced in the United States; the zeal with which they are confronted is not the same everywhere, all the time.

During Chapo Guzman's trial in New York in 2018–19, the American justice system worked to perfection except when the prosecution's witnesses began to denounce former Mexican presidents and drug enforcement officials as corrupt. Then the judge, almost certainly at Washington's behest, banned further discussion or cross-examination of these witnesses. He knew—and so stated—they would create serious foreign policy and national security complications for the executive branch in its relations with Mexico. Bringing Chapo to justice was one thing; going after America's allies, buddies, or cronies in Mexico was quite another. No wonder not everyone takes American protestations of the rule of law and the sanctity of the justice system as literally as its beneficiaries.

American authorities are frequently button-holed by their counterparts, who ask: what about demand, or consumption, in the United States? The answer since President Jimmy Carter's term has always been the same. Yes, we must do something; yes, there is a shared responsibility; yes, we will soon launch a major campaign against drugs in our own country. As of 2019, the composition of American drug consumption has varied significantly. The sources of supply for the United States market have also changed. But the overall dimensions remain similar. None of the efforts to reduce demand, or interdict supply, have achieved anything. The thesis whereby it could have been worse does not fly. There are few examples of the pragmatism-hypocrisy duo that irritate foreigners more than its manifestation in the drug issue, and in Washington's stance on drug enforcement abroad, and drug management internally.

Whither drug enforcement?

There is scarce disagreement regarding the futility of the war on drugs, both domestically and abroad. It has cost, according to some calculations, more than one trillion dollars, and its results are virtually nil.[32] The only argument in its favor is that there is no alternative. In fact, there are many, in various countries, for some drugs or for all, for the entire chain or only for consumption: a regulated, legal marketplace, as in Portugal, Uruguay, Canada, and others. Foreigners can see beyond this unreason, and sense that ultimately, institutional momentum, pandering to conservatism and pragmatic hypocrisy, constitute the true motives behind this tragedy. The case against the prohibitionist stance is so clear that only other considerations could have led nine consecutive American presidents to follow a road that leads nowhere. A splendid summary of the best case against the war on drugs has been made by a historian, rather than a policy maker. Isaac Campos resorts to what scholar Eva Bertram has termed "the profit paradox," whereby increasing efforts to fight the war on drugs simply make the illicit drug industry more attractive. Greater interdiction and eradication of drug supplies produce a rise in prices. Theoretically that should depress demand, but it also has an upward effect on supply. New producers enter the market to benefit from the greater potential for profit. Increased production then decreases prices. All of this is further complicated by the transnational nature of the industry, by the wealth disparities between American consumers and peasant producers, and by the fact that 90 percent of the value added in the market occurs in the United States.[33]

Dismantling the drug enforcement bureaucratic establishment would be a gargantuan task. It has countless federal ramifications (well beyond the DEA), as well as state, county, and city manifestations, all with a vested interest in pursuing a failed policy that nonetheless favors the agencies involved. That establishment includes police unions and the private prison industry, no minor lobbies. American presidents and their closest aides are too well informed and intelligent to not understand this basic drug equation. They also recognize their impotence—political, ideological, administrative—to change course. They resign themselves to business as usual, to the historical inertia they receive when they take office, and adopt the default option. It is the same as with immigration. Blend pragmatism, meaning let things well enough alone, with hypocrisy, meaning pretend you actually believe in what you are doing so the pragmatic part of the policy mix never becomes excessively evident. Is this the best way to run drug and immigration policy? Obviously not. Is it the only way and is it also the typical American way? Almost certainly.

8

Race and religion in America

THERE ARE MANY SALIENT features of American society that distinguish
it from others—rich and less rich ones—as well as a growing number of
commonalities. Two of the United States' most distinguishing characteristics among the affluent countries are race and religion. This might
appear to be an absurd statement: every OECD member nation and
virtually all societies face challenges in these two domains. What is special about America?

To begin with, it is the only rich country where the question of race and
racism stems from a "previously existing condition": slavery. The French,
British, Belgians, Spanish and Portuguese all enforced and exploited slavery
in their former colonies and current possessions, but never at home; Spain
did so in a marginal way until the 16th Century; Brazil, Cuba, Colombia
and the Portuguese former dominions in Africa also experienced slavery
for several centuries, but only Brazil did so as an independent nation.
These nations, including Brazil today, encounter different problems than
America: poverty, inequality, violence, and corruption. They are not comparable to the United States. Although one of Jorge Luis Borge's exegetists
claims that slavery "is the murderous link that unites north and south", in
Historia Universal de la Infamia, the poet enumerates "infinite facts" from
both parts of the hemisphere attributable to slavery.[1]

America must deal with a double challenge: that of the original
sin of slavery on its own territory, and of race and racism specifically
generated by immigration and conquest. Granted, there was another
sin even before slavery and that proceeded after Emancipation: the

expropriation of the lands belonging to the original peoples. But that is a different tragedy. No rich nation has experienced slavery *and* racism over such a sustained period of time. The complexity of the test would be daunting for any society; it is perhaps especially formidable for one in many ways built from scratch. Even more so because the projection of its popular culture across the globe, from film in the early twentieth century to Facebook today, implies that every wrinkle, every blemish, every darkness and horror, every regression, stagnation, or stumble is scrutinized by millions throughout the world.

Religion is somewhat analogous, obviously not in the pernicious and unacceptable connotations of racism, but in its American uniqueness. Or in any case, in view of the traditional consensus: Americans are still considered to be more religious than the peoples of other rich countries, and than an important group of poorer ones. Each metric and measurement throws up varying results and, as we shall see, the definition of religion in America may be broader and more malleable than elsewhere. But even formerly deeply Catholic nations like Ireland vote for "choice" in a referendum, a result that would not necessarily carry the day in the United States; in Spain the church has lost nearly all its power in the past twenty years. The diversity of religions, attendance at religious services, belief in heaven and hell, the emergence of mega-churches in recent decades: all of these traits were unique to America and have been identified as such by countless past observers. The question is whether they continue to be so today.

In other words, I have lumped these two singular American characteristics into one chapter because of their . . . singularity. No other rich country must address the enormous potential and fortune that ethnic diversity brings with it; no other wealthy society must manage the immense challenges it entails. American religiosity has undoubtedly contributed to bringing the country where it is; it may have transformed itself into its opposite: an obstacle to future progress, that America, intuitively, is currently realizing. There is a logic to this method. I am obviously not the only observer to proceed in this fashion. V. S. Naipaul's *A Turn in the South* constitutes essentially a review of race and religion in the Southern states of the country. He knew this pair would surface in his beautifully written travelogue and chose to proceed accordingly: in the South, and in America, race and religion go together, often in unfathomable ways. Naipaul joins them from the beginning, in a purely impressionistic fashion, that I hope conveys his intuition: "So I began to feel the pleasures of the religious meeting: the pleasures of brotherhood, union, formality, ritual, clothes, music . . . . It was the formality—derived by these black people from so many sources—that was the surprise . . . . Torture and tears, luck and grief: these were the motifs of this religion, this binding, this consoling union . . . . Everything happens in the church."[2]

The drama of race as foreigners saw it

As with immigration and drugs, pragmatism and hypocrisy also partly characterize the American approach to one of the most daunting issues for foreigners interested in the United States: race. Although racism is present in innumerable nations, and is often more acute and odious than in America, the contradictions found in the United States make it particularly difficult for outsiders to address. The classic authors dealt with the question of slavery in real time. More recent attempts, from Myrdal to Lévy, have been either monumental and insightful or not worth remembering.

The Swedish economist grasped the question of pragmatism and hypocrisy, lucidly referring to what he called American caste: "They have the political power to make caste legal and orderly, whether with Negro consent or without it. But practically never will whites be heard making such proposals, and still less will they seriously discuss and plan for such a change. They cannot afford to compromise the American Creed. Caste may exist, but it cannot be recognized . . . . The white man can humiliate the Negro; he can thwart his ambitions; he can starve him; he can press him down into vice and crime; he can occasionally beat him and even kill him; but he does not have the moral stamina to make the Negro subjugation legal and approved by society. Against that stands not only the Constitution and the laws which could be changed, but also the American Creed which is firmly rooted in the Americans' hearts."[3]

This was written during World War II, when the contradiction between that American creed and the reality of race relations in the United States grew more blatant than at any time since the Civil War.

America was fighting Nazism with a segregated army. As someone who has lived in many parts of the world since childhood, I have been exposed to the reality of racism on countless occasions. I am familiar with the racism directed against Americans of Mexican origin, against newly arrived Mexicans in the United States, against original peoples in Mexico by mestizo majorities and European minorities, and against Arabs and Africans in Europe. But I belong to the quite un-Mexican-looking elites of my country; I am the object of racist comments in the United States only because of my names. Thus I cannot say that I have come into contact with the drama of race in America, particularly against blacks. Somewhere in my childhood recollections, however, I encountered a powerful strain of anti-racism, particularly involving African Americans. It sprang from my mother.

She was born of Jewish parents near Vilnius, studied in Brussels, and emigrated to Mexico in 1939, where she lived, on and off, till her death in 1984. She was of course familiar with anti-Semitism—her parents were executed by the Nazis in 1941—but had no inkling of anti-black, anti-Asian, or anti-Arab racism. She never chanced upon it until Mexico. There, my mother acquired an intense sensibility regarding the issue during the initial years in her adopted country. She began transmitting it to me later, in New Jersey, Manhattan, and mainly in Egypt, where we lived for three years. My schoolmates at the American School were all from the United States, mostly children of liberal, expat parents, who rarely uttered racist, anti-Arab comments. My best friend there, Bob Bauer, would become Obama's White House counsel half a century later. But some of my playmates *were* racists, and my mother would warn me against them repeatedly, praise me when I argued with them, and defend me when they attacked me.

I only discovered the roots of her potent anti-racism years later. I had been somewhat mystified by her passionate feelings for everything African American in the United States: music, literature, protest, victories, and defeats. During her first years in Mexico, she developed an extremely close relationship with a Haitian writer, poet, and communist leader: Jacques Roumain. He was one of the first poets of the "*negritude*" movement later to flourish in the French Antilles and West Africa, and an exceptionally romantic individual, who died prematurely in 1944. Many of his works were translated into English by Langston

Hughes, the founder of the Harlem Renaissance and icon of African Americans to this day. Roumain and he were close friends, partly, perhaps, since Hughes lived in Mexico in the early 1920s.

The American poet's translation of Roumain's *Les Gouveneurs de la Rosée* (*Masters of the Dew*) became a classic of black Caribbean literature. My mother probably never met Hughes but was struck by Roumain's passion for his country, for the black struggle in the United States, and for his pride in his own "*negritude*." I inherited much of that passion, and though I know it is no substitute for all my gaps and failings in this field, I thank my mother, Roumain, and Hughes for their indirect, distant, and abstract help in understanding racism today. And for introducing me to their successors, from Richard Wright to Paul Beatty.

In her 1954 *America Day by Day*, Simone de Beauvoir devotes nearly fifty pages to what she calls the "black question." She relies on her impressions of traveling on a Greyhound bus from Houston to Savannah and Richmond, and on Myrdal's writings, recently published. Needless to say, she was outraged by what she saw, read, and heard, and rightly concluded, "Everyone, even the racist conservative, recognizes that this is one of the most difficult problems America must face, whatever goals it has in mind."[4] Her descriptions are on occasion lacerating, insightful, and personal, showing once again that foreigners' views of race in the United States are perhaps the greatest condemnation of the American experience, of the most flagrant and hateful contradiction between the promise of the country at birth and its reality nearly two hundred and fifty years later. De Beauvoir sums up her reaction to the beauty and horror of a classic, postcard Southern community: "In the middle of the flowering azaleas, the dormant old houses, and the playing children, the statues of the great slave owners who created the city and fought for it are fixed in glory. But around this dead Savannah, there's another living city, where the grandchildren of slaves live inglorious lives of poverty and hatred: a black belt around a white city."[5]

After Obama and Trump: the case for the original sin

The advent of a black president was expected to change not only the substance of race in American society but also how the rest of the world viewed it. The domestic reaction Obama unleashed despite his best efforts showed that these hopes were ingenuous. As Henry Louis Gates Jr. suggested: "Looking back roughly two years after Donald J. Trump's election, the idea that one black person's occupancy of the White House—and a presidency as successful as his—could have augured the end of race and racism seems both naive and ahistorical . . . . Who could have predicted that the election of the first black president would become a focal point for triggering a dramatic rise in the public expression of some of the oldest, nastiest and most vulgar white supremacist animus about black people?"[6]

Obama was obviously not responsible for this state of affairs; he probably did more to advance the cause of African Americans than any president since Lyndon Johnson. The fact is, however, that he was succeeded by someone who made overt racism acceptable in many circles of American society. Today, the question of race is more present than ever in the United States. The debate about the weight of history and slavery is more current than ever. The public policy discussion about overcoming the so-far insurmountable obstacles to a modicum of equality among races is more intractable than before, if only because so many approaches have been attempted and failed.

While the issue of race touches upon all people of color in the United States, extending to groups well beyond African Americans, to Hispanics, Asian-Americans, and Native Americans, among others, I will concentrate on the question of race as it affects that segment of society that most foreigners have dwelt upon. Excepting the plight of Native Americans that began in the early seventeenth century, racism against blacks is the oldest manifestation of this odious sentiment and ideology on the North American continent. Through slavery, it is the most evil and harmful, which does not mean that Chinese and Mexican immigrants or Native Americans did not receive, at different times in history, treatment that was not equally hateful. A well-versed Mexican observer, in the late 1940s, obsessed with what he called the advent of the "cosmic race," spotted the anti-Asian racism present in many American circles. Vasconcelos described how "In the United States Asians are rejected . . . partly they do not sympathize with the Asian, because they disdain him and would be incapable of intermarrying him. The young women of San Francisco refuse to dance with Japanese naval officers, as proper, intelligent and, in their way, as beautiful as naval officers anywhere in the world. Nevertheless, they will never understand that a Japanese person can be beautiful."[7]

White supremacy attitudes toward African Americans, however, is the least fluid part of the equation, as successive waves of Latino and Asian migrations arrived in the United States and began to climb the social ladder. The disparity between them and whites has diminished, while the gap between whites and African Americans persists, hardly budging over the past fifty years. In 2019, median household income in the United States for all people was 50 percent higher than for blacks, a difference almost identical to half a century before. But for Asian-Americans it was 50 percent higher than for all Americans, and well above that for whites. Latinos, for their part, had surpassed African Americans by nearly 30 percent. The chasm between Latinos and whites has not varied a great deal since 1970—it has diminished by about 5 percent—but this is partly due to the influx of undocumented Mexicans between the late eighties and 2008, who arrive with low income and wealth figures. The numbers for median household *wealth* are analogous.[8] In 2014, the figure for whites was $130,800; for Hispanics, $17,530; for African Americans, $9,590.[9] Another fact shows the same trend: the proportion of Latino families with zero or negative net worth dropped from 40 percent to 33 percent between 1983 and 2016.[10]

Lastly, as Latinos in particular become large minorities or majority-minority groups in many states, and although discrimination persists even in California, undeniable progress has been achieved. This is not self-evident for blacks. It is absurd and painful to even think in terms of "more or less" racism, especially in these anti-Mexican, anti-immigrant times. But the fundamental American dilemma remains what it was eighty years ago with Myrdal, one hundred and fifty years ago after Reconstruction, and four hundred years after the first enslaved peoples were thrown up on the beaches of Virginia. I am not insensitive to the nuances involved in the use of the term African American or black. Teju Cole, the African American novelist who teaches creative writing at Harvard and is of Nigerian parents, sums up some of those nuances eloquently: "'American black' meant slave-descended black. In the terms of US discourse, this wasn't primarily about every black person in the world: it was something else, highly localized to the American situation. To be black in America, that localized tenor of 'black' had to be learned . . . like Obama learned black, like black British living in LA learn black, like Jamaicans in Brooklyn, Haitians in Miami, Eritreans in DC, and Gambians in the Bronx learn black."[11] As with the words Latinos and Hispanics, for the purposes of these passages I use these terms synonymously, without disregarding changing views on the matter.

The original sin versus original virtue argument helps frame the quandary America has faced since the first slaves were delivered by the British to Jamestown, Virginia, in 1619. If slavery was an original sin not only because of its intrinsic evil and indelible nature, but also due to its structural participation in the entire American experiment— from tobacco to sugar to cotton—then the policies needed to erase its consequences are of one type, supposing they are conceivable: radical, extreme, long-lasting as well as immediate. Conversely, if one hundred and sixty years after that first arrival, the Declaration of Independence, the Constitution, and the entire institutional scaffolding erected by the Founders created the conditions whereby that original sin could be eventually expiated, thanks to the extreme virtue of the founding, then there is hope. Gradualism may eventually triumph.

The thesis of the original sin follows the ensuing lines of reasoning. Slavery was ontologically decisive in the tobacco plantations of Virginia, as well as the cotton and sugar plantations in the Deep South until 1865. It was crucial to the emergence of the Industrial Revolution in England—Lancashire looms without cotton were inconceivable; cotton without slavery was too—and to the industrialization of the North in the United States. Exporting enslaved individuals from the upper regions of what became the Confederacy to those farther south became indispensable for the survival of slavery. Expanding the number of slave states—for example, to Texas, after 1847—was a necessary condition for its persistence. Finding a way to square the circle whereby the colonies depending on slavery for their livelihood accepted to join a non-slave majority union was the key to the 1787 compromise that created the United States. More tongue-in-cheek than cynically, Gilberto Freyre, the previously mentioned Brazilian sociologist, made a key point about the complexity of the 1787 compromise: "In the South of the United States, there evolved, from the seventeenth to the eighteenth century, an aristocratic type of rural family that bore a greater resemblance to the type of family in northern Brazil before abolition than it did to the Puritan bourgeoisie of another part of North America, which was similarly of Anglo-Saxon origin, but which had been influenced by a different kind of economic regime. There were almost the same country gentlemen-chivalrous after their fashion; proud of their slaves and lands, with sons and Negroes multiplying about them; regaling themselves with the love of mulattoes; playing cards and amusing themselves with cockfights; marrying girls of sixteen; engaging in feuds over questions of land; dying in duels for the sake of a woman; and getting drunk at great family feasts-huge turkeys with rice, roasted by "old mammies" skilled in the art of the oven, jellies, puddings, dressing, preserved pears, corn-cakes."[12]

After Reconstruction, Jim Crow laws and voter suppression were decisive in maintaining white supremacy rule throughout the South until the Roosevelt era and beyond. A scholar quoted by Henry Louis Gates Jr. points out that global cotton consumption doubled from 1860 to 1890, then doubled again by 1920.[13] The South produced more cotton after the Civil War than before. The trick whereby slavery was practically reinstated was sharecropping, which tied the formerly enslaved freedmen to the cotton plantations, and to a lesser degree, convict-leasing. Sharecropping, in particular, was partly made possible by the decision in Washington to interrupt land reform or applying the right to own land to freedmen. Land there was: more than 850,000 acres confiscated by the federal government, largely by William Sherman in Georgia and South Carolina. It is worth recalling that the 1862 Homestead Act granted millions of acres of land, almost exclusively to whites.[14] Without land, the newly emancipated enslaved peoples were almost condemned to the form of indentured peonage that was sharecropping. So did white supremacy endure in the South.

It also constituted the untold secret of maintaining conservative, business-oriented, anti-labor, and anti-welfare state coalitions in Washington, be they Republican or Democrat. The "solid South" was Democratic until the sixties, but it was also deeply conservative. Even Roosevelt had to accommodate racist congressmen, senators, and Supreme Court justices, and between them, they were able to thwart many of his programs. He excluded farmworkers and domestic employees from the 1935 Social Security Act: in other words two-thirds of the black workers in the South at that time. Not everyone agrees that the explanation for this exclusion purely resided in placating Southern, racist, Democratic congressmen and senators who would have opposed Social Security if it had covered Southern blacks. But many scholars do sustain this point of view. This exclusion remains marginally present in some states today, showing the dastardly effectiveness of the previous exclusion, nearly one hundred years ago.

The notion that the old Confederacy was a different nation, "separate but equal," that did not really affect what occurred in the rest of the country, except through experiences like the Great Migration or World Wars I and II, is from this perspective, totally false. The South was part of the North; racism was present throughout the country; the legacy of slavery did not end at the Mason-Dixon line. The original sin perpetuated itself throughout the politics, economics, and societal attitudes of the entire republic.

Jumping forward, there is a hypothetically logical thread running from slavery to Black Lives Matter and white police brutality against young blacks (and people of color in general) in the twenty-teens. The numbers are staggering and illustrate the following argument. Between 2010 and 2012, "young Black males were twenty-one times more likely to be killed by the police than their white counterparts."[15] Years ago, recruitment for police officers in many, if not all, counties or cities became merit based, resting on entry tests or civil service competition exams and a series of identical standards for all. The purpose was to render recruitment fairer and, particularly, non-discriminatory, given the prevalence of racism in many small and midsize police departments throughout the country. With these practices, it was thought, everyone, including people of color and especially African Americans, would have an equal chance to obtain the job they wanted, without discrimination. Things did not quite turn out that way.

Whites and blacks competed for the same jobs, in the same communities, even if some of the communities were overwhelmingly black, with only a small white minority. Unfortunately, white candidates tended to perform better in these exams than blacks, for the same reasons that whites are better off, do better on SAT scores for college entry, and often make more for the same jobs than blacks. They and their parents received a better education, reside in better neighborhoods, belong to closer-knit families, etc. Exactly the reasons that led to the introduction of affirmative action in many private universities in the late sixties and subsequently in public ones more than fifty years ago.

The outcome of the new police recruitment rules was exceptionally perverse: white cops in black neighborhoods. The best example, because of its high visibility, was Ferguson, Missouri, but certainly not the only one. In large cities, the challenge could be addressed by rotating, or pairing police officers, and affirmative action. In smaller communities, though, if most of the force was white, inevitably the African American neighborhoods would be policed by white officers. But the latter were not equipped to deal with the challenges they faced. Their own educational levels, training, fears, and atavisms, in a nutshell, their racism, nuanced or not, made them poor candidates for policing what were often destitute, violent, black neighborhoods. Hence the killings, hence the movement, hence the difficulties of finding solutions to what appear to be intractable problems.

"The case for reparations"

Tocqueville was prescient in this field as he was in many others (not all, by the way). He never underestimated the enormous weight the history of slavery entailed for America: "The most fearsome of all the ills threatening the future of the United States stems from the presence of the blacks on their soil . . . . In modern times, the insubstantial and temporary fact of slavery is most fatally combined with the substantial and permanent difference of race . . . . The law may abolish slavery but God alone can remove its traces." This is the underlying logic of the case for reparations made by African American writers such as Ta-Nehisi Coates, and Democratic candidates in 2019 like Elizabeth Warren, Cory Booker, and even Marianne Williamson, along with many others. It is also behind HR 40, a piece of legislation calling for a formal study of reparations for African Americans (the 40 stands for "Forty acres and a mule," the unfulfilled promise made to freed slaves after the Civil War). It has been repeatedly introduced (but never passed) in the House of Representatives by former Rep. John Conyers for close to three decades.[16] Its 2019 version, providing 13 million dollars to study the matter, received the support of nearly sixty House

Democrats, including Speaker Nancy Pelosi, and of eleven Democratic presidential candidates.[17] Emancipation eliminated slavery, but not its consequences, or conditions, mainly white supremacy and anti-black racism.

The argument states that for the more than one hundred and fifty years after the Civil War the legacy of slavery has so lastingly endured that only a major overhaul of race relations and public policy will bring about change. The conversation is different from that affecting Asian-Americans or Latinos. There was never an original sin that placed its imprint on everything and distorted every effort to advance gradually and incrementally. In consequence, the numbers reflecting the gap between these minorities and whites have tended to converge, albeit too slowly, especially in the case of Hispanics.

After abolition and Reconstruction, the legacy of slavery was quickly strengthened. First came Jim Crow laws, disenfranchisement, lynching, the Ku Klux Klan, and acute segregation in the South. Then, once the Great Migration was underway and more than 6 million African Americans moved north, "black people across the country were largely cut out of the legitimate home-mortgage market,"[18] the single greatest wealth accumulation in American history. Redlining, neighborhood segregation, school segregation, employment segregation from before World War I to the forties and fifties all guaranteed that even in large cities with Democratic Party hegemony like Chicago, the gap between blacks and whites remained insurmountable and abysmal. According to Coates, "Blacks and whites do not inhabit the same city. The average per capita income of Chicago's white neighborhoods is almost three times that of its black neighborhoods . . . a black neighborhood with one of the highest incarceration rates had a rate more than 40 times as high as the white neighborhood with the highest rate."[19]

Little has changed over the years. The income gap between black and white households has hardly budged since 1970. Even after the Civil Rights and Voting Rights Acts of the sixties, Medicare and Medicaid, affirmative action from the seventies onward, a two-term black president and black mayors in numerous cities from New York to Chicago to Los Angeles, the statistics are stubbornly immobile. A black middle class has emerged, but even it resides in neighborhoods of lower quality of life and services than white families with equal income and wealth.

Black unemployment, for college graduates and those who are not, is far higher than white unemployment. The number of blacks living under the poverty line is incomparably greater than the equivalent figure for whites. With regard to educational levels, national incarceration rates, infant mortality, health statistics and access to health care, and absolutely every additional indicator, blacks and whites live in two different, though not separate, countries. According to a team of economists who surveyed the mobility of Americans born between 1978 and 1983, black sons of wealthy parents suffered astonishing downward mobility compared to whites. There is practically no intergenerational transmission of wealth among blacks.[20]

In 1962, before the great reforms of the sixties, the average *wealth* of white households was seven times greater than that of the black equivalent. In 2019, the mean black household wealth reached \$138,000; for whites, \$933,000, or seven times more—exactly the same multiple as 1962.[21] Home ownership, the classic wealth-building instrument in a middle-class society, also remained unerringly where it stood in 1968: 42 percent, compared to 73 percent of white families who own homes.[22] The median black household *income*, as opposed to wealth, is around \$34,000 per year; for whites, it is \$68,000, exactly double.[23] Coates's conclusion is lapidary: "To ignore the fact that one of the oldest republics in the world was erected on a foundation of white supremacy, to pretend that the problems of a dual society are the same as the problems of unregulated capitalism, is to cover the sin of national plunder with the sin of national lying. The lie ignores the fact that reducing American poverty and ending white supremacy are not the same."[24]

Recalling our exclusion of Asian Americans and Latinos from this brief discussion of race in America, the median white family has forty-one times more wealth than the median black family, but "only" twenty-two times more wealth than the median Latino family.[25] The share of Latino families with zero or negative net worth dropped significantly.[26] One might add that both blacks and whites continue to seriously underestimate the wealth and income gap separating them. According to a 2017 Yale University study, the distance between perception and reality can reach 25 percent: people think the gap is more narrow than it actually is.[27]

Foreigners who have revisited this lacerating question responded in various fashions. Some are more sensitive than others. Myrdal did not formulate the dilemma this way but was clearly of two minds about his hopes for the future. He seemed to think that the idea whereby "the Negro problem would come to solve itself by the lapse of time" was false, even if sincere scholars and politicians had thought so up to that point and afterward. He believed, as one of the creators of the Swedish welfare state, in "social engineering," by which I prefer to think that he meant, back in 1942, a major overhaul of institutions, public policies and something like a new New Deal. Today, he would find himself, I think, on the side of the radical reformers. Not everyone agrees: Cornell University professor of law and author Aziz Rana, for example, considers Myrdal to be a wholehearted supporter and believer in the "creedal" view, whereby the gap between the American reality of race and the American creed of equality will one day, gradually, slowly, painfully but surely, be resolved in favor of the creed.[28] Weber, the more draconian German, in 1904 was "absolutely convinced that the 'color line' problem will be the paramount problem of the time to come, here and everywhere in the world."[29]

A more recent foreign scholar has tip-toed back and forth between the two approaches to race in the United States. Bernard-Henri Lévy initially describes Atlanta, a city he visited on his 2004 trip across America, in glowing terms: "Here I am now in Atlanta, a showcase of peaceful desegregation . . . a symbol of a successful emancipation . . . living proof that racism, stupidity, crime are solvable under capitalism, and where a page has been turned."[30] The subtext is that if this is possible in Martin Luther King's hometown, it can happen anywhere, even if the process might require more time and pain. Then he sustains a lengthy conversation with the *Wall Street Journal*'s bureau chief in Atlanta, who promptly shares with him stories about the perpetuation of slavery after Emancipation through other forms, about Jim Crow, and the way surveys of the last survivors were carried out.

Lévy then wonders: "And what if this happy façade, this image of a black city without bitterness nor complexes, were exactly that: a façade, with an enormous memory hole in its middle?"[31] He provides no answer. Nor did Naipaul, who spent more time in Atlanta and came away with a similar, ambivalent impression: "But here in Atlanta . . . (black) power was circumscribed. And perhaps the very dignity that the politics of the city offered a black man made him more aware of the great encircling wealth and true power of white Atlanta. So that the politics of Atlanta might have seemed like a game, a drawing off of rage from black people. Just as civil-rights legislation gave rights without money or acceptance, so perhaps city politics gave position without strength, and stimulated another, unassuageable kind of rage."[32] Both authors show the same type of doubt about racial progress, even in a supposedly exemplary city like Atlanta. An increasing number of Americans harbor those doubts too.

What do Americans think about the current state of race relations in the United States? They are ambivalent but displaying a trend toward greater concern and division than a decade or two ago. To begin with (and predictably), whites and blacks view matters very differently. In polls undertaken over the past fifty or sixty years, blacks have a consistently and significantly more pessimistic appreciation of race relations, the causes of discrimination and inequality, and policies to improve them, than whites. The year 2017 showed the most negative opinion of both whites and blacks about race relations since the 1992 Los Angeles riots after the Rodney King beatings. At that time, only 20 percent of blacks and 25 percent of whites said race relations were generally good.[33]

The positive figures rose and reached their peak during Obama's first term, when 59 percent of blacks and 65 percent of whites held that optimistic opinion. By 2017, however, only 28 percent of blacks thought so, and 40 percent of whites did. As 2017 ended, whites, Hispanics, and blacks all thought race relations were worse than before, with African Americans, understandably, being most gloomy. The situation becomes more polarized when all Americans are asked if the country needs to continue to make changes for racial equality. During the first fifteen or so years of this century, roughly half thought so, and half did not. But by late 2017, the gap broadened considerably, to 61 percent who believed further changes were needed, and 35 percent supposed the contrary. When broken down among Democrats and Republicans, the polarization sharpened. More than 80 percent of Americans considering themselves Democrats or in that direction thought more changes were necessary; only 32 percent of Republicans did so.

With regard to the key question of whether racial discrimination or what pollsters label "blacks' own condition" is the reason African Americans cannot get ahead in the United States, the difference has widened. In 2010, just after Obama took office, 67 percent of all Americans gave credence to the "blacks' own condition" explanation: only 18 percent attributed the blame to racial discrimination. After Obama left office, in late 2017, the figure for "racial discrimination" had leapt to 41 percent, whereas the total making blacks responsible for their own condition dropped to 49 percent.[34] Obama made a big difference in American life, but not necessarily in leading people to believe that racial discrimination was diminishing in the United States. Finally, after having fallen for several years—through the early twenty-first century—support for affirmative action rose again. In recent times, 71 percent of Americans have concluded that affirmative action programs in colleges are a good thing.[35] Given Supreme Court rulings, some could ask: so what? In fact these shifts in public opinion could lay the groundwork for much broader reform in education or in other fields.

The greatest obstacle facing any kind of radical change in American society to repair at long last the damage wrought by slavery lies in whites' attitudes. In 2014, after Coates's essay was published, half of white Americans believed that slavery was not a factor at all in lower average wealth levels for blacks.[36] Only 14 percent considered slavery to be a major factor.[37] Conversely, half of all black Americans deemed it a major factor, and just 14 percent did not consider it a factor at all.[38] In other words, the two graphs were exactly mirror opposites of each other. And if someone asked whether they desired an extreme solution like reparations through cash payments to descendants of slaves, a tiny 6 percent of white Americans stated so, but nearly 60 percent of blacks did.[39] In 2014, Americans did not like the idea of reparations, for blacks, or for Japanese-Americans interned during World War II, for example. Only German reparations to Jews who survived the Holocaust were found deserving.[40] A recent book by Susan Neiman—*Learning from the Germans*—has delved into this comparison.[41]

To summarize the state of opinion in 2019, a Gallup specialist phrased things the following way: "Only 18 percent of blacks are satisfied with the way they are treated in this country today, compared with half of whites who say they are satisfied with the way blacks are treated. Well over half of blacks believe that they are treated less favorably than whites in dealing with the police, in stores and malls, and on the job. About half of blacks say blacks are treated less favorably in neighborhood shops, in restaurants and in getting healthcare."[42]

Reparations are really a proxy or buzzword for a broader, more ambitious, and more universal approach to correcting previous horrors, atoning for past sins, and working effectively for a better future. They could also just be limited to an acknowledgment of past wrongs, in some interpretations. But mostly it parts from the premise that what has been undertaken thus far, let's say, since the Kennedy and Johnson years, has simply not worked, even if certain specific measures or policies have been more successful than others. Several scholars have attempted to flesh out the details of what a major overhaul of the current state of affairs would entail, although most envisage a new American welfare state, with specific chapters for African Americans, and perhaps for other discriminated minorities. It would include reparations, but not be limited to them.

William Darity, for example, has argued that exclusively offering cash payments without addressing the underlying structures that have restricted black people from building wealth would not succeed. He prefers a "portfolio of reparations." By this he implies a combination of individual payments and race-targeted proposals like vouchers for financial asset building, free medical insurance, or free college education for black people, or a trust fund exclusively for black Americans. He also calls for an education program that would teach Americans the complete story of slavery and its after-effects, which he says would help the country understand the harm wrought.[43] Another of his proposals, formulated together with a colleague, Darrick Hamilton, was praised by *The Economist* for possibly reducing the inheritance gap between blacks and whites. Some economists speculate that herein lies the single most important factor in perpetuating inequality. They, along with Democratic leaders like Cory Booker, suggest "baby bonds," or a trust account for every child born in America.[44] It could not be accessed until adulthood; the government would top it up each year, depositing more for poorer families.

Is such a bold and grand ambition feasible in the medium term? Probably not, unless earth-shattering changes take place in the United States. Karl Marx's summary in his letter to Abraham Lincoln congratulating him on his re-election in 1864 reflects the magnitude of the transformation involved then: "The workingmen in Europe feel sure that, as the American War of Independence initiated a new era of ascendancy for the middle class, so the American Antislavery War will do for the working classes. They consider it a sign of the epoch to come that it fell to the lot of Abraham Lincoln, the single-minded son of the working class, to lead his country through the matchless struggle for the rescue of an enchained race and the reconstruction of a social world."[45] But is also true that the strains on the status quo as far as race are concerned have been growing, perhaps to unsustainable degrees. Obama's election awakened enormous hopes everywhere in the world, but perhaps more for African Americans than anyone else. Some of those hopes were fulfilled, but others have been replaced by frustration and even despair. Which is why it is worth revisiting the other view of the issue, possible personified by Obama himself, and which can be labeled the original virtue approach.

Original virtue or staying the (right) course

Aziz Rana has summed up the second, or original virtue focus quite succinctly: "This model of reform rejected the need for any fundamental break with the past, since greater liberty could be interpreted as a continuation of the arc of American history rather than a radical correction of its course. Rather than restructuring the fabric of American society, the purpose of reform became to make existing goods more broadly accessible—to end formal discrimination, to provide equal opportunity to worthy elements within the black community, to eliminate all glass ceilings based on race or gender."[46] The term original virtue can be utilized sincerely—not tongue in cheek—because the case can be made—and has been—that the Founders, their documents and institutions, their theories and ulterior practice, made it possible to overcome the original sin of slavery.

The Constitution, the Declaration of Independence, the Bill of Rights, the 1787 deal regarding the Electoral College, all enshrined slavery and the role it played in the entire American economy and society. But these documents also rendered change possible, from the Civil War, Emancipation, and Reconstruction, to the New Deal, the Civil Rights Act, and Obama's election. The transformations were woefully slow and partial. They have been largely insufficient, but over the years, the situation of African Americans in absolute terms has improved, even if in relation to whites, or Hispanics and Asian-Americans, it has not.

From this perspective, the major advances that have taken place all derive from the same origin: a political, economic, and legal system that, with time, allowed and actually assured that the outrageous features of the republic's birth would be eliminated. It took a war, the civil rights movement, legal battles and riots, a great deal of pain and sorrow, but in the end justice was purportedly done. A large amount of pending, daunting challenges remain, but the same institutions that permitted progress so far, guarantee further movement in the right direction.

A black middle class has not only emerged but expanded, comprising more than a third of the African American population. More blacks than ever attend college, vote, and get elected, at all levels: cities, state legislatures, governors' mansions, Capitol Hill, and the White House. They are increasingly well represented in business, the media, high-income professions, entertainment, and academia. The cumulative effect of the major reforms of the past half-century has been real and significant. The whole point then is to continue along the same path, repairing what has not functioned effectively, and persevering with what has.

According to its supporters, this approach means, among other policies, that affirmative action in education and government contracts for small businesses should continue and be enlarged. Discrimination in incarceration rates, police recruitment, and policies should be combatted and constantly reviewed. Lingering forms of redlining, mortgage discrimination, and housing segregation should be banned; special attention should be paid to certain highly disadvantaged groups, such as single mothers, young children, or the elderly. But the suggestions by the followers of gradualism and persistence are not limited to recommendations specifically for African Americans.

As importantly, they propose major reforms favoring *all* Americans, as they will have a disproportionately favorable effect on people of color and obvious advantages in building political support. Whether it be Medicare for all; free tuition at public universities or community colleges; decriminalization of certain drugs; universal child-care; parental leave; the end of mandatory sentencing and overhauling the criminal justice system; reviewing police behavior in large cities or having the federal government intervene directly in egregious cases of racism, brutality, or incompetence: all of these reforms of the American welfare state are reasonable, feasible, expensive perhaps, but not something an immensely wealthy society cannot afford.

They require incremental steps, national debates, and time. They are necessary to reduce inequality throughout America: between whites and people of color; among blacks, and among whites. In this view, the fundamental challenge consists in undoing the policies that have aggravated inequality since 1980 and implementing policies that will reduce it for all Americans.

This line of reasoning appears eminently sensible. Moreover, the case for gradualism is strengthened by the resistance or outright opposition to the alternative. There appears to be no imminent consensus, or even a medium-term hope for one, in favor of the more radical perspective. When a foreigner senses the rage and despair of blacks in demonstrations against police brutality, or of Latinos living in conditions not much better than those of their parents or grandparents before they emigrated, it is easy to decry the pragmatism or even cynicism implicit in the reformist, incrementalist approach. On observing the incredible polarization of the American electorate, whereby in 2016 whites voted by huge margins in favor of Trump—by 37 percent among white males without a college education; by 9 percent among white women, running against a white woman—and blacks, Latinos, and Asian-Americans by even greater margins for Clinton, it is difficult to dismiss the need or inevitability of the "original sin" focus.[47]

But simply acknowledging the regrettable state of the status quo is not a sufficient argument in favor of the type of change that is both necessary and desirable. Americans have employed different tools at different moments to enable the changes their society has clamored for. With the exception of the Civil War, those tools have been chiefly moderate, gradual, and late in coming. Some foreign observers, who were both familiar with the United States for having lived there, and with slavery, race, and conquest, for having witnessed it first hand in their own countries, concluded nearly one hundred and fifty years ago that the "original virtue" was not working. So wrote Cuban national hero José Martí in 1894: "What an honest man should observe is not only that the founding elements of different origins and tendencies with which the United States were created have not been forged into one, after three centuries of life in common and one of political occupation, but that a coerced or forced community exacerbates and accentuates these primary differences, and transforms the unnatural federation into a harsh state of violent conquest."[48] The appalling disarray of race relations in America will in all likelihood only be ameliorated with time and patience. This is not the path I would prefer or choose. But it doesn't seem like there is a third way, another path that is neither the radical and impossible course, nor the incrementalist and so far futile one.

Who else considers themselves to be God's country?

I possess no particular insights into the role of religion in the United States, being an atheist with a Jewish mother from a Catholic nation and an anti-clerical father. So, I shall only engage in a few reflective and speculative notes on this subject, lightly structured and not seeking great originality. The omnipresence of the issue is simply too imposing, however, to omit a comment in its regard.

Americans' religiosity has always perplexed visitors or analysts from abroad, partly because of its diversity, its ubiquity, its strength, extending on occasion to stridency, and to the political impact it has always enjoyed. Strangely, Chinese observers had a singular view: "Some Chinese visitors did note that people in America were much less religious than their earlier contact with missionaries in China had led them to expect."[49] Not that the Church, or churches, lack political sway elsewhere. There are few countries in the world—China, Japan, perhaps— where they do not. But most foreigners, and many Americans, would readily admit today that despite the initial and radical, official separation of Church and State in America, in few countries does religion play as important a role in political matters as in the United States. History, intensity, beliefs, and religious pluralism represent an unquestionable factor in explaining this peculiarity.

Originally, nearly every new American was Protestant (Maryland the colony was an exception, and it didn't last; by 1715 it had banned priests, Catholic worship, and Catholic land purchases). Evidently the Native Americans and subsequently the enslaved peoples did not profess that faith, obviously, but those who arrived from Europe were, according to one recent source, 98 percent Protestant.[50] This was a key factor in the creation of American democracy, according to Tocqueville: "Most of English America has peen peopled by men who, having shaken off the authority of the Pope, acknowledged no other religious supremacy; they brought, therefore, into the New World a form of Christianity which I can only describe as democratic and republican. This fact will be exceptionally favorable to the establishment of a democracy and a republic . . . . From the start, politics and religion were in agreement and they have continued to be so ever since."[51] Over the following two hundred years, this homogeneity changed significantly, as did the proportion of Americans who are not religious. By the 1830s, as Tocqueville estimated, there were already more than 1 million Irish and Polish Catholics in the United States. The United States never had it easy in assimilating Catholicism—Irish, Italian, Polish, Mexican—but it managed the task adequately over the last two hundred years. The difference with Islam in Europe is obvious; I suggested a few explanations in the previous chapter.

This did not alter the basic equation for him, as he rejected the notion that this diversity could either weaken religion or democracy. On the contrary. For the French traveler, no great fan of Catholicism in Europe, *American* Catholics were the "most republican and democratic class in the United States."[52] This new original virtue, coupled with another—the purported separation of Church and State—ensured the long-term survival and strength of religion, according to Tocqueville: "its influence is more lasting. It restricts itself to its own resources of which no one can deprive it; it operates within a unique sphere which it occupies entirely and rules effortlessly."[53] Others today, as well as nearly two centuries ago, might phrase the same notion differently. Since no one religion ever had a legal upper hand, or became fully dominant demographically or spiritually, all coexisted more or less in peace. And intensely, by the way, or so it has seemed since time immemorial.

Whenever foreigners are struck by how much more religious Americans seem to be than the citizens of other rich countries, they are correct, in the first instance. Mario Vargas Llosa, who knows the United States well, has expressed his wonder at some data he came across early in this century: "Every weekend, some 120 million American citizens, attend a religious service, more that those who over the course of a year visit stadiums or gyms to see or practice any sport. This statistic does away with the age old cliché whereby this is a materialistic country, where the obsession for money and the worship of the body, has suffocated the life of the spirit."[54] Americans *are* apparently more religious, in every definition of the word, than people in the other rich countries. Much more so than profoundly Catholic nations like Italy, or than societies such as Japan, France, Germany, and Sweden. Compared to Britain, to take an example that culturally at least is perhaps closer to the United States, more than half of all Britons admit they never pray, while only 18 percent of Americans say the same.[55]

Americans are also more religious than the inhabitants of many poor countries. According to the World Values Survey, American religiosity is slightly higher even than Iran's. Only Muslim nations, like Indonesia or Egypt, or poor non-Islamic ones, like India, South Africa, and Brazil, have higher rates of weekly attendance at religious services.[56] Likewise, it would be inconceivable that in 2009, when a poll revealed that nearly 50 percent of all Americans had at one time or another undergone a religious or mystical experience, for a similar statistic to exist in any European country.[57] Not even in Ireland or Poland, perhaps the most religious among them. Similarly, there is, by some accounts, one place of worship for every eight hundred inhabitants, a level of density unheard of elsewhere.

A first balance

Americans' confessed religiosity is deep and intense. According to the Faith Matters Survey carried out by Robert Putnam, 83 percent of the inhabitants of the United States report they belong to a religion; 40 percent say they attend religious services nearly every week or more often.[58] As significantly, perhaps, eight out of every ten Americans are "absolutely sure" there is a God, 60 percent that there is a heaven, and almost one-half that there is a hell.[59] I say more significantly, because there is a serious discussion among specialists in these matters regarding the reliability of self-reporting surveys on actual participation in religious life. One would imagine that people have fewer incentives to lie about their religious *beliefs* than about their religious *practices*.

Once again, these numbers are far higher than their equivalent in the rich countries, and more comparable to those one finds in either non-Islamic poor countries (Brazil, South Africa), or traditional Muslim nations, like Egypt, Iran, or Indonesia. For the highly religious country that Mexico supposedly is, where every time the Pope visits, millions of Mexicans take to the streets to greet him, the figures are the following: 36 percent attending mass at least once a week; half saying hell exists (though not absolutely sure). Only two out of ten Mexicans are guided by their priests in making important decisions. Slightly more than one in two consider themselves to be religious.[60] In contrast to the United States, there is a strong correlation in Mexico between religiosity and educational and income levels: the less educated and more poor are significantly more religious than others.[61]

One of the first foreign visitors ever to comment on American mores, back in 1794, Napoleon's friend and foe, the Duke of Talleyrand, was surprised that America had "thirty religions, but only one dish: meat and potatoes." The culinary judgment was probably false even then (especially if one took into consideration Native Americans and African Americans) but the more substantive one is not. The Faith Matters Survey groups together three religions under the heading of Evangelical Protestant, ranging from the late Billy Graham to megachurches or Pentecostals. They amount to just below 30 percent of the population of the United States; Catholics total around 23 percent; Americans professing no religion number 17 percent and growing; mainline Protestants (among them Baptists, Episcopalians, Methodists, Lutherans, Presbyterians) 13 percent; black Protestants, 8 percent; Jews and Mormons between 2 and 3 percent.[62]

Few countries in the world, not even India, encompass a comparable variety of religions. Brazil, as diverse a nation as the United States in many ways, and where evangelical churches have flourished in recent decades, remains 65 percent Catholic. Only around one-fifth of all Brazilians belong to evangelical churches; these include the same type of diversity as in the United States, although these have become immensely powerful lobbies in recent times. Many American denominations' membership has remained relatively stable over the past half century, with two contradictory exceptions: Evangelical Protestants, and Catholics. The number of non-Latino Catholics is rapidly shrinking, for reasons ranging from demographics to scandal. The Hispanic segment, however, has grown exponentially. Its main sociological support base—Latino immigrants—has broadened enormously. Hispanics are overwhelmingly Catholic, although the translation of beliefs into actual practice is probably as intricate as in their home countries. Six out of every ten Catholics in the United States today are Latinos.[63] Similarly, while the percentage of all Evangelical Protestants began to drop from the mid-nineties onward, the so-called non-denominational or mega-church followers rose, as did the number of those professing no religion. As Putnam puts it, "what the evangelical churches lost in adherents over the last two decades [in 2008] has mostly been made up for by the evangelicals' zeal."[64] Attendance in black Protestant churches has also declined in recent years

The truly complex question about religion in America, which many scholars have asked, with varying replies, is exactly what does religion mean in this context? Is it simply one form of social capital, as Putnam implied in *Bowling Alone*, more than twenty years ago? Is it one more manifestation of Tocqueville's famous "voluntary associations," that he emphasized as one of the most innovative and attractive features of the young republic? Is it in part another expression of money-making prowess, on the one hand, and gullibility, on the other? Is it just one additional "self-help" mechanism, as often seems the case with the mega-churches of Saddleback, Willow Creek, Joel Osteen's Lakewood Church, and many more? Or all of the above?

From an outsider's perspective, it is difficult to admit at face value many of the characteristics of American religiosity, as articulated in the most familiar narratives, both historical and present-day. They often appear as myths, or iconized versions of more complicated trends or junctures. There are exceptions, of course. The unique nature of black Protestantism, for example, is not a myth or a concoction of official, historical, storytelling. Since Emancipation, and before in some cases, the different African American churches were a fundamental source of solace, support, inspiration, and struggle for millions of worshipers. They mainly emerged during Reconstruction, and the period later called Southern Redemption, when the immense hopes awakened by the Northern military occupation of the South were dashed. The end of Reconstruction in the 1870s brought violence against blacks, disenfranchisement, sharecropping and convict-leasing, anti-miscegenation, Black Codes, the color line, and Jim Crow.

In the face of this onslaught, freedmen and -women took refuge in black churches, schools, and colleges. These were singular churches in other ways also. As a Norwegian observer was to notice a century and a half later, with regard to American religion in general, but especially in relation to black Southern churches, "The depth of American religion lay not in visual art, not in representation but, obviously, in music." The same black churches played a crucial role, of course, in the civil rights movement of the sixties as well as the debates during the second decade of the twenty-first century within African American communities, and between them and the rest of the country. But other myths about American religiosity are more difficult to take literally.

Religion may be a feature of American diversity, rather than one additional highlight of uniformity, as many have believed since the early nineteenth century. This would not be due exclusively to the existence and growth of many churches, as well as the non-religious individuals, but also to the varying intensity of religion among different groups of Americans and at different stages in history. Church attendance is one unmistakable indicator of religiosity's intensity, but even that involves self-reporting. Logically, there should be a certain reluctance for people who consider themselves highly religious to admit that they actually attend church infrequently. Scholars take this bias into account, but it is not easy to quantify. It is even more complicated to measure, or qualify, what attendance actually signifies.

When a person attends one of the mega-church Saturday or Sunday events, are they actually "going to Church," in the same way a Jew visits the temple, or a Catholic attends mass, or an African American attends the church of his or her choice? Or is this a family event, a combination of Sunday School for children, meeting friends at a common location, seeking solutions to everyday-life challenges or adversity, and perhaps even political comfort?

This is not meant to imply either that certain groups in the United States are not intensely religious or that a majority of Americans were not so at given moments in time. According to one historian, "The revivals . . . of the 1820s and 1830s (known as the Second Awakening), added a religious underpinning to the celebration of personal self-improvement and self-determination . . . . The revivals' opening of religion to mass participation . . . . resonated with the democratization of politics."[65] Before the Second Awakening began, barely one in ten Americans were church members. By its conclusion, the figure had leapt to 80 percent.[66] Other, analogous junctures surfaced every now and then.

Europeans, Canadians, and Latin Americans—granted, much more Catholic oriented than their northern neighbors—show less church attendance than in the United States, but it is a much more uniform presence. Everybody who attends mass on Sunday pretty much does the same thing on Sunday. Whatever parameter one prefers for measuring religiosity, it calibrates a similar object. Americans undertake multiple activities in their places of worship, depending on ethnicity—African Americans in black Protestant churches, Latinos in Catholic ones—or whether they are mainline Protestants in theirs (similar among themselves, but different from others). Evangelical Protestants and mega-church devotees often immerse themselves in religious practices than can be quite dissimilar to others. From afar, it might appear as if those practices were in fact forms of association to no longer bowl alone. They replace previous forms of civic participation that died out for generational reasons, or instruments of self-help, that could almost as easily dispense with their confessional aspects. But then they would lose the seduction or attractiveness in the "religious market" that appeals to the ingrained American belief in God.

A second glance . . . and a different conclusion

One of the superficial reasons that lead some foreigners, beginning with myself, to believe that part of American religiosity is more skin-deep than the numbers and the mythology suggest, consists in the gap between religious prescriptions for everyday life and the latter's actual nature. There are multiple examples that can be usefully compared with other countries. In 2018, just 30 percent of Americans between the ages of 18 and 34 were married; the number in 1978 was 59 percent.[67] A large part of the shift was toward living with a partner. Thus in 2013, two-thirds of all American married couples had lived together before marriage, the proportion having doubled over the previous twenty-five years.[68] Compared to other nations, the United States falls into the corresponding upper bracket among rich countries.

In Spain, for example, a theoretically very Catholic nation, 48 percent of married couples live together before marrying. In France a bit less than 60 percent of all couples had either lived together before marriage or continued to do so: less than in the United States. Germany showed an equivalent figure of under 50 percent. Great Britain ranks a distant first in these matters: four out of five people in 2010 lived together before marrying. These figures are all for the middle of the second decade of this century.[69] This is the new normal. These numbers include cohabitation couples that did not marry later. The American couples range from young, affluent professionals or even students, to families of scarce resources who cohabit under a common roof for economic reasons, in addition to the affection they may or may not have for each other.

Divorce rates in the United States are also higher than those of rich nations with supposedly lower rates of religiosity, defined in any of the ways I have mentioned above. This is partly due to the proliferation of civil unions in various European countries but is nonetheless symptomatic. America experienced 3.6 divorces per thousand inhabitants in 2016; significantly more than all the other rich nations (France, Germany, and Canada were all at 2.2 or 2.3); the figures for divorces as a percentage of actual marriages, as opposed to civil unions, are similar.[70] Likewise, the number of abortions per woman in child-bearing age is far greater than in most of Western Europe, where in contrast to the United States, the issue has been laid to rest as a matter of policy or controversy for decades. In 2015 there were 17.1 abortions per thousand American women aged between 15 and 39. Of the rich countries, only France (20.7), United Kingdom (20.2), Norway (16.5), and New Zealand (18.1) had comparable numbers.[71] The countries with much higher rates—Russia, Cuba, China—reflect a combination of factors, from abortion as a common form of contraception (Cuba, Russia,

Romania) to China's previous one child per family policy. This is perhaps especially relevant, since the most significant correlation for divorce rates is income parity, and the United States is more unequal today than the European nations, Canada, or Japan.

Cohabitation, divorce, abortion, and same sex-marriage are not necessarily symptoms of non-religiosity, but they tend to be frowned upon by most churches, with the possible exception of liberal Protestants. This is equally the case for same-sex marriages, once they were fully legalized throughout the United States, and where in theory they provoked a generalized rejection by conservative churches, mainly Evangelical Protestants. The rise of the numbers in America closely resembles change in the other North Atlantic nations. In Spain, in 2005, there were 1269 same sex-marriages; the number climbed to 4726 in 2018. In France, that same year, 6000 same-sex marriages were formally registered. For smaller, non-Catholic nations, like Denmark and Holland, there were 480 and 1502 respectively.[72] In the United States, with roughly five to six times the French population, the figure in 2015, according to Gallup, was 123,000, twenty times more than France, thirty times more than Spain.[73] By 2018, the total number in the United States had reached 650,000 by some estimates.[74] The 2020 Census is expected to ask more specific questions on this matter, and more precise statistics will become available.

In the meantime, the trend is undisputable. In other words, Americans may self-report themselves as more religious than their peers in the rich countries. They might actually attend church more frequently than the inhabitants of other OECD members. But actual practices, habits and behavior appear either quite akin to these other societies or indeed significantly "less religious" or more bold in braving the fires of religious orthodoxy. If one wanted to extend this reasoning a bit further, there is a gaping contrast between the existence of explicit dry laws in multiple American cities and tacitly in a few states—Kansas, Mississippi, and Tennessee—and the volumes of alcohol actually consumed in the relevant counties.

Contrariwise, American religiosity contains a well-known peculiarity often absent in other nations. Worshipers in the United States "switch" religions frequently, much more than their affluent counterparts elsewhere. If one includes changes within Protestant options, in 2014,

42 percent of American adults had switched religions at some point in their past. When one regards Protestantism as a single set, 34 percent of Americans identified with a different religious group than the one they were raised in.[75] In countries with less religious diversity than the United States, the figures are understandably much lower: Brazil, 27 percent; Mexico, 12 percent; Argentina, 18 percent.[76] But America ranks below rich countries with more diverse religious configurations.

The reasons behind each switch vary. Sometimes, changes derive from a spouse's different denomination, or people leaving a church more or less for good (the case of Anglo Catholics, for example) due to historical and generational motives, or to scandal. It may involve children of parents with different religions moving from one to the other when they reach adulthood. These figures fluctuate by social segment. African Americans and Latino Catholics are more "faithful" to their initial faith than Protestant whites: the link between religious and ethnic identity holds true. The switching trend rose during the twentieth century according to Putnam, and it stands to reason that it should. The intensity of American's attachment to religion has begun to decline.

Religion is not what it used to be

Putnam and other scrutinizers of the American religious landscape have all detected a fundamental trend at work recently. Barely twenty years ago, foreign scholars did not notice it. French political scientist Denis Lacorne, in his *Religion in America*, almost dismissed it. In reference to "secularism: defined as "the absence of religious belief," he noted that it is fairly rare in America.[77] There *is* a "creeping secularization" underway in the United States, as older, more religious people pass from the scene, and younger demographic cohorts take increasing distance from religion. The same observers have also witnessed how there is a "hollowing out" of the religious center. More Americans move either in the direction of professing no religion, or becoming more devout, engaged or even extreme in their religious beliefs. The moderate, traditional center, with the exception of Latino Catholics, is shrinking rapidly. This trend, or my belief in its existence, should not be confused with any form of regret for the loss of American spiritualism. Many foreigners, from Qutb ("America has forgotten the spirit, which has no value here"[78]) to Aleksandr Solzhenitzyn, have regretted that loss; I applaud it, to the extent the suspicion of the loss is founded in facts.

The question these scholars do not necessarily ask, however, and that perhaps only a foreigner with scant familiarity with the issue might formulate, is the following. Are Americans slowly but surely becoming more secular, or are they reporting attitudes that they were previously reluctant to confess more truthfully and explicitly than before? As we approach the 2020s, are younger Americans, with higher educational levels, more information at their disposal and living increasingly in urban centers, more liable to acknowledge to pollsters that they are not as religious than their parents or grandparents were? Is there a "Bradley effect" in self-reported American views on religion, where just as white voters in California in the 1980s (or in Virginia or the Carolinas) were unwilling to share their true, essentially racist, opinions with pollsters, but once in the voting booth, acted out their true sentiments? They told pollsters they would vote for Thomas Bradley, the former black Democratic mayor of Los Angeles, but then elected a right-wing Republican. The French expert quoted above sensed this years ago when he remarked on the frequency of American church attendance: "Actual weekly observance is thus less than declared observance."[79]

If American attitudes toward religion continue to evolve along the lines the experts have traced, especially among the young; if they begin to track the beliefs and customs of their peers in other rich countries, instead of being outliers; if the current religious polarization becomes more acute, but with the extreme evangelical wing dwindling in size if not in passion; perhaps then it might be useful to ask this question more scientifically. A positive response would imply that even on this score, Americans are becoming more like everybody else in the rich world. It also means that Octavio Paz was mistaken, when he wrote in the 1970s that "the religious base of American democracy is not visible but no less powerful. More than a foundation, it is a buried root; the day it dries, the country will also dry."[80]

Were the answer to be affirmative, a possible explanation may lie in the smaller-than-life nature of one of the vaunted features of American religious exceptionalism, as noted from Tocqueville to Mak. The famous separation of *Church and State*, meaning the absence of a state-sponsored or protected religion as stipulated in the First Amendment, could—arguably—be distinctive of the United States in relation to other countries. It might also have emerged earlier than elsewhere. But there has never been a hermetic, total, iron-clad American separation of *religion and politics*. Indeed, even the first Chinese wall is lower, shorter, and more brittle than one may think.

The Declaration of Independence invokes God (the Creator) as a source and inspiration of rights, goals and guidance. American presidents—as well as almost all public officials, including Supreme Court justices—are sworn in with a Bible (or the equivalent for any other religion). Witnesses, defendants, and jurors appear before a judge and swear to tell the truth, etc., "so help you God." American paper currency after 1957 included the legend "In God we trust." This was also the era when the Pledge of Allegiance all public schoolchildren repeat every day started referring to "one nation under God." And as all naturalized American citizens know, the oath taken when they receive their American citizenship ends "so help me God." We will turn to the question of intelligent design and creationism in the following chapter; suffice it to say here that at a state level, where textbooks are drafted, chosen, and printed in the United States, there are multiple, official, religious views meant for children to read and assimilate.

America established a separation that impedes the consecration of *any one* religion over others. Nonetheless, it also recognized the official, state-sponsored pre-eminence of *religion as such* over non-religion, atheism, or agnosticism. This difference implies that the traditional explanation of American religiosity as the product of state-neutrality is only partially accurate. The tax-exempt status of churches in the United States is one reflection of this ambiguity. All charities are exempt, but churches are so because they are churches. The state-neutrality thesis is only partly valid. Americans were encouraged by the state they constructed to be religious in general, although not to worship in one church in particular. A partial recognition of this fact, and its disapproval by the Supreme Court, was written in a majority opinion by Justice David Souter in 2005, in *McCreary County v. ACLU of Kentucky*: "By showing a purpose to favor religion, the government ends the message to non-adherents that they are outsiders, not full members of the political community, and an accompanying message to adherents that they are insiders, favored members."[81]

So on the one hand, it should seem hardly surprising that after nearly two hundred and fifty years of official, state-sponsorship of religion, Americans should emerge as more religious than others. But on the other hand, given Americans' congenital suspicion and skepticism of all things state-inspired, that religiosity might also not be as ingrained or deep-seated as some might expect. Bryce, despite his cheerleading passages on the supposedly radical separation of Church and State in America, grasped this clearly, though he tended to minimize his own reservations: "There is no established Church . . . . But in several states there still exist qualifications Vermont and Delaware declare that every sect ought to maintain some form of religious worship, and Vermont adds that it ought to observe the Lord's Day. Six Southern states exclude from office anyone who denies the existence of a Supreme Being. Besides these six, Pennsylvania and Tennessee pronounce a man ineligible for office who does not believe in God. Maryland and Arkansas even make such a person incompetent as a juror and witness. The neutrality of the State cannot therefore be said to be theoretically complete."

More transcendent, however, was the imbrication of religion and politics from the very birth of the republic. Over the centuries, religion has placed itself on several sides of multiple ideological and political divides. It has been in favor of abolition, obviously, but also of Prohibition. It has fervently supported the civil rights movement, but also combatted abortion. It has opposed some wars—Vietnam, Central America—but also fought back against gay marriage. To even use the word religion, in the singular, is mistaken. Certain churches have adopted certain stances over the years; others have embraced different or opposing ones.

Mormons have tended to espouse the most conservative causes, as Evangelical Protestants do today. Jews, before 1947, focused on progressive issues, and since then, among other themes, on solidarity with Israel. Black Protestants have logically centered their political participation on the defense and promotion of African American causes, but not necessarily other themes that might be considered analogous: labor rights for all, immigration, or opposition to unjustifiable American foreign policy decisions. But it is almost impossible to find a moment in American history when one religious actor, or one church, was not deeply involved in a political controversy of the time. And politics, of course, is essentially centered on the realm of the state.

Over the years, nearly every one of these churches sought to convince or force the state—in American terms, the government—to intervene on their behalf. They hoped to abolish slavery or impose temperance. To defend civil rights or prohibit abortion and same-sex marriage. To uphold segregation in the South. To mobilize whites and blacks in favor of desegregation in the South. In other words, American churches were constantly searching for the state's engagement, in favor of their causes or beliefs, whatever they might have been, at any one time, for any given church. Perhaps few American churches have endeavored to become an "official" church—the Church of England, the Catholic Church in Italy. But practically all of them have fought to make the state defend, espouse, and materialize their views. This is perhaps more true in recent years than before. And it is easily discernible in American politics now.

There is an enormous identification today among Evangelical Protestants, whites over 45, and Trump voters. To the contrary, a broader alignment of black Protestants, Latino Catholics, non-religious groups, and smaller progressive "mainline Protestants" with the Democratic Party can be detected just about anywhere in the electorate but mainly on the coasts. According to a 2017 Gallup poll, "Americans who are highly religious are much more likely to approve of Donald Trump's performance in office . . . . The relationship between religiosity and Trump approval is mainly among non-Hispanic white Americans. Trump's approval is 64 percent among highly religious whites, twice as high as it is among whites who are not religious."[82] Trump has transformed what were labeled culture wars into political ones, for better or for worse. Ultimately, they were never cultural, but always political; so much so that Ronald Reagan and George W. Bush both resorted to this strategy also, perhaps less intensely. At least now, this is transparent to all.

As the polarization of American politics intensifies, the religious polarization apparently does also, in a well-defined context of shrinking religiosity in society as a whole. Each side struggles to involve the state on behalf of its convictions or interests, be they the choice of a Supreme Court justice, building a wall along the border with Mexico, expelling

Muslims from America, or reversing *Roe v. Wade*. Only the specialists can truly determine whether this politicization of religion is more acute than before. From a distant perspective, that of a foreign observer, it certainly seems so. The questions then remain: is this a product of greater intensity of American religiosity? Is it the result of the so-called creeping secularization that allows more people to admit their self-contradictory religiosity? Is secularization the inevitable consequence of modernity (as Weber put it after his already-cited visit to the United States)?[83] Or the last hurrah of a society that was never as religious as it claimed to be, but that now finds that life itself makes the implementation of its religious beliefs increasingly difficult, if not impossible? Can this final gasp simultaneously coexist with greater political engagement by some extremist religious segments?

In Putnam's phrasing, twenty years ago: "Americans are going to church less often than we did three or four decades ago, and the churches we go to are less engaged with the wider community."[84] *The Economist* concludes likewise: "The United States is now on a path towards secularism that is already far advanced in western Europe . . . . Gallup's numbers suggest Democrats are now about as religious as Britons are."[85] So it seems. America is increasingly resembling other rich countries in religion matters; appearances and one-sided numbers are deceiving in this regard, even in the age of Trump. As the demographics favorable to minorities, to the coasts, and to urban centers advance, the United States will gradually lose what is left of this exceptionality. As a vehicle for promoting outlying political positions and resisting "liberal" social change, America's "religious difference" will unavoidably also lose more of its punch.

In view of its growing convergence with other rich countries in so many fields—some of which we covered, some not—America will be forced to revisit, if not adopt, common solutions to the common challenges it shares with other rich countries. The gist of the previous hundreds of pages consists of one fundamental thread: the United States is slowly but surely becoming similar to everyone else, meaning the rest of the rich world, and the vast middle-class sectors of the not-so-rich nations. It is becoming truly modern and unexceptional. Excluding the most extreme cases of the "American difference"—or exceptions—which we will now examine.

9

The unforgivable: mass incarceration, the death penalty, guns, and intelligent design

THERE ARE FEW CLICHÉS as frequent and superficial as that which claims that *x* people, meaning foreigners, Mexicans, Germans, the French and Irish, etc., have a "love-hate relationship" with the United States. Like most commonplace utterances, this is both true and largely irrelevant. Which does not mean that specific foreigners have not expressed their admiration and affection for the United States over the years and then succumbed to radical disenchantment. After veneration came rejection; after awe came disappointment; after esteem came loathing. Among the many reasons for these drastic reversals of feeling, the American breach of contract with liberalism and tolerance stands out, either directly or implicitly. If these are two of the most attractive and salient traits that endeared America to countless visitors, refugees, immigrants, and simple observers, their dismissal or disrespect have often generated the greatest hostility.

Witness Thomas Mann, who arrived in the United States in 1938 and left, embittered, in 1952. He had already won the Nobel Prize for Literature (in 1929) and was a world-class celebrity when he began teaching at Princeton. His initial feelings about the adopted land of his exile were warm and grateful, according to one of his biographers: "Mann reacted very positively to America and noted, 'it is a blessing to me to sink roots into this soil, and every new tie confirms me in my feeling of being at home . . . . I find people here good-natured to the point of generosity in comparison with Europeans, and feel pleasantly sheltered in their midst.' "[1] He continued to think this way throughout the war and spoke endlessly to convince Americans and FDR (who invited him for dinner and to spend the night at the White House in 1941) to enter it. Mann lived a life of ease in America, first on the East Coast, then in Hollywood, along with a large group of German and European exiles devoted to the arts. His links with the movie industry, and the left, brought him to the attention of the House Un-American Activities Committee as early as 1947. He was subsequently hounded by the FBI and McCarthyism, all the more so after his defense of the Rosenbergs (electrocuted in 1953 for espionage), Paul Robeson, and W. E. B. Dubois.

When he departed, he despised American and America, again according to this biographer: "There was a radical change from Mann's first positive impressions of America to his bitter and furious response to the malicious personal attacks. He privately called them witch-hunts, combining the worst traits in the American character, 'a disgusting exhibition of primitive Puritanism, hatred, fear, corruption and self-righteousness . . . . [T]he sick tense atmosphere of this country oppresses me and I have to steel myself, despite trembly nerves, to ward off detestable and mortally dangerous attacks on me . . . . I have no desire to rest my bones in this soulless soil [to] which I owe nothing, and which knows nothing of me.' "[2]

Or take Jean-Paul Sartre. On the one hand, at the end of the war, during his time in New York as a foreign correspondent for *Le Figaro* and *Combat*, he adored the United States, bending over backward even in regard to racism and segregation: "Yes, blacks from Chicago live in sheds; it is neither fair nor democratic. But many of our white workers live in sheds that are even more miserable. These injustices never seemed to me to be a defect of American society, but rather, a sign of the imperfections of our time."[3] He also praised the country like few before him, mixing in criticisms of Europe, admiration for Faulkner and Dos Passos, and the beauty of America: "What really fascinated us, as European petty-bourgeois that we were, born of parents deeply attached to the land of our farms, intellectuals stuck forever in Paris, was the constant flow of men across an entire continent, the exodus of an entire village toward the orchards of California, the hopeless wanderings of the hero of *Light in August* and of the rootless souls torn this way and that by the storms of *The 42nd Parallel*."[4] On the other hand, the French existentialist philosopher would become, twenty years later, one of the fiercest critics not only of the war in Vietnam, not only of the United States' government, but also of its society itself, devoting many issues of *Les Temps Modernes* to damning everything American.

Other visitors never liked America, and said so vehemently, even stridently, although they spent years in the country, not so much writing as vacationing or ruminating over its fate, and theirs. Rudyard Kipling is a fine example, especially since his *American Notes* are totally devoid of any political correctness, politeness, or even tact. After his first visit, before he settled in Vermont for four years, he traveled from San Francisco to New York and had much to say concerning his voyage. About Chicago, he wrote; "Having seen it, I urgently desire never to see it again. It is inhabited by savages. Its water is the water of the Hooghly, and its air is dirt. Also it says that it is the 'boss' town of America . . . . They told me to go to the Palmer House, which is overmuch gilded and mirrored, and there I found a huge hall of tessellated marble crammed with people talking about money, and spitting about everywhere. Other barbarians charged in and out of this inferno with letters and telegrams in their hands, and yet others shouted at each other."[5] And about the United States in general: "It makes me regard your interesting nation with the same shuddering curiosity, that I should bestow on a Pappan cannibal chewing the scalp off his mother's skull. Does that convey any idea to your mind? It makes me regard the whole pack of you as heathens—real heathens—not the sort you send missions to— creatures of another flesh and blood."[6] Good thing he did not tell his readers what he really thought . . . .

Consider one of the earlier observers, who spent nearly a year in the United States in 1827–8. Frances Trollope had many fine things to say about the new republic, but once she concluded her stay, she made no effort to conceal her state of mind: "I suspect that what I have written will make it evident that I do not like America. Now, as it happens that I met with individuals there whom I love and admire, far beyond the love and admiration of ordinary acquaintance, and as I declare the country to be fair to the eye, and most richly teeming with the gifts of plenty, I am led to ask myself why it is that I do not like it. I would willingly know myself, and confess to others, why it is that neither its beauty nor its abundance can suffice to neutralize, or greatly soften, the distate which the aggregate of my recollections has left upon my mind . . . . I speak not of these, but of the population generally, as seen in town and country, among the rich and the poor, in the slave states and the free states. I do not like them. I do not like their principles. I do not like their manners. I do not like their opinions . . . . But when a native of Europe visits America, a most extraordinary species of tyranny is set in action against him; and as far as my reading and experienced have enabled me to judge, it is such as no other country has ever exercised against strangers."[7] A final diatribe comes from a Mexican anarchist, Ricardo Flores Magón, who was a precursor of the Mexican revolution of 1910, an ally in the United States of the Industrial Workers of the World, or Wobblies, and who died in Leavenworth Prison in Kansas in 1922. In a speech in Texas in 1908, he lambasted his American hosts, who did, repeatedly and undeniably, mistreat him till his death: "Who among you has not received an insult in this country for the mere fact of being a Mexican? Who has not heard tell of the crimes that are committed daily against people of our race? Don't you know that in the South Mexicans aren't allowed to sit in the same table as Americans in restaurants? Have you not walked into a barber shop and, after being looked up and down, been told that Mexicans aren't served there? Don't you know that American jails are full of Mexicans? And have you even counted the number of Mexicans who have been sent to the gallows or been burned by brutal mobs of white people?"[8]

The direct link between these reactions (many more could be added) and America's breaking of its pledge of tolerance and liberalism is neither direct nor obvious. But these sentiments, as well as their roots, are symptomatic, though they may vary over time. Other features of the American experience have been admired or criticized by travelers; few have generated the virulence expressed in these citations. Nearly everything about the United States' two-and-a-half centuries of existence is explainable and understandable—not justifiable or worthy of approval—in both the hearts and the minds of most foreign observers. Each one notes his or her exceptions, naturally enough. For myself, there are four that I cannot countenance. They are, in no particular order, mass incarceration, guns, the death penalty, and intelligent design/creationism. The inclusion of this last notion may surprise some readers, given the less than proportionate damage it wreaks compared to the others. I will explain this anomaly. What follows is one foreigner's rejection of these unfortunate American clashes with what the United State stands for, either as outgrowths of other features or as exceptions *per se*.

I write this at a time when some might consider that there are many other, more objectionable facets of American life. The Trump era has exacerbated many negative aspects of American reality, especially for foreigners subject to his bullying, whether in their country or Trump's. I am forced to agree that infringement of the United States' rules of tolerance and liberalism has gone much further since 2016, extending well beyond the exceptions addressed in the following pages. These are terrible years for America, its neighbors, its friends, and even its adversaries or rivals. Telling the story of these dark times and making a damage assessment is a necessary task that will nonetheless only be undertaken when this period comes to an end. In the meantime, I prefer to concentrate on four critical issues, partly because I fear that they will remain with us even after the storm has passed.

Mass incarceration

Mass incarceration began in the 1970s, partly as a result of a series of laws in various states summed up as mandatory minimum sentencing. So-called three strikes and you're out laws also proliferated. In New York state they came to be known as Rockefeller Laws; elsewhere, they varied in their intensity, but not in their intention. They sought to imprison as many law-offenders as possible, for as many offenses as possible, for as long as possible. They were the symptoms of deeper trends, mainly the law and order, subliminally racist rhetoric introduced by Richard Nixon, and the perceived—and largely real though uneven—crime wave across the United States. As the number of prisons and prisoners rose, the private prison industry's clout did too.

The phenomenon has been widely studied but there are four aspects of this hateful policy that merit comment. First, the increase in mass incarceration from the early seventies through today has been exponential. Second, it is radically exceptional among rich and even poor countries. Third, it affects people of color disproportionately. Finally, it entails long-term consequences, as the prison population, once freed, continues to bear the stigma of time in jail.

In 1972, the overall prison population in the United States totaled somewhat less than 200,000; in 2019 it amounted to 2.2 million, having reached its peak in 2009, at nearly 2.5 million. In the words of one specialist, "The American criminal justice system holds almost 2.3 million people in 1,719 state prisons, 109 federal prisons, 1,772 juvenile correctional facilities, 3,163 local jails, and 80 Indian Country jails as well as in military prisons, immigration detention facilities, civil commitment centers, state psychiatric hospitals, and prisons in the U.S. territories."[9] The increase was almost thirteenfold. Since 2009, a consistent, but slight and gradual drop has occurred: about 7 percent in total, or a bit more than 0.5 percent per year.[10] While many celebrate this decline, it is minuscule compared to the rate that would be necessary for the United States to achieve other rich country levels.

There has been a concomitant increase in the resources spent every year on prisons, the number of prisons (to deal with the overcrowding crisis), the population in the corrections system, the number of life sentences, and the population with some type of criminal history that currently remains under the watch of the correction system (either on probation or parole). All of these statistics have expanded enormously since the early seventies, when Nixon declared his war on drugs, and mainly after 1980, when Ronald and Nancy Reagan declared theirs. There has never been a time in American history with similar totals and analogous increases. It is an unprecedented horror that stems partly from drug-related offenses, mostly of a non-violent, petty nature. The growth of these prison-provoking crimes has approximately tracked that of the incarcerated population over these years. More people are serving more time for more drug-related offenses. Today, 20 percent of all prisoners and 50 percent of those in federal prisons are drug-related offenders.[11] And among drug users or dealers, the mass incarceration racial bias we will describe below is also present: whites are imprisoned for cocaine powder–related offenses; blacks for crack-related ones.

A central explanation resides in the rise of crime during the seventies and eighties; the cycle is not unique to the United States. There was a huge spike of criminal conduct during those decades. Many Americans became so infuriated that they were willing to adopt almost any approach to deal with what they saw as a crisis. Some readers might recall the Willie Horton spot George H. W. Bush used against Michael Dukakis in 1988, associating the Democratic candidate with a convicted murderer who committed other ghastly crimes while on a weekend furlough. A third reason apparently lies in prosecutorial power, even when crime rates begin to diminish. As a recent article on the subject suggested, "by handing enormous discretion to prosecutors—some of them, by the standards of the rest of the world, properly described as politicians, elected to their office and sensitive to voters' needs, including a metric of success linked to putting people in jail—we had given them the freedom to imprison whomever they wished for as long as they liked."[12] These prosecutors, for a series of reasons, including the risky option of going to trial given lengthy sentences, preferred to coerce guilty pleas, even for shorter sentences.

This was an unparalleled trend. No country in the world for which there are reliable statistics suffers from a comparable scourge. The United States includes 5 percent of the world's population and almost a quarter of its prisoners.[13] The incarceration rate is between five and ten times higher than the other wealthy countries: nine times higher than Germany, eight times higher than Italy, five times higher than the UK, and fifteen times higher than Japan. Not even China, with an authoritarian regime as brutal as any other in the world, surpasses the United States. In per capita terms, it jails one-fourth of the people American does; Russia, about two-thirds.[14] At its peak, there were "more people under 'correctional supervision' in America—more than 6 million—than were in the Gulag Archipelago under Stalin at its height."[15]

There are, of course, multiple explanations for the immense gap between European, Canadian, and Japanese incarceration rates, and that of the United States. One is the right to bear arms. The number of assaults in New York and London is roughly the same; the New York figure for murders, mostly with firearms, is much larger. Another factor, probably more relevant, is the length of sentences. According to several sources quoted by *The New York Times* some years ago, "the mere number of sentences imposed here would not place the United States at the top of the incarceration lists. If lists were compiled based on annual admissions to prison per capita, several European countries would outpace the United States. But American prison stays are much longer, so the total incarceration rate is higher. Burglars in the United States serve an average of 16 months in prison, compared with 5 months in Canada and 7 months in England."[16] There is also a correlation between skin color and sentence length, difficult to quantify but real.

Additional elements are mentioned in many of these analyses. The American obsession with drug enforcement is evidently one of them. American democracy's peculiar attribute of electing prosecutors and judges, and subjecting them to public opinion's sensitivities, as already stated, is another. At some level, race is a factor. The question very few want to ask is not if mass incarceration affects African Americans and Latinos disproportionately; obviously it does. The real counterfactual uncertainty is whether in the absence of people of color in the United States, would the incarceration rates be the same? Not because people of color are more prone to breaking the law, but rather because they are incarcerated in greater numbers since they are . . . people of color. The apparently absurd notion might be accurate. Given American racism, if America were all lily-white, the prison population might be similar to that of the other rich countries. Whites wouldn't countenance comparable numbers for themselves, but discriminatory prosecution of crimes, a consequence of police and prosecutorial discretion, are also important factors.

Moreover, a vicious cycle is at work here. The enormous growth of the prison population led to a spectacular increase in the number of privately owned and managed prisons. Once they emerged, the prison business became an interested party, along with prison guard unions and other lobbies, in maintaining a high level of incarceration. Empty prisons don't make money.

Finally, perhaps as a result of higher levels of violence in all walks of life than in the other OECD nations, for historical, social, cultural, and even psychological motives, Americans are willing to pay a higher price for what they believe are remedies to that violence. Canada's crime rates rise and fall in relative symmetry to those of the United States. But the incarceration rates are infinitely lower. Would Canadians countenance American indices? With their budgetary, ethnic, long-term consequences? Apparently not. Citizens of the United States seem willing to accept all of the consequences of mass incarceration. Or rather: white, Anglo, middle-class, non-college-educated, over-50 American voters appear to tolerate having an enormous African American and Hispanic prison population in exchange for lower levels of violence, supposing the tradeoff were valid. I will return to this tradeoff.

Meanwhile, though, the third feature of mass incarceration cannot be sufficiently emphasized, and it has to do, precisely, with race. According to one calculation, one out of every three black boys born today can expect to go to prison in his lifetime, as can one of every six Latino boys—compared to one of every seventeen white boys.[17] This is simply the extreme expression of what everybody knows. Mass incarceration affects African Americans and Latinos not only more than whites, but massively more than their share of the population of the United States. Blacks make up 12 percent of the population; they constitute 33 percent of people in prison. Hispanics constitute 16 percent of the county's inhabitants; their share of the incarcerated pool is 23 percent. Though adult African Americans and Hispanics make up approximately 28 percent of the US population, they comprised 56 percent of all incarcerated people in 2017.[18] Two-thirds of the people sentenced to life in prison are people of color. For all men born in the United States in 2001, the likelihood of imprisonment is one in nine, an extraordinarily high rate compared to other rich countries. For black men, I repeat, *it was one in three!*[19]

No doubt can exist that a racial bias exists in mass incarceration, and a particularly painful one for me: a large share of the imprisoned Hispanic population is of Mexican origin. The reason is evident: Latinos make up a large portion of the people in jail, and Mexican-origin people make up a large share of the Hispanic population. It seems doubtful that anyone would seek to jail Mexican-Americans *per se*. It is simply a fact of life, and a consequence of the overall policy.

There is a discussion of whether the racial bias finds its roots in race, or in class, but that debate is even more troublesome than the racial one. One can make the case that the prison population is predominantly black and Latino because in any country, at any given time, the poor are more likely to be incarcerated than the rest of society. And in American society, as I have stressed repeatedly, along with everyone else, the poor are predominantly black and Hispanic, or blacks and Hispanics are poorer than everyone else. So it can be argued that mass incarceration does not target African Americans or Latinos; it targets the poor, who just so happen to be predominantly black and Hispanic, although incarceration rates for poor whites are also "abnormally" high. Whether it is race, poverty, drugs, inner city neighborhoods, or disunited families, an indisputable racial and/or ethnic bias has characterized law enforcement in the United States since the early seventies. The consequences of this bias are undeniable.

The rate of incarceration of young African American males is so incredibly high that the consequences for black families, women, and children cannot be escaped or dismissed. These are hundreds of thousands of children without fathers, wives without husbands, mothers without sons to assist them as the years go by. The fact that the overall, maddeningly slow downward trend in incarceration has been particularly reflected in Latino and African American rates is welcome. Nonetheless, the gap between people of color and whites is so wide, and the level from which the decline starts so high, that the drop can scarcely bring hope to anyone, even if it is preferable to its contrary. There is simply no country in the world that faces a challenge of this magnitude or impact.

Lastly, mass incarceration has long-lived consequences for the future. Each year, 650,000 men and women nationwide return from prison to their communities. They face nearly 50,000 federal, state, and local legal restrictions that make it difficult to reintegrate back into society.[20] More than 10 million people are admitted to jails (meaning county and city detention centers, often only overnight) in the United States every year.[21] In other words, the number of people who come into contact with prison every year, one way or another, is astounding. But it gets worse.

There is a lively discussion among experts as to what exactly constitutes a criminal record in the United States. Is it just an arrest, without a conviction? Is it a conviction? Is it serving time in jail before bail, the trial, then acquittal? By the broadest definition—not necessarily accurate but the one most widely quoted—nearly a third of the adult working-age population has a criminal record. Two different research centers, the Brennan Center for Justice and The Sentencing Project, have estimated that between 70 million and 100 million American people have records indexed by the FBI's Interstate Identification Index. The Brennan Center states that "America now houses roughly the same number of people with criminal records as it does four-year college graduates. If all arrested Americans were a nation, they would be the world's eighteenth largest, ahead of Canada, France and Australia. The number of Americans with criminal records today is larger than the entire U.S. population in 1900."[22]

In other words, the effects of mass incarceration do not suddenly vanish once someone leaves prison. There is an entire universe of people free in society who continue to pay the price of their earlier imprisonment, at an enormous cost to them and to the country. Foreign students of the American prison, like Michel Foucault, understood this decades ago: "But prison (in the United States) is not only punitive; it is also one of the tools of the process of elimination. Prison is the physical elimination of people who leave it, who die there—sometimes directly, sometimes indirectly—to the extent that they cannot find a job, have no means of subsistence, can no longer form a family. By moving from one prison to another, from one crime to another, they end up being truly physically eliminated."[23]

I mentioned the cost of thousands of restrictions in general. One specific cost consists in the obstacles to employment that ex-felons face constantly. Not everyone with a "criminal record" encounters these difficulties, and in recent times a number of policies have been implemented to eliminate excessively rigorous (or exceedingly superficial) background checks. Nonetheless, it can be excruciatingly complicated for anyone with some type of antecedent to find a job, particularly if the person is African American or Hispanic. One survey shows that five years after leaving prison, two-thirds of former inmates remained unemployed.[24]

A second consequence lies in disenfranchisement, which I discussed in Chapter 4. Somewhat more than 6 million American citizens cannot vote in their country because they are ex-felons or currently incarcerated; the post-prison (or ex-felons) total is roughly half that number.[25] A debate surfaced during the 2019–20 presidential campaign about whether imprisoned citizens should be entitled to vote, as opposed to ex-felons, who obviously should. While the debate is a valid one, the fact that such an enormous pool of people finds itself disenfranchised, knowing that a disproportionate volume is black or Latino, should give pause to many about the electoral consequences of mass incarceration. The only reason so many members of society are disenfranchised for having been incarcerated is because so many were incarcerated.

The entire discussion about voter suppression through ex-felon, or felon, disenfranchisement would end if there were so few felons or ex-felons that their suffrage became irrelevant. Hopefully the successful Florida ballot initiative mentioned earlier can contribute to such a change. We are not there yet.

A third, and particularly pernicious, post-prison consequence of mass incarceration relates to education. In many states, and indirectly at a federal level, "ex-cons" are ineligible for scholarships such as Pell Grants, affirmative action, automatic entry, and other forms of educational support. Sometimes the restrictions are explicit; more frequently, they occur *de facto*. Either way, they can be devastating, and among other factors, lead frequently to recidivism. There are also long-term consequences of mass incarceration in health and family structures. Most importantly, perhaps, the share of mass incarceration that corresponds to non-violent, petty, drug-possession crimes represents an enormous toll for American society. People who were poor, barely educated, perhaps with some type of criminal propensity, but certainly not hardboiled criminals, were incarcerated for minor offenses. In prison, they became what they were not: hardened criminals, who if they were ever released, turned into a small army of "bad *hombres*" through no fault of their own.

There is no justification for this American exception. Some will object that soaring crime rates in the seventies and eighties and their ensuing decline in the nineties and later more than warranted and vindicated mass incarceration. For that to be true, they would have to prove that the drop in crime levels over the past quarter-century is a result of mass incarceration. According to a 2015 study by the Brennan Center for Justice, falling crime rates cannot be ascribed to mass incarceration. Conversely, Steven Levitt showed in a 2004 paper that at least 58 percent of the violent crime drop in the 1990s was due to filling up prisons.

Advocates of mass incarceration would have to demonstrate that the cost of widespread detention outweighed that of crime itself; and that alternative choices were sub-optimum. None of these cases have been made. The causal relationship has not been established. There are so many intervening factors, ranging from the Clinton-era economic boom to mass immigration—implying lower crime rates, as has been well documented—and including better and more numerous police forces in many cities. All we know, nearly fifty years after the experience was initiated, is that no nation in the world followed this path. Some rich countries have worse crime figures than the United States; others, not. The American homicide rate is three to four times higher than for the larger OECD nations. But numbers for robbery, serious assault, theft of private cars are all comparable, with the exception of Japan, which has the lowest rates of any wealthy society.[26] There is, unfortunately, a possible and likely explanation for the United States' homicide data: it is called the Second Amendment, to which I will return below.

The consequences of extensive imprisonment have been devastating for broad swathes of American society. The contradiction between these infamous policies and choices, on the one hand, and classical United States' liberalism and tolerance, on the other, is flagrant, powerful, and inadmissible for the rest of the world. It is one of the remaining and powerful obstacles to modernity for America.

Capital punishment

While different, of course, the death penalty in the United States is inevitably associated with mass incarceration. It seems to expose the same attitude Americans possess with regard to crime and punishment. It reflects their views on retribution and false ideas about what works and what doesn't in a given society, at a given time, on a given issue.

Except for a brief period in the 1970s, the death penalty has been enforced in the United States since Independence. It has been used in military tribunals, outside the framework of the law (through lynchings), for political purposes (the Rosenbergs), to placate mobs as well as to accommodate virulently conservative sectors of society, and in violation of American international commitments (especially the Vienna Convention on Consular Protection). Today, there are 2700 people in the United States awaiting execution.[27]

The only other rich country that implements capital punishment is Japan (and, arguably, Taiwan). All others have *de facto* or *de jure* abolished it over the past thirty or forty years. In addition to Japan, the few democratic countries where it remains in place are India (rarely

used), Jordan, Indonesia, and Jamaica. China is by far the most assid-
uous perpetrator, executing more people every year than all other nations combined. The company the United States finds itself in includes
countries like North Korea, Cuba, Iran, Syria, Sudan, and Saudi Arabia.

The death penalty was *de facto* suspended in the United States between 1972 and 1976 by the Supreme Court, which threw out forty
state statutes establishing guidelines or conditions for its application.
Between 1967 and 1977, when Norman Mailer's Gary Gilmore was
shot by a firing squad in Utah, a virtual moratorium on executions
was upheld in the United States. But from then on, for all practical
purposes, the Supreme Court ruled that the death penalty was constitutional. For federal crimes, it was not applied between 1964 and
2000, but was reinstated in one case in 2003. In recent years, the actual
number of deaths by state government decision has declined sharply,
and a growing number of states have in fact, if not with legal arguments,
barred capital punishment.

Once again, the death penalty in the United States, like mass incarceration, is not color-blind, either for defendants/perpetrators or
victims. Of the roughly 1500 executions carried out between 1976 and
2019, 43 percent were of people of color (34 percent African American,
9 percent Hispanic). Forty-five percent of all prisoners on death row
in 2018 were black or Latino. In 2001 there were more than fifty
Mexicans awaiting execution. When Mexico sued the United States at
the International Court of Justice (ICJ) in The Hague in 2003, one
of its main arguments consisted in the difference of outcomes when
foreigners accused of terrible misdeeds had access to counsel, translation, and consular protection. Mexico won its suit. The Bush administration admitted its defeat, but subsequently Texas, where most of the
death-row Mexicans were located, responded that it was not a party to
the treaty that created the ICJ. The Supreme Court backed the Lone
Star State and punted to Congress. If the latter determined that states be
bound by the international obligations assumed by the federal government, it should say so. Congress hasn't, and probably won't, for years.

The arguments sustained by American advocates of capital punishment have all been rejected by legislators, judges, or voters in other rich
countries. It is not a deterrent to violent crime: as we saw, the murder
rate in the United States is higher than elsewhere. It is not necessarily

popular (as if this were an argument in its favor): Americans have see-sawed between their support and rejection of the death penalty since polls exist. That many states have abolished it in recent years is not truly relevant: the vast majority of executions take place in a limited number of pro-death states, such as Texas, Oklahoma, Florida, Louisiana, and Arkansas. The first state delivers half of all executions in the country.

Other explanations Americans offer when questioned on their outlier status are plain silly. An initial one is just false, in addition to inhuman: execution costs less than life imprisonment. It doesn't, because no condemned man goes to the gallows willingly. Every sentenced criminal fights to the last minute, and the cost for the states of litigation is much higher than that of maintenance. The next one, that this constitutes a state matter, and each state can decide whatever it desires in this regard, is anachronistic and untenable in a globalized world. Since 1648, nation-states have been the only actors in international affairs and international law. Today, the issue of non-state actors has acquired relevance, but "states' rights" in US speak have not. Even the Catalonians do not pretend to isolate themselves from the world. On the contrary, they hope one day—in vain, I think—to join the European Union as a new member. The issue of states' rights regarding fundamental human rights—in one word, slavery—was settled in 1865. That Texas never signed the Geneva Conventions is about as weak and insular an argument as anyone could make.

Another contention is more complicated. It involves three axes: retribution, deterrence, and the violent nature of American society. The extreme case for retribution is the well-known, despicable right some states provide for relatives of a murdered victim: witnessing the execution of the perpetrator. Yes, it is true that the English publicly decapitated or disemboweled criminals they sentenced to death. The French Revolution invented the guillotine to exercise mass terror in public; the Aztecs held human sacrifice rites in the pyramids and shrines in the middle of Tenochtitlán, and Rome crucified early Christians, and others, long before. In the United States the last public execution took place in 1936 in Kentucky, when 20,000 people witnessed the hanging of a black man accused of raping and murdering a white woman. That's the point. No one thinks today these were great ideas, and they were suppressed centuries ago in some countries, decades ago in others. Saudi Arabia and Iran hold public beheadings, hangings, and lapidation, but they are not exactly examples for the rest of the world.

Retribution implies that the crime committed was perpetrated against a victim's entourage, not against society or the state. This is false. The crimes were carried out against society. Only society, through the state and the law, can decide what type of retribution, if any, it requires. Prison is punishment for breaking the law, not retribution for having hurt someone, as painful as it might be to admit it. Revenge or vengeance are not sources of inspiration for the law; nor is an eye for an eye. The proportionality of punishment for the crime committed has limits. No state, not even the most barbaric, punishes torture with torture, rape with rape, or kidnapping with kidnapping.

Deterrence is also a false argument, and for well-known reasons. To begin with, it does not hold up. All of the rich countries that abolished the death penalty enjoy lower rates of violent crime, particularly homicides, than the United States.[28] Only Japan, has both low levels of violence and the death penalty, although capital punishment is rarely resorted to. Moreover, no country that abolished the death penalty over the past half-century witnessed a leap in its crime rate, and particularly in the number of homicides.

The same is true in America. States that eliminated capital punishment *de jure* or *de facto*, like Massachusetts since 1947, have violent crime rates lower or similar to states that are attached to it, like Texas or Oklahoma.[29] Murder rates are actually lower in states without the death penalty.[30] No negative correlation has been established between violent crime, or crime at all, and the death penalty within the United States. Which makes sense: the fear factor that underlies the notion of deterrence does not seem relevant to the type of criminals who commit crimes punishable by death. They don't Google various possible crimes before committing them to see which ones are not subject to fatal injections. Moreover, the fact that a relatively small percentage of murder convictions actually lead to the death penalty undercuts its effect as a deterrent. Thankfully.

Lastly, there is history. America is a land attached to certain traditions that are part of its national character, it is argued (by those who for this purpose sustain that history *does* matter). This may make it an outlier, but that is the way it is. Historical explanations exist for the persistence of the death penalty, and they are pretty much perennial, or unmovable, in this view. The rest of the world may not like it, but Americans will continue to apply the death penalty whenever and for whatever reasons they see fit. In its own peculiar fashion, capital punishment forms part of the American creed. This is not a straw man, but a line of reasoning implicit in much of the narrative in Mailer's "The Executioner's Song," written back in 1979, when Gary Gilmore's execution in Utah marked the renewed use of the death penalty in the United States. Most significantly, according to this narrative, the United States is a more violent society than others, for myriad reasons of all natures.

This is all hogwash. Depending on the moment, half the population of the United States, or slightly more, is in favor of the death penalty; half, or slightly less, opposes it. This is roughly analogous to the proportions in other rich countries, before abolition. Some saw the ratio vary after suspension; others witnessed its constancy. There is nothing special about the United States in this regard. Furthermore, America itself has experienced relatively long periods when no executions took place. It lived through phases—the thirties, for example—when many were carried out, but there were also other eras characterized by a moderate number of executions. There is no clear, historical pattern, one way or another, except for the fact of capital punishment itself. Similarly, there are states where no gassings, hangings, electrocutions, or injections have occurred for more than a century, like Michigan, Wisconsin, and Maine, and others that still practice them frequently. The inhabitants of Rhode Island, Connecticut, or Oregon are as typically American as those of Florida or Nebraska (which outlawed the death penalty, by the way, in 2017).

And American society is no more violent than other rich nations. It simply accepts policies, attitudes, and anachronisms that others have eliminated. It might seem nasty to bring it up in this fashion, but Germany does not exactly have a history of non-violence, for example. The British in Northern Ireland, the French in Algeria, the Belgians in the Congo, the Dutch in Indonesia were not precisely choir boys as far as violence was concerned. Not to mention Russia, at practically every stage in its history, a country that abolished the death penalty in 1999. In addition, these countries all employed capital punishment before abolition, and with minor exceptions, none are the worse for it or regret it.

Finally, the best refutation of American exceptionalism as the reason for retaining the death penalty resides in a simple fact. More and more American states are jettisoning executions. Over the past decade, one way or another, Connecticut, Delaware, California, Pennsylvania, Colorado, Illinois, Maryland, Nebraska, New Mexico, and Washington, among others, have banned executions. Soon half the states—with more than half the population—will be no-death-penalty states; the only populous ones conserving it will be Texas and Florida. The trend seems unmistakable. If it were contrary to the American way, it would not be underway.

There is no American historical or congenital violent DNA that justifies this aberration. If anything, the application of the death penalty overwhelmingly to poor, or black, or Latino defendants makes it more acceptable to many Americans; one can question whether it would survive if everyone who murdered were to be executed. The only real explanation stems from inertia, and the inability to change that in turn emanates from a dysfunctional political system. The Supreme Court will not have an anti-death penalty majority for years to come. The Congress, for all the reasons reviewed in Chapter 4, will not move in this direction. No president will dare act unilaterally, supposing he or she could. So capital punishment will endure like marijuana penalization, until state by state it withers and disappears; this would perhaps be a logical outcome for such a decentralized, federalist, diverse nation. As Stephen Pinker puts it, "The American death penalty is not so much being abolished as falling apart piece by piece."[31] Meanwhile, it remains as one of America's pending *aggiornamenti*: another example of its penchant for insisting on being out of step with the rest of the modern world.

Guns

Weapons possession self-evidently represents a possible root cause of the two previous themes. Mass incarceration—at least the part springing from violent crime—and the death penalty for murder are hard to separate from the current application of the Second Amendment and the American right to bear arms.

Apparently, the only other country in the world to enshrine gun ownership in its constitution is Guatemala. Mexico has a similar provision, but it is totally ignored by the millions of Mexicans who own guns illegally. If there is one American characteristic besides race that foreigners tend to deplore and be baffled by it is the availability and proliferation of all types of guns in the United States, the number of Americans who own them, and the incredible growth of mass shootings by people who may or may not have purchased them legally. There is no explanation for it, in the eyes of those who report on, analyze, and speculate about tragic episodes from Columbine to Newtown. That similar tragedies take place elsewhere—in Norway, in New Zealand, in London—is a different matter. They occur despite gun control, not as a result of its absence. American historian Richard Hofstadter regretted half a century ago "the uniqueness of the United States as the only modern industrial nation that persists in maintaining a gun culture."[32] It has a historical origin, as one of the essential technological devices of nation-building and westward expansion, along with the railroads and barbed wire. It is difficult to imagine the conquest of Mexico, the West, and the Southwest without a collective and individual gun culture.

Americans were not always so attached to guns. It is only after 1850 that households began to harbor them on a large scale, partly thanks to technological changes: the first Colt revolvers and Remington rifles; repeating guns; rimfire cartridges. The Civil War required mass production, lowering prices because of increasing returns to scale. Between 1860 and 1865 prices shrank by a quarter. It was one thing to have the right to bear arms, but another to actually exercise that right. "Research into domestic inventories from 1765 and 1790 has shown that only 15 percent of the households studied were in possession of firearms."[33] The Second Amendment did not become law because everyone already had guns. On the contrary, people began to acquire guns only many years after its adoption.

The numbers are staggering and familiar. Regarding all types of weapons, there may be more firearms in the United States than people, including children. Estimates for the total number of weapons range from 265 million to 390 million. If we stick to handguns, by definition not owned for hunting, Americans possess nearly 120 small arms for every one hundred individuals. The next two countries in line, excluding nations at war like Yemen, that is, Canada and Finland, reach the low thirties. Most non-northern, low-hunting rich countries are much further down the list: the United Kingdom with five guns per hundred inhabitants, Japan, virtually none.[34] The United States has around 5 percent of the world's population, and 42 percent of the civilian-owned guns on the globe.[35]

These figures correlate closely with gun-related homicides. As I already described in relation to crime in general, the United States has the highest homicide rate with guns of any rich country, and by far.[36] Only nations at war or Latin American countries like Honduras, Venezuela, Colombia, Mexico, and Brazil, for example, have higher gun-homicide figures; Turkey, Iran, Jordan, even Iraq, all have lower numbers.[37] The causal relationship can be argued endlessly. America experiences higher homicide rates because it has more guns, or it owns more guns because it suffers from more homicide rates. But regardless of the direction in which the causality runs, the two figures are radical exceptions in the wealthy nations.

The same type of correlation exists among states. Those that have the highest percentage of gun ownership—Alaska, Arkansas, Idaho, and Wyoming—also feature the greatest number of gun deaths per 100,000 residents. This is especially revealing if one considers the fact the United States does not suffer from an exceptionally high non-violent or non-gun crime rate; it is only when gun violence is included that the data change. I mentioned the comparison between New York and London as far as assaults and burglaries are concerned. New York has fewer of these that do not entail guns than London, but astonishingly more crimes with guns than the British capital. More guns equals more gun violence seems to be a fair assessment. The most tragic correlation appears to involve suicides: the greater the number of guns, the larger the total of suicides. In sum, as a study by the Harvard School of Public Health concluded: "Gun availability is a risk factor for homicide, both in the United States and across high-income countries . . . where there are more guns, both men and women are at a higher risk for homicide, particularly firearm homicide . . . . [S]tates with higher levels of household gun ownership had higher rates of firearm homicide and overall homicide." [38]

Therefore there is also a far greater number of mass shooting incidents in the United States than in any other comparable country. The petty arguments sometimes espoused by gun advocates, including

Donald Trump, that these tragedies took place because no one had a gun available to stop them, or that the killer would have been allowed to buy a gun even with background checks, or "people kill people, guns don't kill people," are all unsustainable to a non-US audience. Suffice it to say that according to an authoritative source, there is around one mass shooting every day in America, defined as shootings where four or more people were shot at, regardless of the number of actual deaths.[39] Each mass shooting generates a minor—or powerful—wave of public reaction in favor of gun control. The wave dissipates as quickly as it emerged, and nothing is done. Even the Clinton assault weapons bill of 1994 was allowed to expire by George W. Bush and Congress in 2004.

Still, given the number of guns in the hands of people who should not possess them, one can reasonably ask: why aren't Americans killing themselves in far greater numbers? There are at least two conceivable answers. One is Trump's: the fact that so many people are armed explains why there is not even more violence than already prevails. The other is somewhat less cynical. Americans do respect the rule of law and know full well that, with a few very tightly defined exceptions, shooting people is illegal. Scant consolation perhaps, but it could be worse.

Many observers and governments outside the United States feel that the US arms industry, particularly the small arms chapter, has a disproportionate impact on gun laws. It is true that during Obama's first term, for example, gun manufacturers doubled their production.[40] Between 2006 and 2017, civilians in the United States purchased 122 million new or imported firearms.[41] It would stand to reason that these business results and prospects would move the industry toward a rabid, entrenched opposition to any kind of gun control. Similarly, other lobbies, mainly the National Rifle Association (NRA), fight controls to the bitter end. The NRA's outsized influence on American politics has undoubtedly contributed significantly to the gun epidemic. Single-issue lobbies, combined with unwitting though warranted identity politics peculiarities, are a distinguishing feature of today's political system.

The dysfunctional nature of the American political system practically guarantees that change in this field, as with the death penalty, is not around the corner. Over-representation of rural states and conservative, under-populated ones still subsists and neutralizes any chance of repealing the Second Amendment. Too much money is sloshing around in opposition to more modest measures, such as reinstating the assault weapons ban, significant background checks, eliminating bump-stocks (effected by an executive decree, but not by congressional action), or cracking down on illegal US arms exports to Mexico. After the "Fast and Furious" scandal, whereby the Obama Administration allowed an illegal shipment of arms to be sent to Mexico in order to track and arrest the perpetrators and beneficiaries, much has been said about illegal arms sales to Mexico. While on the one hand it is scandalous to see how the United States does very little about it, on the other hand the notion that large American arms manufacturers profit immensely from these sales is somewhat far-fetched.

The issue has been transformed into a new and, additionally, ideological and polarized debate, which was not necessarily the case thirty or forty years ago. Republican presidents and governors, including Richard Nixon and Ronald Reagan, signed gun control measures into law that Congress previously approved, regardless of who held a majority. The NRA itself supported certain restrictions after the 1968 assassinations of Robert Kennedy and Martin Luther King, the Newark and Detroit riots of that summer, and the Black Panthers' strident defense of gun possession and "open carry," in the defense of African Americans.

This began to change dramatically in the late seventies and eighties. According to various historians, only then did the Second Amendment come to be interpreted—though not by the Supreme Court—as guaranteeing an *individual's* right to own arms, not as "the people's right to form militias for the common defense,"[42] nor for hunting purposes. No one has ever shot a rabbit with an AR-15 or an M-16. This interpretation was transformed into a litmus test of conservatism, or Republicanism, and loyalty to an "originalist" interpretation of the Constitution. The blossoming of these sentiments coincided with a rapid expansion in the number of Americans with guns.

Americans are hunters, like many other peoples. Canadians, Norwegians, even the French who have on occasion given a surprising percentage of their votes to "*chasseur*" candidates, feel that hunting is a legitimate, entertaining, safe, and popular hobby or sport. One may not share these views, but in the world we live in, with the exception of endangered species, to ban hunting is not an imminent option. Likewise, other than in nations supremely affected by their history, like Japan by

World War II and Hiroshima, or inward-looking and reflexive ones such as the United Kingdom, the abolition of the "freedom" to possess handguns is not in the cards. But to allow even the mentally deranged to obtain automatic or semi-automatic weapons with which to carry out mass shootings that have caused the death of hundreds, and soon thousands of innocent victims, is simply unfathomable to foreigners.

Americans' personal reasons for possessing arms have changed. If polls twenty-five years ago showed that two-thirds of US citizens who owned weapons said they did so for recreational purposes (hunting, collecting, and sporting use), by 2015 the National Firearms Survey found that 63 percent of Americans answered that "protection against people" was the primary reason for owning a gun.[43] The chief historical explanations for this additional American exception, however, do not quite make the grade.

There are logical roots to the American idiosyncrasy. The frontier and the decimation of the Native American peoples meant that danger did indeed lurk close by for settlers early on, as it was in the West after the Civil War and the completion of the Trans-Continental railroad. The Army was unable to "defend" everyone, and many civilians were forced to defend themselves, often against attacks that they had instigated. Before the Civil War, assaults against abolitionists in border or Northern slave states (Kentucky, Missouri) obliged newspaper publishers, activists, and writers to own weapons in self-defense against the wrath of the pro-slavery fanatics. The author of *The War before the War* describes one such incident in the 1840s: "a pro slavery mob assembled across the river from St. Louis in the Illinois town of Alton, set fire to the house of the abolitionist newspaper editor Elijah Lovejoy, shot him to death, and threw his printing press into the river. John Quincy Adams called it 'the most atrocious case of mob rioting which ever disgraced this Country'. . . . In 1845, pro-slavery thugs drove the *True American* edited by Cassius Clay in Lexington, Kentucky, out of the state despite his having fortified the office with a cache of rifles and gunpowder."[44]

Blacks—free or enslaved—were prohibited from owning weapons before Emancipation. After the Civil War, freedmen who had served in the Union Army, or even those who had not, could acquire guns, or retain the ones they had fought with, as a historian of gun rights explains: "Prior to the Civil War, blacks and mulattoes, free and slave, were excluded from military service. Yet when the war was over 200,000 blacks and mulattos had taken up arms in defense of the Union, many former slaves from the South."[45]

Obviously, they took those arms home with them after the conflagration, and although there is scant evidence of a spike in gun-related violence in the South of armed blacks against whites, the latter feared the consequences of freedmen weapon-ownership. So they went out and "got their guns." Some of them rode horses, put on robes and masks, and became the Ku Klux Klan. Black Codes reinstated gun-possession prohibitions for African Americans; enraged whites launched disarmament posses. According to one study of this process, "In January 1866, *Harper's Weekly* reported that in Mississippi such groups have seized every gun and pistol found in the hands of the so-called freedmen."[46] Another historian summarizes the process and the paradox the following way: "The systematic, and often times violent manner in which Freedmen were disarmed by all-white Southern militias was disturbing, especially to Northern Republicans, who found it utterly dumbfounding how it was politically expedient for Southern states to count Freedmen as part of their federal apportionment, yet denied Freedmen the opportunity to serve in the militia or possess and use arms, using the justification that they were not citizens of the United States."[47]

Today, citizens of many lands who receive real-time information about mass shootings in the United States cannot but wonder what makes Americans so different. They are also bewildered by the apparent impossibility of change. After each tragedy, a president speaks, prays, grieves, and attempts to heal. He promises to do something and fails, immediately, or shortly after. And so on until the next horror. As with the two previous outlying American aberrations, the fascination with guns remains incomprehensible. As does our next and final reflection, the strangely American notion of intelligent design or contemporary creationism and the debates it arouses in the United States.

Intelligent design or creationism

Intelligent design rests on the idea that the complexity of life on earth is such that it could not have occurred haphazardly, but required the design and action of an intelligent agent: God. Certain readers may protest that a series of beliefs, no matter how deep-seated or aberrant they may seem, are not in the same league with the previous three banes. They would be correct if the measuring rod applied only to actual damage wrought. This one does not. My point here is that these traits are profoundly disturbing, objectionable, and exceptional. They make America an outlier with regard to other rich nations; the exact harm each one does is not central to my argument.

Intelligent design emerged in the late 1980s, when a sector of traditional American creationism grasped that the religious path to destroying the educational "monopoly" held by evolution was closed. Instead of insisting on religion as a valid alternative, which the Supreme Court rendered impossible in its 1987 *Edwards v. Aguillard* ruling, some creationists opted for a science vs. science approach. They even accepted many of the conclusions reached by the natural sciences about the age of the earth, the evolution of species, and modern genetic theory.

In their view, however, there were many scientific theories of life, none less controversial or more proven than others, and all should be taught in public schools. Following that choice, dozens of bills were introduced in state after state, seeking to include "intelligent design" theories in science classes, as opposed to teaching creationism in religion classes or social studies. Most of the bills were defeated—except for the Louisiana Science and Education Bill in 2008—but the struggle continues.

In relatively recent times (after the year 2000), bills were tabled or passed in at least one house of a state legislature in Alabama, Florida, Iowa, Maryland, Michigan, New Mexico, Oklahoma, and South Carolina. They all failed to be approved by both houses or were vetoed. None is actually on the books in any state, except Louisiana. Similarly, in 2001, the Senate in Washington, DC, passed—by ninety-one to eight votes—what came to be known as the Santorum Amendment—in fact a Sense of the Senate Resolution—that established a certain legislative validation of these theories through an education funding bill: "The Conferees recognize that a quality science education should prepare students to distinguish the data and testable theories of science from religious or philosophical claims that are made in the name of science. Where topics are taught that may generate controversy (such as biological evolution), the curriculum should help students to understand the full range of scientific views that exist, why such topics may generate controversy, and how scientific discoveries can profoundly affect society."[48] The resolution, however, was not included in George W. Bush's "No Child Left Behind" law.

At a state level, the Kansas Board of Education approved a notorious guideline in 1991. It voted to eliminate any mention of evolution from the state's science curriculum—one of the most far-reaching efforts to challenge the teaching of evolution in public schools. After the Supreme Court ruled states could not compel the teaching of creationism, its supporters appear more active, attempting to get around the constitutional issues. Creationists are increasingly trying to keep Darwin out of the classroom or ensure that evolution is presented as merely one more unproved theory.[49] From the mid-1980s through the second decade of this century, creationists have shifted their theoretical stance toward intelligent design, and their legal strategy from state legislatures and federal courts to school boards and textbook companies. But the theory is the same, as is the goal: to eliminate or limit the teaching of evolution in public schools. The shift sprang from a series of setbacks the movement suffered from the early eighties onward.

The first was perhaps the landmark ruling against the so-called Act 590 of the state of Arkansas, signed into law in 1981 by Governor Frank White. It was one of the first state statutes to enshrine balanced treatment for the "science of creation" and the "science of evolution," although it excluded the introduction of any religious instruction. The purpose of this exclusion was to get around the Establishment Clause of the First Amendment, which in effect bans religious instruction in public schools. The constitutionality of Act 590 was quickly questioned; it went to federal court, where among others, Stephen J. Gould testified against it. In January 1982, federal Judge William R. Overturn struck it down. With regard to these debates, Ronald Reagan, during his 1980 campaign, had stated, "If we have to teach evolution, which is only a theory, we should also teach biblical creation."[50]

A similar defeat occurred in 2005, for the first time explicitly involving the intelligent design version of creationism: the *Kitzmiller v. Dover Area School District* decision, in Pennsylvania.[51] This was the first direct challenge brought in United States federal courts testing a public-school district policy that required the teaching of intelligent design. In 2004, the Dover Area School District modified its biology curriculum and required that intelligent design be taught as an alternative to evolution. That decision was challenged in court among others by the ACLU, arguing that intelligent design was a form of creationism, and that the school board, as in Arkansas, violated the Establishment Clause.

Dominique Lecourt, a French epistemologist and philosopher who has studied the history of creationism and intelligent design in the United States, noted before the Dover ruling that the link to the Scopes Trial in 1925 was obvious. He seized the logic of the new creationist offensive during the last quarter of the twentieth century: "The fundamentalists know that America today is not the country of the years before the Great Depression . . . . They will not utter the word 'theology' . . . . In a society where scientific efficiency is king, they will only utter the word 'science' even if they actually and surreptitiously seek their arguments in the theology of the nineteenth century. Their rule is to do without saying."[52]

In more recent reviews of these matters, the National Center For Science Education—admittedly a rabid anti-intelligent design/creationism (IDC) organization—rephrases the same idea: "IDCs currently concentrate their efforts on attacking evolution. Under innocuous-sounding guises such as 'academic freedom,' 'critical analysis of evolution,' or 'teaching the strengths and weaknesses of evolution,' IDCs attempt to encourage teachers to teach students wrongly that there is a 'controversy' among scientists over whether evolution has occurred. So-called 'evidence against evolution' or 'weaknesses of evolution' consist of the same sorts of long-discredited arguments against evolution which have been a staple of creationism since the 1920s and earlier."[53]

The debate does date back to the Scopes Trial in the twenties, and much before, to nineteenth-century theological discussions. It always comprised an educational connotation—Thomas Scopes was sentenced to a one hundred dollar fine for *teaching* evolution in a Dayton, Tennessee, public school—as well as religious, political, and legal implications. This mixture is what makes creationism and intelligent design so incomprehensible to foreigners. The problem does not lie in religious beliefs themselves—every country embraces one or another. Nor does it involve any one individuals' preference for a particular theory on the origin of life versus another. At stake here is the attempted imposition, through education, of one set of beliefs as opposed to other beliefs. Foreign indignation stems from the injection of religious beliefs into educational and scientific discussions, as opposed to limiting them to the study of religion and the practice of faith.

At the peak of the creationist/intelligent design struggles to influence school boards, courts, and the US Congress, European institutions considered themselves obligated to take a stand. A Council of Europe committee produced a document on the "dangers of Creationism in education." It concluded that "Creationism in any of its forms, such as 'intelligent design,' is not based on facts, does not use any scientific reasoning and its contents are pathetically inadequate for science classes."[54] Soon after the report was published, the Council of Europe's Parliamentary Assembly urged European schools to "resist presentation of creationist ideas in any discipline other than religion," including "intelligent design," which it described as "the latest, more refined version of creationism," "presented in a more subtle way." It did not seek to question a belief, but to "warn against certain tendencies to pass off a belief as science."[55] There is another danger lurking that should be mentioned in passing. In many high schools and even community colleges in the United States, including California, there is a trend toward accentuating the "methodological" nature of science. In this view, somewhat associated with the logical positivism or logical empiricist school of epistemology, science is not characterized by its conclusions, but rather by the "scientific method." On occasion, this approach tilts toward relativism: it does not really matter what conclusions one arrives at, as long as they are reached "scientifically." The next step is to relativize method, and creationism sneaks in again through the back door.

The United States systematically places last in favor of evolution among rich countries in recent polls seeking to ascertain whether people believe in evolution or creation. Only nations like Turkey, Saudi Arabia, and Indonesia (all Islamic) believe widely in creation or reject evolution.[56] In an older poll, undertaken by *Science Magazine* in 2006, in response to the statement "Human beings, as we know them, developed from earlier species of 'animals,'" only 40 percent of Americans agreed—the lowest number among seventeen OECD rich countries.

Similarly, Americans continue to believe in creation by meaningful margins. In the peak years of IDC, at the turn of the century, 47 percent thought that God had created man in his present form, and only 9 percent thought God had no part in the process. The rest subscribed to the view that "Man developed, with God guiding," a view that could be interpreted as equivalent to intelligent design. The Gallup figures have since evolved, with a lower 40 percent equally considering either the purely creationist conviction or the ID equivalent one. The strictly evolutionist opinion rose to 22 percent.[57] It is worth restating here that in these matters, self-reporting polls can be contradictory, or partly unreliable. Not everyone likes confessing to a stranger what they think of God or mankind.

The creationist/intelligent design movement has suffered various undeniable defeats in recent years. It has not disappeared, however, and quite logically, received new wind in its sails with the advent of Donald Trump. Nevertheless, as Americans become less religious, and as the zealots who progressively conquer the remaining religious space also shrink in number and influence, one can expect that IDC will equally retreat. It has done so before, only to re-emerge when circumstances favor its expansion.

In the meantime, the same reflection provoked by the three previous unintelligible traits is valid for this one. No possible explanation— historical, psychological, cultural, or materialistic—can justify the illogical and anomalous conduct described in the case of creationism and intelligent design. Again, the issue is not whether any group of people in the United States holds these beliefs; they are respectable. Isaac Newton, a while back, of course, owned them fully: "This extraordinary arrangement of the Sun, the planets and comets could have no other source than the design and oversight of an intelligent and powerful being."[58]

The question is why certain Americans, with undeniable support in their society, have sought to ban science in education, to impose their beliefs as an equivalent to what everyone else considers science, and why they have actually been able to achieve some of their aims, some of the time. This should not happen in a nation with the educational levels, wealth, information, connectivity, and social capital that all abound in America. The checks and balances function at the end of the day, but only at the end: after debates, trials, legal recourse, and legislative restraint that normally would be unnecessary, and that are costly for everybody.

Eccentric and fringe groups exist everywhere, many of them in the United States; some refuse interventionist medicine; others ultimately advocate the substitution of myth for science. For one reason or the other, they refuse blood transfusions, vaccinations, transplants, or chemotherapy, or subscribe to strange theories about Martians or the after-life. Occasionally, they implement their convictions, and produce great damage to others: children, cult members, innocent victims, and "deserters." None of this is exclusive to the United States. The uniqueness of America, in this case for the worst, is that these beliefs have the possibility of entering into law, or customs and guidelines, or acquire respectability in broad sectors of American society. In a sense, it is that respectability or acceptance that is most shocking. There is truly no explanation for it.

From anachronism to modernity

A common thread runs through the four peculiarities I reviewed in this chapter. It is not geographical or political. The practices I cite do not belong exclusively to the fly-over regions. California and New York had some of the toughest mandatory sentencing laws. Senator Bernie Sanders of Vermont, unquestionably one of the most left-wing members of his chamber, doesn't like gun control; his state, possibly the most progressive in the nation, includes a large number of hunters. But by and large, it is American conservatism that most heavily supports mass incarceration, guns, the death penalty, and creationism. Not everyone who does is conservative, and not all conservatives back these unnerving American opinions. But there is a connection.

It is a conservatism based on fear of the "other," on the need to protect one's family, community, race, and religion. There is an obvious inability, perhaps along racial divides, to identify with victims (of mass incarceration or the death penalty, for example). The approach to life it represents harks back to the frontier and the West, as many have observed. But it also involves American insularity and isolationism, as well as the mistrust of the unknown, despite the fact that Americans have always shown the necessary courage to deal with the unknown. It is partly the consequence of an absence of government capability, of government reach and acceptance of government itself for those Americans who espouse these absurd convictions.

Those who always disliked, mistrusted, and rejected the state and its hypothetical overreach wanted to arm *themselves*, do justice *themselves*, protect *themselves*, and try to impose their religious beliefs on others, by-passing the state. The Army cannot protect me, because it is not present, or is run by Northerners; I need weapons to protect myself. We must execute people or lock them up indefinitely because if we don't, they will become recidivists and come back to haunt us. We must protect our religion and traditions because if we don't, the "others" will destroy them, and us.

It is a supremely anachronistic world-view which has yet to overcome its past. In a sense, the American indifference to history leads to a Freudian "return of the repressed." When one does not acknowledge that beliefs, practices, and dogma are a reflection of their time within certain material conditions, it is not easy to abandon them when those conditions cease to exist. Unlike other characteristics of American life which have evolved from their original contours to more "modern" ones, these four have stubbornly survived, and have been exacerbated under Trump. They evoke the proverbial dinosaur that outlived the extinction of its species, or the Japanese soldiers who, unaware that World War II had ended, hid out in the jungle for half a century. They run directly counter to the process I have attempted to describe in these pages: America's arduous journey toward becoming modern and "unexceptional." If such a welcome change occurs in the coming years, it might indeed mark the end of the American difference.

10

A final word: an end to American difference?

THE OVER-ARCHING THEME OF these pages consists in the simple thought that most of what could be said about the United States since the first foreigners began to wonder about it can be boiled to one dis-tinguishing feature: a middle-class society. Not an ordinary one: rather, a society that allowed and encouraged equality for many, and exclusion for the rest. Who the rest were is no secret: Native Americans; enslaved peoples from Africa; disenfranchised, dispossessed, and discriminated-against women; African Americans; Mexicans and subsequently other Latinos; plus Chinese; Muslims of many lands; and more.

With time, different cohorts of the excluded were brought into fold, or elbowed their way into it. By now, some are closer to equality, though still far removed: women in general, white women in particular. Others are still waiting. But for those inside the fold, a majority of the population enjoyed a common trait, and it was not poverty. It was the fact of equality, though not the aspiration to it or the thought of it.

Over the years, that equality was transformed by the gradual inclu-sion of groups of the once excluded, and distorted by the appearance of immense wealth for a few, particularly from the Gilded Age onward. These two processes, however, did not fundamentally alter the basic equation. This boiled down to a large middle class; a small, fabulously affluent minority; and enough poor people brought into the system to promise a minimum of social mobility but also to provide the low-skill, low-wage labor indispensable in a market economy.

The country constructed a political system to match this configuration. Little by little, it established the holding of relatively free and fair elections for most executive and legislative offices. Everyone inside the system participated on equal grounds, while those on the outside did not participate at all. Gradually, the franchise was extended: to non-property-owning males, to freed slaves (only for them to be *de facto* deprived of it soon after), to women, and Hispanics, and other newcomers. Those in the system were, once again, pretty much all alike. Those who were different found themselves for long periods denied entry to that system.

Until the early sixties of the twentieth century, and with the exception of certain New Deal reforms (for example, Social Security), given limitless available resources, an immigration spigot that could be turned on and off at will, and a weak labor movement, the great American middle class functioned as a substitute for a welfare state comparable to that of other rich countries. With full employment, high wages, and the exclusion of broad minorities with scant political clout, there was no real need for health care for all, a decent pension for everyone, proper unemployment compensation, etc. In the sixties, Medicare, Medicaid, and food stamps joined Social Security as the scaffolding of the bare-bones American welfare state in the late sixties and seventies, constituting the three-odd decades starting with the end of World War II: the American equivalent of France's "*trente glorieuses*."

Then the spell was broken. For a series of reasons including Ronald Reagan's economic and social policies, globalization, and a relative loss of American competitiveness—and with the rising influence of lobby groups—inequality began to rise starting from the Nixon years, wages and real overall income stagnated, and the middle class ceased to expand, and perhaps even to shrink. These trends have persisted until today. They partly explain Donald Trump's election in 2016.

The need for a plain-vanilla welfare state like elsewhere else became apparent, as American society started resembling everybody else's. Figures 10.1 and 10.2, comparing inequality rates in France and the United States over the past hundred years, show this evolution. Both countries were roughly as unequal before the Depression; inequality rose enormously during the thirties. But after World War II the United States became significantly more egalitarian than France. Then came

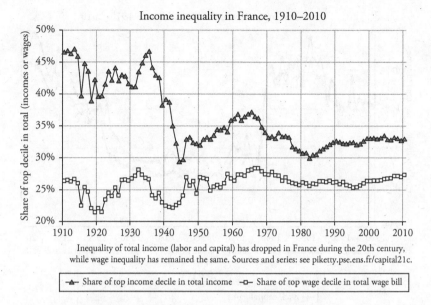

Income inequality in France, 1910–2010

Inequality of total income (labor and capital) has dropped in France during the 20th century, while wage inequality has remained the same. Sources and series: see piketty.pse.ens.fr/capital21c.

—▲— Share of top income decile in total income   —□— Share of top wage decile in total wage bill

FIGURE 10.1. Income inequality in France 1910–2010

Source: "Data–WID–World Inequality Database." WID. Accessed October 12, 2019. https://wid.world/data/#countrytimeseries/sptinc_p90p100_z/FR/1900/2014/s/k/p/ yearly/a; Piketty, Thomas. Top Incomes over the 20th Century: A Contrast between Continental European and English-Speaking Countries. Oxford: Oxford University Press, 2014.

1980. Inequality began to rise dramatically in the United States but remained relatively stable in France. The trend has persisted.

But this was not evident to everybody in mainstream American politics. In fact, the middle-class substitute for a cradle-to-grave welfare state was quickly disappearing. In 2019, however, something changed. In one way or another, the principal Democratic contenders for the presidency in 2019–20—even Joe Biden—espoused many of the tenets of a modern version of that welfare state. So much so that Trump and the Republican Party centered their attacks on them for seeking to bring socialism to America, something that conservatives believe should never be allowed to occur.

As we emphasized in Chapter 8 in the section devoted to race, the "case for reparations" can be visualized as a proxy discussion for the advent of a new—or actually the first—American welfare state. Similarly, the programmatic proposals offered by many of the

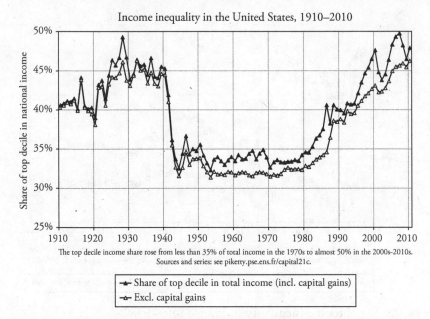

FIGURE 10.2. Income inequality in the United States, 1910–2010

Source: Data for the US retrieved from "Data–WID–World Inequality Database." WID. Accessed October 12, 2019. https://wid.world/data/#countrytimeseries/sptinc_p90p100_z/US/1913/2014/eu/k/p/yearly/s.

presidential contenders in the 2019–20 Democratic campaign also pointed in that direction. The most obvious example was Medicare for All, or a National Health Service, or a single-payer health care system. They did not all mean exactly the same thing; several candidates— Sanders, Warren, Harris, O'Rourke—did not agree on the details or simply did not spell them out. But they had all learned the lesson of Barack Obama's attempt to fix the American health care disaster with half-way measures, albeit the only ones possible at the time. Now Democratic politicians seeking the White House took far more ambitious stances in this on this issue. Previously existing fringe positions entered the mainstream.

The same is true for other issues. Elizabeth Warren proposed the creation of universal childcare and parental leave. Almost as interestingly, she suggested financing it with a wealth tax on fortunes over $50 million. If one recalls, as Robert Reich often does, that the United States has imposed a terribly regressive asset tax since time immemorial—property taxes—that affects those whose only asset is their homes, the idea should not be so revolutionary. It is.

Free college tuition for all; raising marginal income taxes back to levels pre-dating Ronald Reagan, George W. Bush, and Donald Trump; imposing a carbon tax on non-renewable energy sources; almost doubling the minimum wage: all of these promises were exciting, innovative, disruptive, and would have been considered appropriate only for the extreme fringe as recently as 2016. They would not create an American welfare state overnight, but as the conservatives said, tended to reshape the United States as Denmark, or Scandinavia and Europe in general. The Green New Deal also fits this narrative.

The reinvigorated debate about eliminating the Electoral College as well as other reforms to the currently dysfunctional political system is also part of this process. No welfare state or deep "systemic" changes in the United States today are conceivable without a political system that can achieve them democratically. Those profound changes include a response to challenges such as the one China represents for the United States, and in continuing to extend and consolidate American civilization. I am strongly optimistic about that, and the edification, at last, of a full-fledged American welfare state, regardless of the outcome of the 2020 presidential elections.

This optimism has several sources. First is the current political and ideological leanings of young Americans. More than half of United States millennials considered themselves consistently liberal or mostly liberal in a 2018 poll. That same year, more than two-thirds of the under-30 electorate voted for Democratic House candidates (the equivalent of a national election). The next generation of voters—the so-called generation Z, born after 1996—is even more progressive. They may change their minds as the years go by, but there is an underlying degree of permanence in these convictions that cannot be underestimated. There *has* been a long-term trend, at least since Ronald Reagan, and in the South, since the sixties, of no-longer-so-young *conservative* Democrats deserting to the Republican Party. But many *moderate* Democrats have become liberals, and many liberals have moved further left. These are all lasting changes, at least for a generation.

A second consideration lies in the demographic shifts in American society and in the American electorate. As we have noted, the voting universe was 61 percent white and 39 percent minority in 2018. Today, however, 44 percent of the millennial generation, belongs to a minority. By the early 2040s, barely twenty years from now, the United States will become a majority-minority country. There is no reason to believe that the current, immense tilt toward the Democratic Party among minority voters will not persist.

Latinos, whom some expect to become more conservative over time, given their views on social issues, and their heavily Catholic roots, have a long memory, on the one hand, and a short Cuban half-life on the other. The Republican Cuban-Americans in Dade County, Florida, are passing from the scene. After Republican California Governor Pete Wilson attempted to pass Proposition 187 in 1994, seeking to bar any undocumented individual in California from having access to public services, Hispanics in that state gave up on the GOP. They continue to vote massively for Democrats. In 2018, the percentage was an astounding 75 percent. The same seems true of the African American and Asian-American electorate. Why would they stray away from the liberal attitudes—at least on political issues—that they and their parents espoused for years, as they gradually see the growth in their turn-out, the number of their elected officials, and their overall presence in society? There are no guarantees in politics, but this appears to be a safe bet to make, even with the damage done to the judicial branch under Trump.

This constituency for a "proper" welfare state is complemented by the evolution of white, younger, college-educated Americans. On race matters, for example, Trump's policies and attitudes generated a "white-liberal backlash" in favor of less racially resentful stances. According to one study, between 1988 and 2016, "while the proportion of racially resentful white Republicans grew only slightly, . . . Trump . . . raised the salience of race. Democrats, by contrast, grew increasingly liberal (on race)."[1]

Retooling the political system and building this new welfare state, which might appear illusory or naive, is probably a necessary condition for dealing with three major challenges the United States must face in the coming years. Two are of an international nature but with huge domestic consequences. The first and foremost is climate change.

The Trump years notwithstanding, it seems increasingly clear, in Washington state and California or Germany and Holland, that there is an effective national and international approach to climate change, and Trump's totally useless, impotent approach. Disbelieving climate change, leaving its diminishment to the market, or seeking purely national solutions to it—what many have done over the past half-century—leads nowhere. The global essence of the issue, its public goods nature, and the cost of any of the conceivable tools necessary to face the challenge, all demand a level of social and governmental coordination such as is emerging in Western Europe and on the American West Coast. The Chinese solution—supposing it is one—is simply unacceptable to societies accustomed to democratic governance.

Taxes, international cooperation and enforcement, stringent regulation, civil society participation, and major public sector investment in renewable energy and new technologies are all better suited to a modern welfare state than to the more free-market, laissez-faire, deregulated American status quo. In this case it is not the stagnation of the middle class that brings upon the need for change; it is a new phenomenon singularly unsuited to the old American scheme. The relative success California has enjoyed on environmental matters in general, and in combatting climate change in particular, can be partly attributed to the coastal "state of mind," but much more so to state legislation approved and paid for by Californians for decades now. In this regard, and all power to it, California is a bit like Denmark, Germany, Holland, and Washington state. All of these entities are combatting climate change effectively, ambitiously, and through a comprehensive approach. It is difficult to envisage a *national, American* approach to this immense threat to everyone's well-being, and notably that of the younger generations, that can be much different. Which implies building a truly American version of a modern welfare state.

Secondly, unlike the fears of previous "declinists" during the twentieth century, which mostly turned out to be exaggerated, there is a long-term issue with China, accompanied by short- and medium-term implications. Demographics are not mechanical nor automatic, but a nation with four to five times more inhabitants than the United States, and a growing industrial and technological base, is bound eventually to catch up with its rival. The key question is obviously the word "eventually": next month, next year, or thirty to forty years from now. If, as most experts surmise, America has sufficient time to adapt to this approaching challenge, the sticker shock of Chinese parity should be more than manageable.

Militarily, even while practically half of all Americans think their country is "only one of several leading military powers," they are wrong.[2] China, in particular, possesses nowhere near the American capacity to project power on the seas, the air, space, and even on land away from its own perimeter or in cyberspace. Its economy, measured in per capita terms, thus controlling for population, is infinitely smaller than the American one. Technologically, despite ambitious plans for the future and undeniable advances in recent years, Chinese firms and/ or the state are not yet in the United States' league. Washington harbors undoubted vulnerabilities today, especially in the financial field, but most extrapolations of past growth into the future have proved unreliable. Lastly, Chinese soft power, while rising, is light years away from the potency of American civilization, despite significant efforts such as the Belt and Road Initiative, the International Infrastructure Bank, Chinese-language missions in Africa, the String of Pearls plan, and multiple bilateral agreements. China, in these areas of international endeavor, is not yet ready for prime time.[3]

None of which implies that the challenges are not real, nor that psychologically and even culturally Americans are ready to navigate these uncharted waters. The United States has not faced a perceived threat to its hegemony since the Cold War; there has been no real menace to that hegemony since World War I. The Soviet Union did not pass muster as a credible rival, brouhaha, Red Scares, and all. Addressing this unfamiliar experience is not something great powers manage easily: witness Britain, France, and, mainly, Russia today.

On occasion, this implies sacrifice, not necessarily in human lives— though that too can take place—but in resources and burdens many Americans do not want to shoulder. Surveys by the Center for American Progress and the Eurasia Group in 2019 discovered what American foreign policy priorities should be and are in the minds of ordinary citizens. The rivalry with China did not truly figure; almost all of the top issues were "negative": stopping bad things from happening. The young were the most adamant. They were particularly—and perhaps counter-intuitively—reluctant to see the United States attempt to prevent human rights abuses.[4] Even Trump's tariffs on Chinese exports to

America were not well received by consumers and were disapproved by US exporters to China hurt by Beijing's reprisals. As time passes, the adjustments to the end of single-power hegemony will become more painful, though none that can be foreseen today will be fatal. But without fixing the store at home, they will be much more difficult to face.

Thirdly, after responding to the challenges of climate change and China, consolidating, deepening, and strengthening American civilization represents an additional pending task. Defining it remains complicated; describing it is often simpler. Fatimah Asghar, a Pakistani-American writer and poet, gets it right when she attempts to define her belonging to that civilization when it is viewed from abroad, instead of when she is seen from within: "I both belong and don't belong to America. When I'm in America I'm constantly reminded that I'm not actually from here. But when I'm abroad, I feel the most American I've ever felt: hyperaware that my cultural reference points are American, that I can't shake my American entitlement, that once I open my mouth and talk, I am perceived as an American."[5] She is perceived as a member, representative, and expression of American civilization, even if in her own country he feels not part of it.

American civilization will encounter new threats or challenges, starting with those that began on 9-11; though present before, they became dangerously evident after that date. Inevitably, resistance to the growing presence of American civilization will swell. As societies that for different reasons seemed amenable to the influence of American civilization are transformed—partly by that civilization—some will react negatively to what they view as *excessive* proximity.

As we have all seen with Trump, now and then what the world may consider as the most unattractive features of American civilization will come to the fore. They will provoke responses even among those nations closest to the United States. There will be issues of inclusion and exclusion within the *limes*. The strongest traits of this civilization—a certain type of economy, representative democracy, respect for human rights, freedom of expression, a large, though shrinking middle class, mass culture and consumption—may be either criticized or rejected on their own merits. Or some societies might discard them precisely because they are inherent to American civilization.

America will find the appropriate answers to these questions and conflicts if and only if it is able to show the world that among its many virtues, the inherent capacity to constantly reinvent itself is perhaps the most seductive one. This implies addressing the age-old challenges still awaiting a solution—racism, violence, an aggressive and unilateral defense of perceived national interests abroad, insularity and retrenchment when things go awry at home, disrupting the environment. Reinventing itself also entails jettisoning exceptionalities that have no place in the modern world, much less so in American civilization: guns, mass incarceration, the death penalty, the recurrent war on drugs. These are, by definition, anachronisms that should no longer have a place in a society that claims to be world's most modern, and probably is.

The lasting triumph and enhanced longevity of American civilization will come when Americans themselves acknowledge the decline and end of their difference with the rest of the world, or at least with its rich countries. Accepting that it has become like every other wealthy nation is both an arduous task for any society, and one that has been underway for some time in the case of the United States. It is especially strenuous for a society that was born with the ingrained notion of exceptionality, and that has sought to reproduce it from generation to generation

This is, obviously, a two-way street. As the classic author Mary Beard described a previous process: "the interaction between Rome and other cultures in the empire is striking for the variety of forms it took and for the very diverse hybrid versions of Roman . . . culture . . . that were the result."[6] Affluent European and Asian countries are also changing and converging with the United States, whether in regard to issues of climate change, poverty, inequality, immigration, violence, drugs, rights for all, or many others. The narrowing and gradual elimination of differences does not mean that all countries will become the same. It signifies that their self-defining traits take on board how their importance diminished and how commonalities are increasingly emphasized. I believe this has been occurring in the rich world over the past decades, and even in some countries geographically with, say, Mexico and economically with East Asia.

The process involving greater proximity to American civilization will not be exempt from perils and unpleasant consequences. Those nations that do not participate in it are increasingly likely to resent it and react negatively to its progress. The gap, if not the clash, between civilizations, might be exacerbated by this evolution. This exacerbation may incorporate forms of exclusion and rejection that no one should approve of or countenance. It is also an uneven process. American civilization is rapidly expanding into China and India, which comprise more than a third of the world's population, but where it is also generating anti-bodies. Which brings us to a final point about the *limes* and civilization.

I return to my French friend's analogy. Régis Debray stresses how Rome—the civilization as such, not the republic or the empire—transformed itself over the centuries, in the eastern and western empires, as well as how it uniquely adapted to new circumstances. As he reasons: "Caracalla (for whom the famous baths of Rome are named) was mad, but extending citizenship to all of the Empire's free men (in 212) was wise."[7] The extension of the *limes* changed Rome, and Rome of course changed the location and nature of the *limes*. A civilization *is* influenced by those beyond the *limes*; the exchange works both ways. The main point, as a recent historian of the *Pax Romana* framed it, is "that people living as far apart as the Tyne and the Euphrates may have watched the same stories and hummed the same tunes."[8] Or from the Hudson to the Yalu.

American civilization and the United States as a nation are both being modified by what lies beyond the borders and the hinterland of the "empire"; like Rome, at least until the very end, for the better. It could not be otherwise, if we are to take the notion of an American civilization seriously. From the most immediate, nearest, and simplest impact—i.e. the growth of Hispanic influence on the mores of American society: language, cuisine, music, sports—to the more complex and contradictory—how the United States responds to climate change, and domestically and in foreign policy to China's rise and its gradual Americanization—America is less of an island than ever before. Being Rome means extending the language, taxes, the roads, the legal code, military practice and aqueducts, hygiene and amphitheaters across the world, but also receiving the inspiration and impulse of the northern neighbors, the Christians, and eventually the eastern empire.

Will American civilization last as long as Rome, either the empire or civilization? Certainly not, if only for demographic reasons. But it has a long way to go still, especially if it shows Rome's adaptability, and understands what American civilization is, and what it still lacks to consolidate it. A fulfilled modernity would perhaps be the best name for what is missing. The journey toward that modernity—and full-fledged civilization—is underway. It will be arduous, but ultimately successful.

NOTES

<hr>

Introduction

1. Naipaul, V. S. *A Turn in the South*. New York: Vintage International, 1990, p. 222.

Chapter 1

1. Dickens, C., and P. Ingham. *American Notes*. London: Penguin, 2004, p. 176.
2. Knausgaard, Karl Ove. "My Saga," part 1. *The New York Times*. February 25, 2015.
3. Bryce, J. V. *The American Commonwealth*, vol. 2, 3rd ed. London: The Macmillan Company, 1904, p. 816.
4. Tocqueville, A. D. *Democracy in America: And Two Essays on America*. London: Penguin, 2003, p. xxv.
5. St. John De Crevecoeur, J. Hector. "What Is an American?" In *Letters from an American Farmer*. 1782.
6. Sitaraman, G. *The Crisis of the Middle Class Constitution: Why Economic Inequality Threatens our Republic*. New York: Alfred A. Knopf, 2017.
7. Ibid., p. 63.
8. Mak, G. *In America: Travels with John Steinbeck*. London: Harvill Secker, 2014, p. 149.
9. Ibid., p. 205.
10. Lepore, Jill. *These Truths: A History of the United States*. New York: W. W. Norton & Company, 2018, p. 79.
11. Ibid., p. 163.

12. Trotsky, Leon. "CHAPTER XXII NEW YORK." In *Leon Trotsky: My Life*, vol. 22. New York. Accessed March 2, 2019. https://www.marxists.org/archive/trotsky/1930/mylife/ch22.htm.

13. Mathur, Anurag. *The Inscrutable Americans*. Calcutta: Rupa, 2004, p. 125.

14. Baudrillard, J. *Amérique*. Paris: Grasset, 1986, p. 109.

15. Mathur, *The Inscrutable Americans*, p. 13.

16. "Human Development Reports." Human Development Reports. Accessed July 25, 2019. http://hdr.undp.org/en/composite/IHDI. "World Happiness Report 2019." Accessed July 20, 2019. https://worldhappiness.report/ed/2019/.

17. "Inequality by Country." The Chartbook of Economic Inequality. Accessed October 15, 2018. https://www.chartbookofeconomicinequality.com/inequality-by-country/usa/.

18. Ibid.

19. Sartre, Jean-Paul. "Sartre on the American Working Class: Seven Articles in Combat from 6 to 30 June 1945." *Sartre Studies International* 6.1 (2000): 10–11.

20. Tocqueville, *Democracy in America*, p. 370.

21. Mak, *In America*, p. 75.

22. Fuentes, Carlos. *En esto creo*. México: Editorial Planeta Mexicana, 2002, p. 255.

23. Temin, Peter. *The Vanishing Middle Class: Prejudice and Power in a Dual Economy*. Cambridge, MA: MIT Press, 2017, p. 4.

24. Ibid., pp. 9–10.

25. Piketty, T., E. Saez, and G. Zucman. "Distributional National Accounts: Methods and Estimates for the United States." NBER. December 15, 2016. Accessed March 19, 2019. https://www.nber.org/papers/w22945.

26. Lévi-Strauss, Claude. *The View from Afar*. Chicago: The University of Chicago Press, 1985, p. 267.

27. Sombart, Werner. "The Cost of Living in America and Germany." In *Why Is There No Socialism in the United States?* London: The Macmillan Press, 1976, pp. 75–92.

28. Ibid., p. 37.

29. Liang Qichao. "The Power and Threat of America." In *Land without Ghosts: Chinese Impressions of America from the Mid-Nineteenth Century to the Present*. Ed. Arkush, R. David, and Leo Ou-fan Lee. Berkeley, CA: University of California Press, 1989, p. 87.

30. "Apuntes De Martí." Lente Latinoamericano. January 30, 2019. Accessed July 2, 2019. https://lentelatinoamericano.wordpress.com/2019/01/30/apuntes-de-marti/.

31. Parker, Stephen R. *Bertolt Brecht: A Literary Life*. London: Bloomsbury Methuen Drama, 2015, p. 433.

32. Duus, Peter, and Kenji Hasegawa. *Rediscovering America: Japanese Perspectives on the American Century*. Berkeley, CA: University of California Press, 2011: Maida Minoru, "The Characteristics and Pecularities of the Americans" (1925), p. 101.

33. Borges, Jorge Luis. "Autobiographical notes Argentine writer." *The New Yorker*, September 19, 1970 issue, p. 95.

34. Zhengkeng Xu, "Things about America and Americans." In Arkush and Lee, In *Land without Ghosts*, p. 130.

35. Tocqueville; *Democracy in America*, p. XXXIII.

36. Ibid., p. 135.

37. "Taxes." Gallup.com. Gallup, June 5, 2019. Accessed March 20, 2019. https://news.gallup.com/poll/1714/taxes.aspx.

38. Santayana, G. *Character & Opinion in the United States*. Scholar select. New York: Charles Scribner's Sons, 1920, p. 185.

39. Long, Jason, and Joseph Ferrie. "Intergenerational Occupational Mobility in Great Britain and the United States since 1850." American Economic Review. Accessed October 19, 2018. https://www.aeaweb.org/articles?id=10.1257/aer.103.4.1109.

40. Chetty, R., D. Grusky, M. Hell, N. Hendren, R. Manduca, and J. Narang. "The Fading American Dream: Trends in Absolute Income Mobility since 1940." NBER. December 8, 2016. Accessed March 20, 2019. https://www.nber.org/papers/w22910.

41. "U.S. Kids Now Less Likely to Earn More Than Their Parents." NPR. December 18, 2016. Accessed March 20, 2019. https://www.npr.org/2016/12/18/506076733/u-s-kids-now-less-likely-to-earn-more-than-their-parents.

42. Ibid.

43. Isaacs, J. B., I. V. Sawhill, and R. Haskins. *Getting Ahead or Losing Ground: Economic Mobility in America*. Publication. The Brookings Institute/Economic Mobility Project. Accessed August 20, 2019. https://www.brookings.edu/wp-content/uploads/2016/06/02_economic_mobility_sawhill.pdf, p. 62.

44. Mak, *In America*, p. 109.

45. Ibid., p. 169.

Chapter 2

1. Tocqueville, A. D. *Democracy in America*, p. xxv, vol. 2, part 1. pp. 525–6.

2. Bulmer-Thomas, Victor. *Empire in Retreat: The Past, Present, and Future of the United States*. New Haven, CT: Yale University Press, 2018, p. 57.

3. Judt, Tony. Foreword to *Religion in America: A Political History*, by Denis Lacorne. New York: Columbia University Press, 2014, p. XIII.

4. Mak, G. *In America*, p. 67.

5. Sitaraman, G. *The Crisis of the Middle Class Constitution*, p. 121.

6. Marx, Karl. *Surveys from Exile*, vol. 2. London: Penguin Books, 1973, p. 341.

7.   Ibid.

8.   Lepore, J. *These Truths*, p. 157.

9.   "Elecciones Nacionales." Resultados Electorales 2018. Accessed March 14, 2019. http://resultados2018.tse.go.cr/resultados2darondadefinitivos/#/presidenciales.

10. Bulmer-Thomas, *Empire in Retreat*, p. 28.

11. Ibid., p. 50.

12. "America's Devious Dream: Roosevelt and the Panama Canal." History Extra. November 19, 2018. Accessed December 12, 2018. https://www.historyextra.com/period/modern/americas-devious-dream-roosevelt-and-the-panama-canal/.

13. Immerwahr, D. *How to Hide an Empire: A History of the Greater United States*. New York: Farrar, Straus, and Giroux, 2019, p. 95.

14. Ibid., p. 107.

15. Williamson, Chilton. *American Suffrage: From Property to Democracy 1760–1860*. Princeton, NJ: Princeton University Press, 2019.

16. "1860 Census Results." Accessed August 15, 2019. http://www.civil-war.net/pages/1860_census.html. "Slave, Free Black, and White Population, 1780–1830." Accessed August 15, 2019. https://userpages.umbc.edu/~bouton/History407/SlaveStats.htm.

17. Irwin, Douglas A. *Clashing over Commerce: A History of US Trade Policy*. Chicago: University of Chicago Press, 2017, p. 277.

18. Mazzucato, Mariana. *The Entrepreneurial State: Debunking Public vs. Private Sector Myths*. New York: Public Affairs, 2015.

19. Tregarthen, Timothy D., and Libby Rittenberg. *Macroeconomics*, 2nd ed. New York: Worth Publishers, 1999, p. 177. Black, Conrad. *Flight of the Eagle: A Strategic History of the United States*. Toronto: Signal, 2014.

20. Brown Tindall, George, and David E. Shi. *America: A Narrative History*, vol. 2. W. W. Norton & Company, 2012, p. 589.

21. Fraser, Steve. *The Age of Acquiescence: The Life and Death of American Resistance to Organized Wealth and Power*. New York: Little, Brown, and Company, 2015, p. 66.

22. Ibid.

23. Piketty, Thomas, *Capital in the Twenty-First Century*. Cambridge, MA: Belknap Press, 2014, pp. 348–350, 506.

24. Tear sheet by Coatsworth, John H. "U.S.–Latin American Relations: WWII to the Present." Lecture.

25. Fuentes, C. *Nuevo tiempo mexicano*. México, DF: Aguilar, Altea, Taurus, Alfaguara, 1994, p. 86.

26. Sachs, J. D. *A New Foreign Policy: Beyond American Exceptionalism*. New York: Columbia University Press, 2018.

27. McCormack, J. W. "The Story of Oscar Wilde in America." Culture Trip. March 28, 2018. Accessed April 4, 2019. https://theculturetrip.com/north-america/usa/articles/the-story-of-oscar-wilde-in-america/.

28. "The Trouble with Putting Tariffs on Chinese Goods." *The Economist.*
     May 16, 2019. Accessed May 19, 2019. https://www.economist.
     com/special-report/2019/05/16/the-trouble-with-putting-tariffs-
     on-chinese-goods. "Trade Can No Longer Anchor America's
     Relationship with China." *The Economist.* May 16, 2019. Accessed
     May 19, 2019. https://www.economist.com/special-report/2019/05/16/
     trade-can-no-longer-anchor-americas-relationship-with-china.

Chapter 3

1.   Debray, R. *Civilisation: comment nous sommes devenus Américains.*
     Paris: Gallimard 2017, p. 21.
2.   "Obituary: Juan Gabriel Died on August 28th." *The Economist.* September
     10, 2016. Accessed October 3, 2018. https://www.economist.com/
     obituary/2016/09/10/obituary-juan-gabriel-died-on-august-28th.
3.   Llosa, Mario Vargas. "Tribuna: Librerías Y Libródomos." EL PAÍS.
     January 11, 1997. Accessed July 2, 2019. https://elpais.com/diario/1997/01/
     12/opinion/853023603_850215.html.
4.   Vasconcelos, José. *Ulises Criollo.* México: Porrúa, 2006, p. 26.
         Also see: Pineda Buitrago, Sebastián. "Entre El Desprecio
     Y La Admiración: Visión De Estados Unidos En Ulises Criollo
     De José Vasconcelos." Latinoamérica. Revista De Estudios
     Latinoamericanos. http://www.scielo.org.mx/scielo.php?script=sci_
     arttext&pid=S1665-85742013000200006.
5.   Beauvoir, Simone De. *America Day by Day.* Berkeley, CA: University of
     California Press, 2000, p. 43.
6.   *The Last of the Mohicans. A Narrative of 1757.* Historical Introduction by
     James Franklin Bear. Albany: State University of New York Press, 1983,
     pp. XXVII–XXVIII.
7.   McCrum, Robert. "The 100 Best Novels: No 16—The Scarlet Letter by
     Nathaniel Hawthorne (1850)." *The Guardian.* January 6, 2014. Accessed
     May 14, 2019. https://www.theguardian.com/books/2014/jan/06/
     scarlet-letter-nathaniel-hawthorne-100-best-novels.
8.   Díaz Hernán. *Borges, between History and Eternity.*
     London: Continuum, 2012, p. 102.
9.   Bryce, J. V. *The American Commonwealth.* (Third edn, Vol. 2).
     London: The Macmillan Company, 1904, p. 766.
10. Ibid., p. 783.
11. Díaz Hernán. *Borges, between History and Eternity.*
     London: Continuum, 2012, p. 116.
12. Nolan, James L. *What They Saw in America: Alexis De Tocqueville,
     Max Weber, G. K. Chesterton, and Sayyid Qutb.* New York: Cambridge
     University Press, 2016, p. 71.
13. Fuentes, C. *Myself with Others: Selected Essays.* New York: Farrar, Straus
     and Giroux, 1990, p. 205.

14. Ortega y Gasset, José. *Obras Completas*. Vol. IV. Madrid: Alianza Editorial, 1983, pp 369–79.

15. Borges, Jorge Luis. "Autobiographical Notes Argentine Writer." *The New Yorker*, September 19, 1970 Issue, p. 42.

16. Kaplan, Justin. "Born to Trouble. One Hundred Years of Huckleberry Finn," ERIC. September 11, 1984, Fort Lauderdale, Florida, Broward County Library, p. 15. files.eric.ed.gov/fulltext/ED262416.pdf. Anderson, Frederick, ed. *Mark Twain's Notebooks & Journals*. Vol. III *(1883–1891)*. Berkeley, CA: University of California Press, 1979, p. 115.

17. Maixner, Paul, ed. *Robert Louis Stevenson: The Critical Heritage*. London and New York: Routledge, 1971, p. 22.

18. Xiaotong Fei, "The Shallowness of Cultural Tradition." In Arkush and Lee, *Land without Ghosts*, p. 179.

19. Gordon, Robert J. *The Rise and Fall of American Growth: The U.S. Standard of Living since the Civil War*. Princeton, NJ: Princeton University Press, 2016, p. 174.

20. Ibid., p. 176.

21. Orozco Nuñez, Miriam. "El Nacimiento de La Prensa De Masas En Europa: El Caso De España." Master's thesis, Universidad De Cádiz, 2016, p. 7. Accessed July 3, 2019. https://rodin.uca.es/xmlui/bitstream/handle/10498/18558/TFG El nacimiento de la prensa de masas en Europa.pdf?sequence=1&isAllowed=y.

22. "Daily, Sunday, and Weekly Newspaper Circulation Increased from 7 Million in 1870 to 39 Million in 1910 . . . " Gordon, *The Rise and Fall of American Growth*.

23. Severgnini, Beppe. *Ciao, America! An Italian Discovers the U.S.* New York: Broadway Books, 2003, p. 175.

24. Roser, Max, and Esteban Ortiz-Ospina. "Literacy." Our World in Data. September 20, 2018. https://ourworldindata.org/literacy.

25. "La Alfabetización a Través De La Historia." La alfabetización a través de la historia, n.d. http://jesusgonzalezfonseca.blogspot.com/2011/08/la-alfabetizacion-traves-de-la-historia.html.

26. Gordon, *The Rise and Fall of American Growth*.

27. Ibid., p. 176.

28. Ibid.

29. Bryce, *The American Commonwealth*, p. 751.

30. Bruun, Erik, and Jay Crosby, eds. *The American Experience: The History and Culture of the United States through Speeches, Letters, Essays, Articles, Poems, Songs and Stories*. New York: Black Dog & Leventhal Publishers, 2012, p. 250.

31. Meyers, Jeffrey. "Thomas Mann in America." *Michigan Quarterly Review*. Fall 2012. Accessed April 16, 2019. https://quod.lib.umich.edu/cgi/t/text/text-idx?cc=mqr;c=mqr;c=mqrarchive;idno=act2080.0051.419;view=text;rgn=main;xc=1;g=mqrg.

32. Weissmann, Jordan. "The Decline of the American Book Lover." *The Atlantic*. May 26, 2018. Accessed March 22, 2019. https://www.theatlantic.com/business/archive/2014/01/the-decline-of-the-american-book-lover/283222/.

   Brown, Brendan. "The Ultimate Guide to Global Reading Habits (Infographic)." Global English Editing. February 11, 2019. Accessed March 22, 2019. https://geediting.com/world-reading-habits/.

   Suárez, Michael J. F., S. J., and H. R. Wooudhuysen. *The Book: A Global History*. Oxford: Oxford University Press, 2013, p. 669.

33. Gordon, *The Rise and Fall of American Growth*, p. 200.

34. "Film History of the 1920s," n.d. Accessed October 27, 2018. https://www.filmsite.org/20sintro.html. Accessed October 27, 2018.

35. Fleishman, Jeffrey. "A New 'Birth of a Nation' Dredges up the Complicated, Ugly Legacy of the Groundbreaking 1915 Film." *Los Angeles Times*. September 30, 2016. Accessed July 5, 2019. https://www.latimes.com/projects/la-ca-mn-birth-nation/.

36. Hirabayashi Hatsunosuke, "Motion Pictures: The Americanization Machine." In Duus and Kenji, *Rediscovering America*, p. 119.

37. Gordon, *The Rise and Fall of American Growth*, pp. 186–90.

38. Ibid., p. 193.

39. Mitchell, B. R. *European Historical Statistics 1750–1970*. London: MacMillan Press, 1975.

   D'Lugo, Marvin, Ana M. López, and Laura Podalsky, eds. *The Routledge Companion to Latin American Cinema*. New York: Routledge, 2018, p. 319.

40. Haskell, Barbara, "América: Mexican Muralism and Art in the United States, 1925–1945," p. 1. Essay will appear in the book accompanying the Whitney Museum's upcoming exhibition "Vida American: Mexican Muralists Remake American Art, 1925–1945."

41. Ibid., p. 6.

42. Llosa, Mario Vargas. "Tribuna: El Látigo Del Zorro." EL PAÍS. June 26, 1999. Accessed July 2, 2019. https://elpais.com/diario/1999/06/27/opinion/930434406_850215.html.

43. Parker, S. op. cit., p. 432.

44. Ibid.

45. Foucault, Michel. *1980–1988*. Vol. IV. Paris: Gallimard, 1994, p. 781.

46. Lévi-Strauss Claude. *The View from Afar*. Chicago: The University of Chicago Press, 1985, p. 262.

47. Nolan, op. cit., p. 197.

48. Mak, op. cit., p. 30

49. Ibid.

50. Gordon, *The Rise and Fall of American Growth*, pp. 415–16.

51. Kansteiner, Wulf. "Nazis, Viewers and Statistics: Television History, Television Audience Research and Collective Memory in West

Germany." *Journal of Contemporary History*, Oct. 2004, pp. 575–98. https://www.jstor.org/stable/4141411?read-now=1&seq=3#page_scan_tab_contents, p. 577.

52. "Histoire De La Télévision: Une Exception Française?" La Revue des Médias, n.d. https://larevuedesmedias.ina.fr/histoire-de-la-television-une-exception-francaise.

53. Ibid.

54. Ibid.

55. Ramírez Bonilla, Laura Camila. "La Hora De La TV: Incursión De La Televisión Y La Telenovela En La Vida Cotidiana De La Ciudad De México (1958–1966)." *Historia Mexicana*, Colmex, July–September 2015. http://www.scielo.org.mx/scielo.php?script=sci_arttext&pid=S2448-65312015000300289#fn8. *Statistics on Radio and Television, 1950–1960*. Statistical Reports and Studies. Paris: UNESCO, 1963, p. 74.

56. Ibid., p. 75.

57. Ibid.

58. Ibid. and Gordon, *The Rise and Fall of American Growth*, p. 415.

59. Bunyol, Josep Maria. "Las Series Que Contraprogramaron El Franquismo." Serielizados. April 16, 2018. Accessed July 4, 2019. https://serielizados.com/series-contraprogramaron-franquismo/.

60. "A View from Japan: An Interview with Motoyuki Shibata by Linh Dinh." June 6, 2016. Accessed April 16, 2019. https://www.countercurrents.org/dinh060616.htm.

61. Vargas Llosa, Mario. " 'Faulkner En El Laberinto.' " *La Vanguardia*. http://hemeroteca.lavanguardia.com/preview/1981/05/23/pagina-5/32926503/pdf.html.

62. Nolan, *What They Saw in America*, p. 204.

63. Baudrillard, *Amérique*, p. 199.

64. *Da Outra América: Gilberto Freyre's Racial Formation in the United States* by Jonathan Michael Square. Accessed October 5, 2019. http://lanic.utexas.edu/project/etext/llilas/ilassa/2008/square.pdf.

Chapter 4

1. Floquet, Michel. *Triste Amérique: le vrai visage des États-Unis*. Paris: Les Arènes, 2016, pp. 206, 211.

2. Most recently in Sitaraman, Ganesh. *The Crisis of the Middle Class Constitution: Why Economic Inequality Threatens Our Republic*. New York: Alfred A. Knopf, 2017.

3. Drutman, Lee. "American Politics Has Reached Peak Polarization." *Vox*. March 24, 2016. https://www.vox.com/polyarchy/2016/3/24/11298808/american-politics-peak-polarization.

4. Lepore, J. *These Truths*, p. 325.

5. Mak, G. *In America*, p. 245.

6. Britannica, The Editors of Encyclopaedia. "United States Presidential Election of 1912." *Encyclopaedia Britannica Online.* https://www. britannica.com/event/United-States-presidential-election-of-1912.

7. Levitsky, Steven, and Daniel Ziblatt. "Why Republicans Play Dirty." *The New York Times.* September 20, 2019. https://www.nytimes.com/2019/ 09/20/opinion/republicans-democracy-play-dirty.html?searchResultPosit ion=1.

8. Britannica, The Editors of Encyclopaedia. "United States Presidential Election of 1932." *Encyclopaedia Britannica Online.* https://www. britannica.com/event/United-States-presidential-election-of-1932.

9. Gates, Henry Louis, prod. "Reconstruction: America after the Civil War." Public Broadcasting Service (PBS). April 2019.

10. Jackson, Brooks. "Blacks and the Democratic Party." FactCheck.org. June 3, 2019. https://www.factcheck.org/2008/04/blacks-and-the-democratic-party/.

11. Ibid.

12. Ibid.

13. "Two-Thirds of Hispanic Voters Identify with or Lean toward the Democratic Party." Pew Research Center's Hispanic Trends Project, n.d. https://www.pewresearch.org/hispanic/2016/10/11/democrats-maintain-edge-as-party-more-concerned-for-latinos-but-views-similar-to-2012/ph_2016-10-11_politics_4-02/.

14. "Hispanic Voters More Engaged in 2018 than in Previous Midterms." Pew Research Center, n.d. https://www.pewresearch.org/fact-tank/2018/11/02/hispanic-voters-more-engaged-in-2018-than-in-previous-midterms/.

15. Nolan, J. *What They Saw in America,* p. 113.

16. Flippen, Alan. "Black Turnout in 1964, and Beyond." *The New York Times.* October 16, 2014. https://www.nytimes.com/2014/10/17/upshot/black-turnout-in-1964-and-beyond.html.

17. "How Groups Voted." Roper Center for Public Opinion Research. https://ropercenter.cornell.edu/data-highlights/elections-and-presidents/how-groups-voted.

18. Board, The Editorial. "Why Are Florida Republicans So Afraid of People Voting?" *The New York Times.* August 10, 2019. Accessed August 12, 2019. https://www.nytimes.com/2019/08/10/opinion/sunday/florida-vote.html.

19. Lichtman, A. J. *The Embattled Vote in America: From the Founding to the Present.* Cambridge, MA: Harvard University Press, 2018, p. 234.

20. Ember, Sydney, and Matt Stevens. "Bernie Sanders Opens Space for Debate on Voting Rights for Incarcerated People." *The New York Times.* April 27, 2019. https://www.nytimes.com/2019/04/27/us/politics/bernie-sanders-prison-voting.html.

21. "California." GovTrack.us. Accessed February 16, 2019. https://www.govtrack.us/congress/members/CA#representatives.

22. Zurcher, Anthony. "US Election 2016 Results." BBC News. Accessed February 22, 2019. https://www.bbc.com/news/election/us2016/results.

23. Nagourney, Adam, and Robert Gebelof. "In Orange County, a Republican Fortress Turns Democratic." *The New York Times*. December 31, 2018. Accessed January 2, 2019. https://www.nytimes.com/2018/12/31/us/orange-county-republicans-democrats-demographics.html.

24. "Majority-Minority Districts." Ballotpedia. Accessed May 23, 2019. https://ballotpedia.org/Majority-minority_districts.

25. "1990 Census of Population. California Part 1." US Bureau of the Census. Accessed February 12, 2019. https://www2.census.gov/library/publications/decennial/1990/cp-2/cp-2-6-1.pdf.

26. Mak, *In America*, p. 341.

27. Leighley, Jan E., and Jonathan Nagler. *Who Votes Now?: Demographics, Issues, Inequality and Turnout in the United States*. Princeton, NJ: Princeton University Press, 2014, p. 1.

28. Judt, Tony. *Ill Fares the Land*. London: Penguin Books, 2010, p. 88.

29. Naipaul, *A Turn in the South*, p. 29.

30. Ferguson, Niall. "America Is Exhausted by This New Civil War." October 21, 2018. http://www.niallferguson.com/journalism/miscellany/america-is-exhausted-by-this-new-civil-war.

31. "OECD Statistics." OECD Statistics. Accessed March 22, 2019. https://stats.oecd.org/.

32. Piketty, Thomas. *Le capital au XXIe siècle*. Paris: Éditions du Seuil, 2013, pp. 501–5.

33. Graham, Carol. *Happiness for All?: Unequal Hopes and Lives in Pursuit of the American Dream*. Princeton, NJ: Princeton University Press, 2017.

34. Mak, *In America*, p 115.

35. Sitaraman, *The Crisis of the Middle Class Constitution*, p. 204.

36. Fallows, James, and Deborah Fallows. *Our Towns: A 100,000-Mile Journey into the Heart of America*. New York: Vintage Books, 2019, p. 49.

37. Judt, *Ill Fares the Land*, p. 64.

38. For identity politics, see *Foreign Affairs* 97.5 (September–October 2018) and *Foreign Affairs* 98.2 (March–April 2019).

39. Myrdal defines the American Creed as follows: "Americans of all national origins, classes, regions, creeds and colors, have something in common: a social ethos, a political creed. It is difficult to avoid the judgement that this 'American Creed' is the cement in the structure of this great and disparate nation . . . . America, compared to every other country in Western civilization, large or small, has the most explicitly expressed system of general ideals and reference to human interrelations. The American Creed is not merely—as in some other countries—the implicit background of the nation's political and judicial order as it functions . . . . But as principles who ought to rule, the Creed has been made conscious to everyone in American society." Myrdal, Gunnar, and Sissela

Bok. *An American Dilemma: The Negro Problem and Modern Democracy*. Volume I. Transaction Publishers, 1996, pp. 3, 6. According to Samuel P. Huntington, "Americans, it is often said, are a people defined by and united by their commitment to the political principles of liberty, equality, democracy, individualism, human rights, the rule of law, and private property embodied in the American Creed." Huntington, Samuel P. *Who Are We?: The Challenges to America's National Identity*. New York: Simon & Schuster Paperbacks, 2005, p. 46.

40. Mak, *In America*, p. 349.
41. "Demographics of the U.S. Military." Council on Foreign Relations. Council on Foreign Relations, n.d. Accessed March 28, 2019. https://www.cfr.org/article/demographics-us-military. Accessed March 28, 2019.
42. Lepore, *These Truths*, p. 157.
43. Ibid., p. 123.
44. Wegman, Jesse. "The Man Who Changed the Constitution, Twice." *The New York Times*. March 14, 2019. Accessed March 15, 2019. https://www.nytimes.com/2019/03/14/opinion/birch-bayh-constitution.html.
45. Ibid.
46. "American Democracy in Crisis: The Challenges of Voter Knowledge, Participation, and Polarization." *PRRI*. www.prri.org/research/american-democracy-in-crisis-voters-midterms-trump-election-2018/.
47. Ortega y Gasset. *Obras Completas*. Madrid: Alianza Editorial, p. 160.

Chapter 5

1.   Mak, *In America*., p. 63.
2.   Wilde, O. "The American Man." *The Court and Society Review* 4.145. April 13, 1887.
3.   Paz, O *The Labyrinth of Solitude; and, the Other Mexico; Return to the Labyrinth of Solitude; Mexico and the United States; the Philanthropic Ogre*. New York: Grove Press, 2001, p. 362.
4.   Ibid.
5.   Ashida Hitoshi. "America on the Rise." In Duus and Kenji, *Rediscovering America*., p. 93.
6.   Lepore, Jill. "A New Americanism." *Foreign Affairs*. June 28, 2019. https://www.foreignaffairs.com/articles/united-states/2019-02-05/new-americanism-nationalism-jill-lepore.
7.   Lepore, *These Truths*., p. 10.
8.   /@indarktimes. "Hannah Arendt: America Is Not a Nation—In Dark Times." *Medium*. October 27, 2018. Accessed April 23, 2019. https://medium.com/@indarktimes/hannah-arendt-america-is-not-a-nation-9e3905b2dfde.
9.   Santayana, G. *Character & opinion in the United States*, p. 169.
10. Valéry, Paul. *Notes sur la grandeur et décadence de l'Europe*. Biblioteque de la Pléiade. *Oeuvres*, volume II. Paris: Ed. Gallimard, 1960, p. 930.

11.   Fuentes, C. *Myself with others*, p. 202.

12.   Nolan, *What They Saw in America*, p. 8.

13.   Lévy, Bernard-Henri. *American Vertigo*. Paris: Grasset, 2006, p. 386.

14.   McCormack, J. W. "The Story of Oscar Wilde in America." Culture Trip. March 28, 2018. Accessed April 04, 2019. https://theculturetrip.com/ north-america/usa/articles/the-story-of-oscar-wilde-in-america/.

15.   Fleming, C. M. *How to Be Less Stupid about Race: On Racism, White Supremacy, and the Racial Divide*. Boston, MA: Beacon Press, 2018, p. 30.

16.   Remarks by the President at Naturalization Ceremony. December 15, 2015. Retrieved from https://obamawhitehouse.archives.gov/the-press-office/2015/12/15/remarks-president-naturalization-ceremony.

17.   Weiss, Bari. "San Francisco Will Spend $600,000 to Erase History." *The New York Times*. June 28, 2019. Accessed July 19, 2019. https:// www.nytimes.com/2019/06/28/opinion/sunday/san-francisco-life-of-washington-murals.html.

18.   Schmidt, Benjamin M. "The History BA since the Great Recession." November 26, 2018. Accessed March 2, 2019. https://www.historians. org/publications-and-directories/perspectives-on-history/december-2018/ the-history-ba-since-the-great-recession-the-2018-aha-majors-report.

19.   Ibid.

20.   Beauvoir, *America Day by Day*, p. 67.

21.   DelBanco, A. *The War Before the War*.New York: Penguin Press, 2018, pp. 135, 144.

22.   Schama, Simon. *The American Future: A History*. New York: Ecco, 2010, p. 326.

23.   Severgnini, *Ciao, America!*, p. 200.

24.   Yagoda, Ben. *Will Rogers: A Biography*. Norman, OK: University of Oklahoma Press, 2000.

25.   "Will Rogers Quotes." BrainyQuote. Xplore. Accessed September 10, 2019. https://www.brainyquote.com/quotes/will_rogers_103996.

26.   Twain, Mark. *Roughing It*. Place of publication not identified: Digireads. com Publishing, 2018, p. 100.

27.   Twain, Mark. *The Innocents Abroad*. Place of publication not identified: Empire Books, 2012, p. 80.

28.   Mencken, H. L., and A. Cooke. *The Vintage Mencken*. New York: Vintage Books, 1990, pp. 129–30, 132.

29.   MacHale, Des. *Wit*. Kansas City: Andrews McMeel Publishing, 2003, p. 36.

30.   "H. L. Mencken Quotes." BrainyQuote. Xplore. Accessed September 10, 2019. https://www.brainyquote.com/quotes/h_l_mencken_137231.

31.   "Forbes Quotes." Thoughts on the Business of Life. Accessed July 24, 2019. https://www.forbes.com/quotes/3725/.

32.   Watkins, Mel. *African American Humor: The Best Black Comedy from Slavery to Today*. Chicago, IL: Lawrence Hill Books, 2002.

33. Gordon, Dexter B. "Humor in African American Discourse: Speaking of Oppression." *Journal of Black Studies* 29.2 (November 1998), p. 256.

34. Banks Mason, Cheryl. *The Dynamics of Black Humor from Africa to America and the Transformation from Slavery to the Twentieth Century.* Master's thesis, Clark Atlanta University, 2008. Atlanta: ETD Collection for AUC Robert W. Woodruff Library, 2008. Accessed June 20, 2019. https://core.ac.uk/download/pdf/9420431.pdf.

35. Ibid., p. 54.

36. "Chris Rock Quotes." BrainyQuote, n.d. Accessed June 17, 2019. https://www.brainyquote.com/quotes/chris_rock_129973.

37. "Dave Chappelle: Somebody Broke into My House Once, This Is a Good Time to Call the . . ." SComedy. Accessed September 10, 2019. https://scomedy.com/quotes/Dave-Chappelle.

38. "Dave Chappelle Quotes." BrainyQuote, n.d. Accessed June 17, 2019. https://www.brainyquote.com/quotes/dave_chappelle_564197.

39. "Stand-Up Comedy Quotes and Jokes." SComedy, n.d. http://scomedy.com/quotes?search=I enjoy my own thoughts sometimes.

40. Beatty, Paul. "Black Humor." *The New York Times.* January 22, 2006. https://www.nytimes.com/2006/01/22/books/review/black-humor.html.

Chapter 6

1. "The Trouble with Putting Tariffs on Chinese Goods." *The Economist.* May 16, 2019. Accessed May 19, 2019. https://www.economist.com/special-report/2019/05/16/the-trouble-with-putting-tariffs-on-chinese-goods.

2. Nye, Joseph. "China Will Not Surpass America Any Time Soon." *Financial Times.* February 19, 2019. Accessed February 20, 2019. https://www.ft.com/content/7f700ab4-306d-11e9-80d2-7b637a9e1ba1.

3. Stokes, B., J. Poushter, L. Silver, J. Fetterolf, and K. Devlin. "Trump Approval Worldwide Remains Low Especially among Key Allies." December 6, 2018. Accessed March 10, 2019. https://www.pewresearch.org/global/2018/10/01/trumps-international-ratings-remain-low-especially-among-key-allies/.

4. "Employment-Hours Worked." OECD Data. n.d. https://data.oecd.org/emp/hours-worked.htm.

5. America still leads in technology, but China is catching up fast. May 16, 2019. Retrieved from https://www.economist.com/special-report/2019/05/16/america-still-leads-in-technology-but-china-is-catching-up-fast

6. Mazzucato, *The Entrepreneurial State*, p. 29.

7. Lbelanger225. "Fortune 500." *Fortune.* July 30, 2019. Accessed August 5, 2019. https://fortune.com/fortune500/. Lbelanger225. "Global 500." *Fortune.* July 30, 2019. Accessed August 5, 2019. https://fortune.com/global500/2019. The six American non-extraction companies are Walmart, Apple, Berkshire Hathaway, Amazon, United Health Group, and McKesson.

8. "The Three Greatest American Companies of All Time." The American Business History Center. July 26, 2019. https://americanbusinesshistory. org/the-three-greatest-american-companies-of-all-time/. Britannica, The Editors of Encyclopaedia. "United States Steel Corporation." Encyclopaedia Britannica. https://www.britannica.com/topic/United-States-Steel-Corporation. "American Telephone and Telegraph Company." International Directory of Company Histories. 2019. https://www.encyclopedia.com/ books/politics-and-business-magazines/american-telephone-and-telegraph-company. "Standard Ogre." The Economist. December 23, 1999. https:// www.economist.com/business/1999/12/23/standard-ogre.

9. Hualong, Tang. "The Contradictory American Character." In Land without Ghosts: Chinese Impressions of America from the Mid-Nineteenth Century to the Present. Ed. R. David Arkush and Leo Ou-fan Lee. Berkeley, CA: University of California Press, 1989, p. 126.

10. Gordon, The Rise and Fall of American Growth, p. 455.

11. "A Matter of Timing: Yellow Fever and the Mosquito Hypothesis." Small Things Considered. Accessed August 19, 2019. https://schaechter. asmblog.org/schaechter/2009/12/a-matter-of-timing-yellow-fever-and-the-mosquito-hypothesis.html

12. Mazzucato, The Entrepreneurial State, p. 75.

13. Intellectual Property Statistics. Accessed April 24, 2019. https://www. wipo.int/ipstats/en/

14. "Apple iPhone Sales by Year 2007–2018." Statista. Accessed May 15, 2019. https://www.statista.com/statistics/276306/global-apple-iphone-sales-since-fiscal-year-2007/. McDermott, Jennifer. "US iPhone Sales Statistics 2012–2016." Finder US. June 2, 2019. Accessed May 15, 2019. https://www. finder.com/iphone-sales-statistics. Faigle, Philip, Julian Stahnke, and Paul Blickle. "Apple: Why the iPhone Costs Us Billions." ZEIT ONLINE. October 23, 2015. Accessed May 5, 2018. https://www.zeit.de/wirtschaft/ unternehmen/2015-10/iphone-apple-taxes-europe. González, Carlos. "Las ventas de iPhone caen en Europa ¿es esto lo que quiere ocultar Apple?" ADSLZone. November 6, 2018. Accessed May 15, 2019. https://www. adslzone.net/2018/11/06/apple-ventas-caida-europa-18/.

15. "Las grandes bolsas del mundo: BBVA." BBVA NOTICIAS. April 17, 2018. Accessed April 13, 2019. https://www.bbva.com/es/grandes-bolsas-mundo/. Cots, Pepe. "10 principales bolsas de valores del mundo y sus índices." Rankia. January 25, 2019. Accessed April 13, 2019. https://www.rankia.mx/blog/mejores-opiniones-mexico/ 3479166-10-principales-bolsas-valores-mundo-sus-indices.

16. "Hong Kong slips behind New York and Nasdaq in five-month global IPO rankings, as trade war takes a toll on sentiment." South China Morning Post. June 4, 2019. Accessed June 21, 2019. https://www.scmp.com/business/banking-finance/article/3012950/ hong-kong-slips-behind-new-york-and-nasdaq-five-month.

17.   Akcigit Ufuk, John Grigsby, and Tom Nicholas. "Immigration and the Rise of American Ingenuity." *American Economic Review: Papers and Proceedings* 107.5 (May 2017), pp. 327–31.

18.   "United States—OECD Data." *The OECD*. Accessed August 21, 2019. https://data.oecd.org/united-states.htm. "QS Higher Education System Strength Rankings (HESS) 2018." *Top Universities*. August 7, 2018. Accessed May 21, 2019. https://www.topuniversities. com/system-strength-rankings/2018?utm_source=website&utm_medium=blog&utm_campaign=rankings. "Digest of Education Statistics, 2013." National Center for Education Statistics (NCES) Home Page, a part of the US Department of Education. Accessed August 21, 2019. https://nces.ed.gov/programs/digest/d13/tables/dt13_326.10.asp. "Federal Government Publishes More Complete Graduation Rate Data." *College Search & Scholarships: College Decision Resources*. Accessed June 21, 2019. https://www.cappex.com/articles/blog/government-publishes-graduation-rate-data.

19.   Mellow, Gail O. "The Biggest Misconception about Today's College Students." *The New York Times*. August 28, 2017. https://www.nytimes.com/2017/08/28/opinion/community-college-misconception.html.

20.   H. B. Cavalcanti. *Almost Home: A Brazilian-American's Reflections on Faith, Culture, and Immigration*. University of Wisconsin Press, 2012, p. 97.

21.   "PISA Results in Focus." PISA 2015, *OECD* 2018. Accessed April 20, 2019. www.oecd.org/pisa/pisa-2015-results-in-focus.pdf.

22.   "Digest of Education Statistics." National Center for Education Statistics (NCES) Home Page, a part of the US Department of Education. Accessed August 21, 2019. https://nces.ed.gov/programs/digest/d11/tables/dt11_241. asp.

23.   Chen, Grace. "The Catch-22 of Community College Graduation Rates." *Community College Review*. November 18, 2010. Accessed February 16, 2019. https://www.communitycollegereview.com/blog/the-catch-22-of-community-college-graduation-rates.

24.   "Digest of Education Statistics, 2017." National Center for Education Statistics (NCES) Home Page, a part of the US Department of Education. Accessed August 21, 2019. https://nces.ed.gov/programs/digest/d17/tables/dt17_311.40.asp?current=yes.

25.   Fallows, *Our Towns*, pp. 126–7.

26.   Mellow, Gail O. "The Biggest Misconception about Today's College Students." *The New York Times*. August 28, 2017. https://www.nytimes.com/2017/08/28/opinion/community-college-misconception.html.

27.   Ibid.

28.   "Unraveling America?" The James G. Martin Center for Academic Renewal. June 13, 2016. https://www.jamesgmartin.center/2012/09/unraveling-america/.

29. Dillinger, Jessica. "Nobel Prize Winners by Country." *WorldAtlas*. October 30, 2015. Accessed August 21, 2019. https://www.worldatlas.com/articles/top-30-countries-with-nobel-prize-winners.html.

30. Joffe, J. *The Myth of America's Decline: Politics, Economics, and a Half Century of False Prophecies*. New York: W. W. Norton & Company, 2014, p. 205.

31. Ibid., 203.

32. Snyder, Thomas. " 120 Years of American Education: A Statistical Portrait." National Center for Education Statistics (NCES) Home Page, a Part of the U.S. Department of Education. January 19, 1993. https://nces.ed.gov/pubsearch/pubsinfo.asp?pubid=93442. Table 24

33. The Condition of Education—Postsecondary Education—Postsecondary Students—Undergraduate Enrollment—Indicator May (2019). Accessed August 22, 2019. https://nces.ed.gov/programs/coe/indicator_cha.asp. Figure 5.

34. "The 10 Best Universities in America." *U.S. News & World Report*. U.S. News & World Report. Accessed July 11, 2019. https://www.usnews.com/best-colleges/rankings/national-universities.

     "Brown University." Factbook, Office of Institutional Research. Accessed August 22, 2019. https://www.brown.edu/about/administration/institutional-research/factbook.

     "Everyone." Registrar's Office. Accessed August 22, 2019. https://registrar.stanford.edu/everyone.

     "Harvard at a Glance." Harvard University. Accessed August 22, 2019. https://www.harvard.edu/about-harvard/harvard-glance. "Historical Enrollment." University Registrar. Accessed August 22, 2019. https://registrar.uchicago.edu/data-reporting/historical-enrollment/.

     Person. "6,665 Degrees and Certificates Awarded at Harvard's 368th Commencement." *Harvard Gazette*. May 29, 2019. Accessed August 22, 2019. https://news.harvard.edu/gazette/story/2019/05/6665-degrees-and-certificates-awarded-at-harvards-368th-commencement/.

     "University Enrollment Statistics, Office of the Registrar." Princeton University. Accessed August 22, 2019. https://registrar.princeton.edu/enrollment.

35. Sachs, *A New Foreign Policy*, p. 158

Chapter 7

1. Vasconcelos, José. *Ulises Criollo*. México: Porrúa, 2006, p. 288.

2. "Yearbook 2009." Department of Homeland Security. June 6, 2019. Accessed June 22, 2019. https://www.dhs.gov/immigration-statistics/yearbook/2009.

3. "Table 25. Nonimmigrant Admissions by Class of Admission: Fiscal Years 2015 to 2017." Department of Homeland Security. November 6, 2018.

Accessed June 22, 2019. https://www.dhs.gov/immigration-statistics/ yearbook/2017/table25.

4. "Yearbook 2000." Department of Homeland Security. Table 38. June 6, 2019. Accessed June 22, 2019. https://www.dhs.gov/immigration-statistics/yearbook/2000. "Yearbook 2009." Department of Homeland Security. Table 32. June 6, 2019. Accessed June 22, 2019. https://www.dhs.gov/immigration-statistics/yearbook/2009. "Table 32. Nonimmigrant Temporary Worker Admissions (I-94 Only) by Region and Country of Citizenship: Fiscal Year 2017." Department of Homeland Security. November 8, 2018. Accessed June 22, 2019. https://www.dhs.gov/immigration-statistics/yearbook/2017/table32.

5. "Table 25. Nonimmigrant Admissions by Class of Admission: Fiscal Years 2015 to 2017." Department of Homeland Security. November 6, 2018. Accessed June 22, 2019. https://www.dhs.gov/immigration-statistics/yearbook/2017/table25. US Department of State. Table XVI(B). Accessed June 22, 2019. https://travel.state.gov/content/travel/en/legal/visa-law0/visa-statistics/annual-reports/report-of-the-visa-office-2018.html.

6. "Table 1. Persons Obtaining Lawful Permanent Resident Status: Fiscal Years 1820 to 2016." Department of Homeland Security. December 18, 2017. Accessed June 22, 2019. https://www.dhs.gov/immigration-statistics/yearbook/2016/table1.

7. "Yearbook 2008." Table 32D. Nonimmigrant admissions 2008. Department of Homeland Security. June 6, 2019. https://www.dhs.gov/immigration-statistics/yearbook/2008.

    "Table 32. Nonimmigrant Temporary Worker Admissions (I-94 Only) by Region and Country of Citizenship: Fiscal Year 2017." Department of Homeland Security. November 8, 2018. https://www.dhs.gov/immigration-statistics/yearbook/2017/table32.

8. "Crece Migración Legal a EU." Reforma. May 9, 2019, p. 4.

9. "Ingresos por remesas." Banco de México. Accessed May 28, 2019. www.banxico.org.mx/SieInternet/consultarDirectorioInternetAction.do?accion=consultarSeries.

10. "Census Profile: Allentown, PA." Census Reporter, n.d. https://censusreporter.org/profiles/16000US4202000-allentown-pa/.

11. "Many Worldwide Oppose More Migration—Both into and out of Their Countries." Pew Research Center, n.d. https://www.pewresearch.org/fact-tank/2018/12/10/many-worldwide-oppose-more-migration-both-into-and-out-of-their-countries/.

12. H. B. Cavalcanti, *Almost Home*, p. 97.

13. Chin, R. C. *The Crisis of Multiculturalism in Europe: A History*. Princeton: Princeton University Press, 2017, p. 82.

14. Ibid., p. 303.

15. Ferguson, Niall. "Paris and the Fall of Rome." *The Boston Globe.* November 16, 2015. https://www.bostonglobe.com/opinion/2015/11/16/ paris-and-fall-rome/ErlRjkQMGXhvDarTIxXpdK/story.html.

16. Chin, R. C. *The Crisis of Multiculturalism in Europe: A History.* Princeton: Princeton University Press, 2017, pp. 82, 174.

17. Ibid., p. 199.

18. "Table 3. Persons Obtaining Lawful Permanent Resident Status by Region and Country of Birth: Fiscal Years 2015 to 2017." Department of Homeland Security. October 2, 2018. https://www.dhs.gov/immigration-statistics/yearbook/2017/table3.
       https://travel.state.gov/content/dam/visas/Statistics/Non-Immigrant-Statistics/NIVDetailTables/FY17NIVDetailTable.pdf.

19. Goldbaum, Christina. "Trump Crackdown Unnerves Immigrants, and the Farmers Who Rely on Them." *The New York Times.* March 18, 2019. Accessed March 18, 2019. https://www.nytimes.com/2019/03/18/nyregion/ ny-farmers-undocumented-workers-trump-immigration.html.

20. "Countries by Median Age 2018." Accessed May 7, 2019. http:// worldpopulationreview.com/countries/median-age/.

21. "Reports and Detailed Tables from the 2017 National Survey on Drug Use and Health (NSDUH)." CBHSQ. Accessed August 22, 2019. https:// www.samhsa.gov/data/nsduh/reports-detailed-tables-2017-NSDUH.

22. Kilmer, Beau, Susan S. Sohler Everingham, Jonathan P. Caulkins, Gregory Midgette, Rosalie Liccardo Pacula, Peter Reuter, Rachel M. Burns, Bing Han, and Russell Lundberg. *How Big Is the U.S. Market for Illegal Drugs?* Santa Monica, CA: RAND Corporation, 2014. https:// www.rand.org/pubs/research_briefs/RB9770.html.

23. Global Drug Survey. "Cokeinoes! Cocaine Delivered Faster than Pizza. Global Drug Survey." Accessed July 22, 2019. https://www. globaldrugsurvey.com/gds-2018/cokeinoes-cocaine-delivered-faster-than-pizza/.

24. Gallup, Inc. "Illegal Drugs." Gallup.com. July 25, 2019. Accessed July 30, 2019. https://news.gallup.com/poll/1657/illegal-drugs.aspx.

25. Coyne, Christopher J., and Abigail R. Hall. "Four Decades and Counting: The Continued Failure of the War on Drugs." *Cato Institute* 12. April 2017. Accessed April 24, 2019. www.cato.org/publications/policy-analysis/four-decades-counting-continued-failure-war-drugs#full.

26. Jiang, Steven. "China Lectures the US on Opioid Crisis." CNN. June 26, 2018. Accessed January 30, 2019. https://edition.cnn.com/2018/06/25/asia/ china-us-opioid-crisis-intl/index.html.

27. Beletsky, Leo, and Corey S. Davis. "Today's Fentanyl Crisis: Prohibition's Iron Law, Revisited." *International Journal of Drug Policy* 2017. http:// fileserver.idpc.net/library/Todays-fentanyl-crisis-prohibitions-iron-law-revisited.pdf.

28.   Dwf_admin. "Prevalence of Illegal Drug Use in the US among People Aged 12 or Older." *Drug War Facts*. September 16, 2018. Accessed May 16, 2019. https://www.drugwarfacts.org/node/2593.

29.   Balsamo, Michael. "Schumer Announces Fentanyl Sanctions Bill before China Talks." *PBS, Public Broadcasting Service*. February 10, 2019. Accessed April 24, 2019. www.pbs.org/newshour/nation/schumer-announces-fentanyl-sanctions-bill-before-china-talks.

30.   Wee, Sui-lee. "Trump Says China Will Curtail Fentanyl. The U.S. Has Heard That Before." *The New York Times*. December 3, 2018. Accessed April 26, 2019. www.nytimes.com/2018/12/03/business/fentanyl-china-trump.html.

31.   Myers, Steven Lee. "China Cracks Down on Fentanyl. But Is It Enough to End the U.S. Epidemic?" *The New York Times*. December 1, 2019. Accessed December 5, 2019. https://www.nytimes.com/2019/12/01/world/asia/china-fentanyl-crackdown.html?smid=nytcore-ios-share.

32.   Coyne, Christopher J., and Abigail R. Hall, *Four Decades and Counting*.

33.   Campos, Isaac. *Home Grown: Marijuana and the Origins of Mexico's War on Drugs*. Place of publication not identified: University of North Carolina Press, 2014, p. 230.

Chapter 8

1.   Díaz Hernán. *Borges, between History and Eternity*, p. 93. Borges, Jorge Luis. *Obras Completas*. Vol. 1. Buenos Aires: Sudamericana, 2011, p. 577.

2.   Naipaul, *Turn in the South*. p. 15.

3.   Myrdal, G., and B. Sissela, *An American Dilemma*, p. 1009.

4.   Beauvoir, S., *America Day by Day*, 248.

5.   Ibid., p. 235.

6.   Gates, Henry Louis. Stony the Road: Reconstruction, White Supremacy, and the Rise of Jim Crow. New York: Penguin Group USA, 2019, pp. 2, 4.

7.   Vasconcelos, José. La Raza Cósmica. México: Editorial Porrúa, 2017, p. 16.

8.   "Claritas-Median-HHI-by-Race-Ethnicity-Feb2019." Marketing Charts. https://www.marketingcharts.com/charts/median-household-income-raceethnicity-2019/attachment/claritas-median-hhi-by-race-ethnicity-feb2019.

9.   Amadeo, Kimberly. "How to Close the Racial Wealth Gap in the United States." The Balance. June 25, 2019. Accessed April 22, 2019. http://www.thebalance.com/racial-wealth-gap-in-united-states-4169678.

10.   "Report: Dreams Deferred." Institute for Policy Studies. March 22, 2019. Accessed April 19, 2019. https://ips-dc.org/racial-wealth-divide-2019/.

11.   Cole, Teju. "On the Blackness of the Panther." In The Good Immigrant: 26 Writers Reflect on America. New York: Little Brown, 2019, p. 40.

12.   Gilberto Freyre, *The Masters and the Slaves*, p. 355.

13. Gates, H. L., *Reconstruction: America After the Civil War*, p. 16.
14. Fleming, C. M., *How to Be Less Stupid about Race*.
15. Kendi, Ibram X. Stamped from the Beginning: The Definitive History of Racist Ideas in America. New York: Nation Books, 2016, p. 1.
16. Lockhart, P. R. "The 2020 Democratic Primary Debate over Reparations, Explained." Vox. June 19, 2019. www. vox.com/policy-and-politics/2019/3/11/18246741/ reparations-democrats-2020-inequality-warren-harris-castro.
17. Stolberg, Sheryl Gay. "At Historic Hearing, House Panel Explores Reparations." *The New York Times*. June 19, 2019. Accessed June 30, 2019. https://www.nytimes.com/2019/06/19/us/politics/slavery-reparations-hearing.html.
18. Coates, Ta-Nehisi. "The Case for Reparations." The Atlantic. June 22, 2018. Accessed March 8, 2019. https://www.theatlantic.com/magazine/ archive/2014/06/the-case-for-reparations/361631/.
19. Ibid.
20. "The Sons of Slaveholders Quickly Recovered Their Fathers' Wealth." The Economist. April 4, 2019. Accessed April 28, 2019. https://www.economist.com/united-states/2019/04/04/ the-sons-of-slaveholders-quickly-recovered-their-fathers-wealth.
21. "The Black-White Wealth Gap Is Unchanged after Half a Century." The Economist. April 6, 2019. Accessed April 12, 2019. https://www.economist.com/united-states/2019/04/06/ the-black-white-wealth-gap-is-unchanged-after-half-a-century.
22. Ibid.
23. "EPI Analysis of Current Population Survey Annual Social and Economic Supplement Historical Poverty Tables (Table H-5 and H-9) Figure A." From: "E. (n.d.). Real Median Household Incomes for All Racial Groups Remain Well Below their 2007 Levels." Retrieved March 3, 2019. https:// www.epi.org/blog/real-median-household-incomes-racial-groups/
24. Coates, "The Case for Reparations."
25. Collins, Chuck. "New Study Says the Median Black Family Will Have Zero Wealth by 2082." In These Times. January 31, 2019. Accessed June 10, 2019. https://inthesetimes.com/working/entry/21705/ race-wealth-gap-black-family-inequality-white-economy-united-states.
26. "Wealth Gaps Rise to Record Highs between Whites, Blacks, Hispanics." Pew Research Center's Social & Demographic Trends Project. April 15, 2014. https://www.pewsocialtrends.org/2011/07/26/wealth-gaps-rise-to-record-highs-between-whites-blacks-hispanics/. Board of Governors of the Federal Reserve System. "Recent Trends in Wealth-Holding by Race and Ethnicity: Evidence from the Survey of Consumer Finances." Accessed August 22, 2019. https://www.federalreserve.gov/econres/notes/feds-notes/ recent-trends-in-wealth-holding-by-race-and-ethnicity-evidence-from-the-survey-of-consumer-finances-20170927.htm.

27. "How Fair Is American Society?" Yale Insights. September 18, 2017.
     Accessed August 22, 2019. https://insights.som.yale.edu/insights/
     how-fair-is-american-society.

28. Rana, Aziz. "Race and the American Creed." no. 1. September 28, 2016.
     https://nplusonemag.com/issue-24/politics/race-and-the-american-creed/.

29. Nolan, *What They Saw in America*, p. 88.

30. Lévy, B., *American Vertigo*, p. 265.

31. Ibid., p. 268.

32. Naipaul, *Turn in the South*, p. 58.

33. "Most Americans Say Trump's Election Has Led to Worse Race Relations
     in the U.S." Pew Research Center for the People and the Press. December
     26, 2018. https://www.people-press.org/2017/12/19/most-americans-say-
     trumps-election-has-led-to-worse-race-relations-in-the-u-s/.

34. "Views on Race, Immigration and Discrimination." Pew Research Center
     for the People and the Press. September 18, 2018. Accessed June 22,
     2019. https://www.people-press.org/2017/10/05/4-race-immigration-and-
     discrimination/.

35. Newport, Frank. "The Harvard Affirmative Action Case and Public
     Opinion." Gallup.com. August 5, 2019. Accessed August 20, 2019. https://
     news.gallup.com/opinion/polling-matters/243965/harvard-affirmative-
     action-case-public-opinion.aspx.

36. "Overwhelming Opposition to Reparations for Slavery and Jim Crow."
     YouGov, n.d. https://today.yougov.com/topics/politics/articles-reports/
     2014/06/02/reparations?utm_source=link_newsv9&utm_campaign=item_
     247178&utm_medium=copy.

37. Ibid.

38. Ibid.

39. Ibid.

40. Ibid.

41. Neiman, Susan. *Learning from the Germans: Race and the Memory of Evil.*
     New York: Farrar, Straus, and Giroux, 2019.

42. Newport, Frank. "Reparations and Black Americans' Attitudes about
     Race." Gallup.com. March 1, 2019. Accessed April 2, 2019. https://news.
     gallup.com/opinion/polling-matters/247178/reparations-black-americans-
     attitudes-race.aspx.

43. Lockhart, P. R., "The 2020 Democratic Primary Debate over Reparations,
     Explained."

44. "The Black-White Wealth Gap Is Unchanged after Half a
     Century." The Economist. April 6, 2019. Accessed May 2,
     2019. https://www.economist.com/united-states/2019/04/06/
     the-black-white-wealth-gap-is-unchanged-after-half-a-century.

45. Marx. "Marx's Letter to Abraham Lincoln." https://www.marxists.org/
     history/international/iwma/documents/1864/lincoln-letter.htm.

46. Aziz Rana, *Race and the American Creed.*

47. Coates, Ta-Nehisi. "The First White President." The Atlantic. May 22, 2018. Accessed November 19, 2018. https://www.theatlantic.com/magazine/archive/2017/10/the-first-white-president-ta-nehisi-coates/537909/.

48. "The Truth about the United States by José Martí." Reading the Periphery.org. December 18, 2017. Accessed April 10, 2019. http://readingtheperiphery.org/marti/.

49. Arkush, R. David, and Leo Ou-fan Lee. Land without Ghosts: Chinese Impressions of America from the Mid-Nineteenth Century to the Present. Berkeley, CA: University of California Press, 1989, p. 6.

50. Waldman, Steven. Sacred Liberty: Americas Long and Bloody Struggle for Religious Freedom. New York: HarperOne, 2019, p. 33.

51. Tocqueville, *Democracy in America*, p. 336.

52. Ibid., vol. 1, part 2, p. 337.

53. Ibid., p. 349.

54. Llosa, Mario Vargas. "Tribuna: A Dios Rogando." EL PAÍS. April 30, 2005. Accessed June 17, 2019. https://elpais.com/diario/2005/05/01/opinion/1114898407_850215.html.

55. Davies, Bess Twiston. "Half of Britons Pray, Says Survey." The Times. January 13, 2018. Accessed August 22, 2019. https://www.thetimes.co.uk/article/half-of-britons-pray-says-survey-5hlm95brv.

56. Putnam, R. D., D. E. Campbell, and S. R. Garrett. American Grace: How Religion Divides and Unites Us. New York: Simon & Schuster, 2012, p. 9. "How Often Do You Attend Religious Services." WVS Database. Accessed April 15, 2019. http://www.worldvaluessurvey.org/WVSOnline.jsp?WAVE=6&COUNTRY=875.

57. "Many Americans Mix Multiple Faiths." Pew Research Center's Religion & Public Life Project. February 11, 2014. Accessed July 21, 2019. https://www.pewforum.org/2009/12/09/many-americans-mix-multiple-faiths/.

58. Putnam, R. D., D. E. Campbell, and S. R. Garrett. *American Grace*, p. 7.

59. Ibid., p. 9.

60. Julia Isabel. Sentimientos y resentimientos de la nación. Universidad Nacional Autónoma de México-Instituto de Investigaciones Jurídicas. (Los mexicanos vistos por sí mismos. Los grandes temas nacionales.) México: Universidad nacional autonoma de México, 2015, pp. 330–41.

61. Ibid., p. 329.

62. "Religion in America: U.S. Religious Data, Demographics and Statistics." Pew Research Center's Religion & Public Life Project. May 11, 2015. Accessed August 19, 2019. https://www.pewforum.org/religious-landscape-study/.

63. Putnam, R. D., D. E. Campbell, and S. R. Garrett. *American Grace*, p. 300.

64. Ibid., p. 107.

65. Foner, E. The Story of American Freedom. New York: W. W. Norton &
     Company, 1999, pp. 55, 57.
66. Lepore, J., These Truths, p. 190.
67. U.S. Census Bureau. "For Young Adults, Cohabitation Is Up, Marriage Is
     Down." United States Census Bureau. November 15, 2018. Accessed May
     9, 2019. https://www.census.gov/library/stories/2018/11/cohabitaiton-is-
     up-marriage-is-down-for-young-adults.html.
68. Manning, Wendy D. "Cohabitation and Child Wellbeing." The Future
     of Children. 2015. Accessed May 9, 2019. https://www.ncbi.nlm.nih.gov/
     pmc/articles/PMC4768758/.
69. Aunión, J. A. "El Matrimonio En España Es Solo Cuestión De Tiempo."
     EL PAÍS. October 15, 2015. Accessed May 12, 2019. https://elpais.com/
     politica/2015/10/12/actualidad/1444669104_299557.html.
     "Le couple dans tous ses états non-cohabitation, conjoints de même
     sexe, pacs . . . ." Le Couple dans tous ses états—insee première—1435.
     Accessed May 12, 2019. https://www.insee.fr/fr/statistiques/1281436.
     "Cohabitation, Marriage, and Union Instability in Europe." Institute
     for Family Studies. Accessed May 13, 2019. https://ifstudies.org/blog/
     cohabitation-marriage-and-union-instability-in-europe.
70. "What Do Marriage and Fertility Have to Do with the Economy?"
     Sustain Demographic Dividend. Accessed April 26, 2019. http://
     sustaindemographicdividend.org/wp-content/uploads/2012/07/SDD-
     2011-Final.pdf.
71. Abortion Rates by Country (list by Country). Accessed August 16, 2019.
     http://www.johnstonsarchive.net/policy/abortion/wrjp336abrate2.html.
72. "Homosexual Marriages in France 2013–2018." Statista. Accessed April
     17, 2019. https://www.statista.com/statistics/464227/number-same-sex-
     marriages-france/. "Instituto Nacional De Estadística." Instituto Nacional
     De Estadística (National Statistics Institute). Accessed April 17, 2019.
     https://www.ine.es/dynt3/inebase/index.htm?padre=1128&capsel=3650.
     Instituto Nacional De Estadística. "Notas De Prensa." Movimiento
     Natural De La Población (MNP), Indicadores Demográficos Básicos
     (IDB). June 19, 2019. Accessed July 22, 2019. ine.es/prensa/mnp_2018_
     p.pdf. "Denmark: Number of Marriages between Two Same-Sex Partners
     2012–2018." Statista. Accessed July 30, 2019. https://www.statista.com/
     statistics/578822/marriages-between-two-same-sex-partners-in-denmark/.
     "Netherlands: Number of Marriages, Straight and Same-Sex 2008–2018."
     Statista. Accessed August 13, 2019. https://www.statista.com/statistics/
     520171/number-of-straight-vs-same-sex-marriages-in-the-netherlands/.
73. AP. "Same-Sex Marriages in U.S. since Supreme Court Ruling Estimated
     to Be 123,000." CBS News. June 22, 2016. Accessed April 16, 2019.
     https://www.cbsnews.com/news/same-sex-marriages-us-supreme-court-
     ruling-estimate/. Jones, Jeffrey M. "In U.S., 10.2 percent of LGBT Adults
     Now Married to Same-Sex Spouse." Gallup.com. February 7, 2018.

Accessed April 16, 2019. https://news.gallup.com/poll/212702/lgbt-adults-married-sex-spouse.aspx.

74. "LGBT Demographic Data Interactive." January 2019. Los Angeles, CA: The Williams Institute, UCLA School of Law.

75. Lipka, Michael. "10 Facts about Religion in America." Pew Research Center. August 27, 2015. https://www.pewresearch.org/fact-tank/2015/08/27/10-facts-about-religion-in-america/.

76. "A Change of Heart?" Pew Research Center's Religion & Public Life Project. November 10, 2014. https://www.pewforum.org/2014/11/13/chapter-1-religious-switching/pr_14-11-13_latinamerica-01-01/.

77. Lacorne, Denis. Religion in America: A Political History. New York: Columbia University Press, 2014, p. 147.

78. Nolan, *What They Saw in America*, p. 201.

79. Ibid., p. 209.

80. Paz, Octavio. México en la obra de Octavio Paz. Volume 1: El peregrino en su patria : Historia y política de México. México: Fondo de Cultura Económica, 421.

81. Lacorne, D., *Religion in America*, p. 159. Also see: McCreary County v. American Civil Liberties Union of Ky., 545 U.S. 844 (2005). Justia Law.

82. Newport, Frank. "2017 Update on Americans and Religion." Gallup.com. March 14, 2018. Accessed July 3, 2019. https://news.gallup.com/poll/224642/2017-update-americans-religion.aspx.

83. Nolan, *What They Saw in America*, p. 101.

84. Putnam, R. D. Bowling Alone: The Collapse and Revival of American Community. New York: Simon & Schuster, 2000, p. 79.

85. "American Religion Is Starting to Look Less Exceptional." The Economist. April 27, 2019. https://www.economist.com/united-states/2019/04/27/american-religion-is-starting-to-look-less-exceptional.

Chapter 9

1. Meyers, J. n.d. "Thomas Mann in America." Retrieved April 4, 2019. http://hdl.handle.net/2027/spo.act2080.0051.419.

2. Ibid.

3. Mathy, J. n.d. "L'Américanisme' est—il un humanisme? Sartre aux Etats-Unis (1945–46)." http://www.academicroom.com/article/lamericanisme-est-il-un-humanisme-sartre-aux-etats-unis-1945-46.

4. Ibid.

5. Kipling, R. *American Notes*, V.

6. Ibid., VII.

7. Trollope, F. M. *Domestic Manners of the Americans*. Mineola, NY: Dover Publications, 2003, pp. 251, 253.

8. Lomnitz, Claudio. *The Return of Comrade Ricardo Flores Magón*. New York: Zone Books, 2014, p. 432.

9.   Sawyer, Wendy, and Peter Wagner. "Mass Incarceration: The Whole Pie 2019." Prison Policy Initiative, n.d. https://www.prisonpolicy.org/reports/pie2019.html.

10.   "Criminal Justice Facts." The Sentencing Project, n.d. https://www.sentencingproject.org/criminal-justice-facts/.

11.   "Nation behind Bars. A Human Rights Solution," n.d. Accessed May 2, 2019. https://www.hrw.org/sites/default/files/related_material/2014_US_Nation_Behind_Bars_0.pdf.

12.   Gopnik, Adam. "Who Belongs in Prison?" *The New Yorker*. June 25, 2019. https://www.newyorker.com/magazine/2019/04/15/who-belongs-in-prison.

13.   "Mass Incarceration." Equal Justice Initiative. July 29, 2019. https://eji.org/mass-incarceration.

14.   "Criminal Justice Facts." The Sentencing Project, n.d. https://www.sentencingproject.org/criminal-justice-facts/.

15.   Gopnik, Adam. "The Caging of America." *The New Yorker*. November 16, 2018. https://www.newyorker.com/magazine/2012/01/30/the-caging-of-america.

16.   Liptak, Adam. "Inmate Count in U.S. Dwarfs Other Nations'." *The New York Times*. April 23, 2008. https://www.nytimes.com/2008/04/23/us/23prison.html.

17.   "Mass Incarceration." American Civil Liberties Union, n.d. https://www.aclu.org/issues/smart-justice/mass-incarceration.

18.   Gramlich, John. "The Gap between the Number of Blacks and Whites in Prison Is Shrinking." Pew Research Center. April 30, 2019. Accessed May 5, 2019. https://www.pewresearch.org/fact-tank/2019/04/30/shrinking-gap-between-number-of-blacks-and-whites-in-prison/.

19.   "Criminal Justice Facts." The Sentencing Project, n.d. https://www.sentencingproject.org/criminal-justice-facts/.

20.   "Mass Incarceration." American Civil Liberties Union, n.d. https://www.aclu.org/issues/smart-justice/mass-incarceration.

21.   Saneta deVuono-powell, Chris Schweidler, Alicia Walters, and Azadeh Zohrabi. *Who Pays? The True Cost of Incarceration on Families*. Oakland, CA: Ella Baker Center, Forward Together, Research Action Design, 2015. https://ellabakercenter.org/sites/default/files/downloads/who-pays-exec-summary.pdf.

22.   "Just Facts: As Many Americans Have Criminal Records as College Diplomas." Brennan Center for Justice. November 17, 2015. https://www.brennancenter.org/blog/just-facts-many-americans-have-criminal-records-college-diplomas.

23.   Foucault, M., *1980–1988*, vol. II, p. 531.

24.   "The Costs of Incarceration Run Deeper than Budget Line Items and Sentences Served." Who Pays?, n.d. http://whopaysreport.org/key-findings/.

25. "6 Million Lost Voters: State-Level Estimates of Felony Disenfranchisement, 2016." The Sentencing Project, n.d. https://www. sentencingproject.org/publications/6-million-lost-voters-state-level- estimates-felony-disenfranchisement-2016/.

26. "Crime Data, Statistics and Data." United Nations. Accessed May 22, 2019. https://dataunodc.un.org/crime.

27. Kristof, Nicholas. "When We Kill." *The New York Times*. June 14, 2019. Accessed June 15, 2019. https://www.nytimes.com/2019/06/14/opinion/ sunday/death-penalty.html.

28. "Abolitionist and Retentionist Countries." Death Penalty Information Center. Accessed June 13, 2019. https://deathpenaltyinfo.org/policy-issues/ international/abolitionist-and-retentionist-countries. "Murder Rate by Country 2019." Accessed June 13, 2019. http://worldpopulationreview. com/countries/murder-rate-by-country/.

29. "Murder Rate of Death Penalty States Compared to Non-Death Penalty . . . ." Death Penalty Information Center. Accessed June 15, 2019. https:// deathpenaltyinfo.org/facts-and-research/murder-rates/murder-rate-of- death-penalty-states-compared-to-non-death-penalty-states.

30. Kristof, *When We Kill*.

31. Pinker, Steven. *Enlightenment Now*. New York: Penguin Books Ltd., 2019, p. 212.

32. Yamane, David. "The Sociology of U.S. Gun Culture—." *Sociology Compass*. June 16, 2017. Accessed April 28, 2019. https://onlinelibrary. wiley.com/doi/10.1111/soc4.12497.

33. Mak, *In America*, p. 139.

34. "Small Arms Survey—Public Information on All Aspects of Small Arms." November 6, 2019. http://www.smallarmssurvey.org/fileadmin/docs/ Weapons_and_Markets/Tools/Firearms_holdings/SAS-BP-Civilian-held- firearms-annexe.pdf.
      http://www.smallarmssurvey.org/fileadmin/docs/T-Briefing-Papers/ SAS-BP-Civilian-Firearms-Numbers.pdf.

35. "Americans Own Nearly Half World's Guns in Civilian Hands: Survey." Reuters. June 18, 2018. https://www.reuters.com/article/us-usa-guns/ americans-own-nearly-half-worlds-guns-in-civilian-hands-survey- idUSKBN1JE220.

36. Groll, Elias. "America's Exceptional Gun Culture." *Foreign Policy*. December 19, 2012. Accessed May 19, 2019. https://foreignpolicy.com/ 2012/12/19/americas-exceptional-gun-culture/.

37. Aizenman, Nurith. "Deaths from Gun Violence: How the U.S. Compares with the Rest of the World." NPR. November 9, 2018. Accessed May 19, 2019. https://www.npr.org/sections/goatsandsoda/2018/11/09/666209430/ deaths-from-gun-violence-how-the-u-s-compares-with-the-rest-of-the- world.

38. "Homicide." Harvard Injury Control Research Center. June 30, 2016. Accessed May 6, 2019. https://www.hsph.harvard.edu/hicrc/firearms-research/guns-and-death/.

39. "Gun Violence Archive." Accessed July 30, 2019. https://www.gunviolencearchive.org/reports/mass-shooting.

40. Horsley, Scott. "Guns in America, by the Numbers." NPR. January 5, 2016. Accessed April 15, 2019. https://www.npr.org/2016/01/05/462017461/guns-in-america-by-the-numbers.

41. "Small Arms Survey—Public Information on All Aspects of Small Arms." November 6, 2019.
    http://www.smallarmssurvey.org/fileadmin/docs/T-Briefing-Papers/SAS-BP-Civilian-Firearms-Numbers.pdf.

42. Lepore, J., *These Truths*, p. 673.

43. Yamane, *The Sociology of U.S. Gun Culture*, pp. 3, 5.

44. DelBanco, A. *The War Before the War*, pp. 135, 144.

45. Charles, Patrick J. *Armed in America: A History of Gun Rights from Colonial Militias to Concealed Carry*. S.l.: PROMETHEUS, 2019, p. 138.

46. Winkler, Adam. "The Secret History of Guns." *The Atlantic*. October 6, 2017. Accessed April 27, 2019. https://www.theatlantic.com/magazine/archive/2011/09/the-secret-history-of-guns/308608/.

47. Charles, P., *Armed in America*, p. 138.

48. "Farewell to the Santorum Amendment?" NCSE. March 16, 2016. Accessed May 4, 2019. https://ncse.com/library-resource/farewell-to-santorum-amendment.

49. Belluck, Pam. "Board for Kansas Deletes Evolution from Curriculum." *The New York Times*. August 12, 1999. Accessed April 28, 2019. https://www.nytimes.com/1999/08/12/us/board-for-kansas-deletes-evolution-from-curriculum.html?searchResultPosition=1.

50. Lecourt, D. *L'Amérique entre la Bible et Darwin: suivi de intelligent design: science, morale et politique*. Paris: Presses universitaires de France, 2007, p. 14.

51. Berkley Center for Religion, and Georgetown University. "Kitzmiller v. Dover Area School District." Berkley Center for Religion, Peace and World Affairs. Accessed May 20, 2019. https://berkleycenter.georgetown.edu/cases/kitzmiller-v-dover-area-school-district.

52. Lecourt, *L'Amérique entre la Bible et Darwin*, p. 98.

53. "What Is 'Intelligent Design' Creationism?" NCSE. March 17, 2016. https://ncse.com/creationism/general/what-is-intelligent-design-creationism.

54. Brasseur, Anne. "The Dangers of Creationism in Education." Committee on Culture, Science and Education. Parliamentary Assembly. September 17, 2007. http://assembly.coe.int/nw/xml/XRef/X2H-Xref-ViewHTML.asp?FileID=11751.

55. Reilhac, Gilbert. "Council of Europe Firmly Opposes Creationism in School." Reuters. October 4, 2007. https://uk.reuters.com/article/science-europe-creationism-dc/council-of-europe-firmly-opposes-creationism-in-school-idUKL0417855220071004.

56. "Polling Creationism and Evolution Around the World." NCSE. August 19, 2012. https://ncse.com/news/2011/04/polling-creationism-evolution-around-world-006634.

57. Brenan, Megan. "40 percent of Americans Believe in Creationism." Gallup.com. August 5, 2019. Accessed August 9, 2019. https://news.gallup.com/poll/261680/americans-believe-creationism.aspx.

58. Lecourt, *L'Amérique entre la Bible et Darwin*, p. 230.

Chapter 10

1.   Edsall, Thomas. "Trump Is Changing the Shape of the Democratic Party, Too." *The New York Times*. June 19, 2019. Accessed June 20, 2019. https://www.nytimes.com/2019/06/19/opinion/trump-racial-resentment.html.

2.   Gallup, Inc. "U.S. Position in the World." Gallup.com. July 3, 2019. Accessed July 25, 2019. https://news.gallup.com/poll/116350/position-world.aspx.

3.   Castañeda, Jorge G. "Not Ready for Prime Time." *Foreign Affairs*. September 16, 2010. Accessed July 2019. https://www.foreignaffairs.com/articles/south-africa/2010-09-01/not-ready-prime-time.

4.   Brooks, David. "Voters, Your Foreign Policy Views Stink!" *The New York Times*. June 13, 2019. Accessed June 13, 2019. https://www.nytimes.com/2019/06/13/opinion/foreign-policy-populism.html.

5.   Asghar, Fatimah. "On Loneliness." In *The Good Immigrant*, p. 87.

6.   Beard, Mary. *SPQR: A History of Ancient Rome*. New York: Liveright Publishing Corporation, 2015, p. 497.

7.   Debray, R., *Civilisation*, p. 187.

8.   Goldsworthy, Adrian. *Pax Romana: War, Peace, and Conquest in the Roman World*. New Haven, CT: Yale University Press, 2016, p. 298.

INDEX

For the benefit of digital users, indexed terms that span two pages (e.g., 52–53) may, on occasion, appear on only one of those pages.